From Elvis to Trump, Eyewitness to the Unraveling: Co-Starring Richard Nixon, Andy Warhol, Bill Clinton, The Supremes, and Barack Obama!

Eric Rozenman

From Elvis to Trump, Eyewitness to the Unraveling: Co-Starring Richard Nixon, Andy Warhol, Bill Clinton, The Supremes, and Barack Obama!

Eric Rozenman

Academica Press
Washington~London

Library of Congress Cataloging-in-Publication Data

Names: Rozenman, Eric (author)
Title: From elvis to trump, eyewitness to the unraveling : co-starring
richard nixon, andy warhol, bill clinton, the supremes, and barack
obama! | Rozenman, Eric
Description: Washington : Academica Press, 2021. | Includes references.
Identifiers: LCCN 2021950641 | ISBN 9781680537369 (hardcover) |
9781680537376 (paperback) | 9781680537383 (e-book)

For Melinda, a Woman of Valor

Contents

Preface:
Hidden in Plain Sight

Sixty-five Peculiar Years

From Elvis to Trump, Eyewitness to the Unraveling; Co-Starring Richard Nixon, Andy Warhol, Bill Clinton, The Supremes and Barack Obama! blends bits of memoir, celebrity vignettes and shards of U.S. history from 1956 to 2020 to achieve something unique: An often wry, quirky but substantive answer to the questions how did we get here and where are we going.

From Elvis to Trump is an eyewitness's meditation on the past 65 years, from the incandescent arrival and impact of Elvis Presley and rock n'roll on American and international culture through the disruptive—or better, accelerant—election of Donald Trump as the 45th president of the United States and its continuing ripple effects.

By a series of sometimes Zelig-like coincidences (some Chasidic rabbis maintain there are no coincidences) the author, as newspaper reporter, congressional press secretary, lobbyist of sorts and newspaper and magazine editor found himself eyewitness to the famous and the influential, and sometimes the infamously influential. In addition to the main title characters, other players appearing in this pageant of the second half of the 20th century and first two decades of the 21st include: Gov. George Wallace, CBS-TV's Mike Wallace, President George H. W. Bush, Bob Hope, Miss America Jacqueline Mayer, The Beatles, Arnold Schwarzenegger, Ambassador Shirley Temple Black, Prime Minister Yitzhak Rabin, The Rolling Stones, Nobel Peace Prize Laureate Elie Wiesel and Secretary of State Hillary Clinton.

The 1967 March on the Pentagon, the Woodstock dress rehearsal known as the 1969 Atlanta International Pop Festival; the first Palestinian *intifada* in 1988 (a Molotov cocktail in every alley); and

Donald Trump's bizarre rally outside the U.S. Capitol in 2015 are among events witnessed and endured. Comic relief pitchers include F.B.I. agents investigating the author, an alphabetically challenged U.S. Army sergeant and a No-Doz fueled tow-truck driver. Foreboding arrives with Wiesel's renewed fears of Jew-hatred in unstable societies and America's self-inflicted instability.

Among those left on the cutting room floor, not for lack of intrinsic interest but rather because not every digression furthers discourse, were Ohio's four-term Gov. James A. Rhodes (R); Stripper Blaze Starr ("Burlesque Comes to Campus!"); Speaker of the House Thomas Phillip "Tip" O'Neill, Jr. (D), ("That's some outfit your wife's wearing …"); *Hustler* magazine's Larry Flynt; Sen. John Glenn—fighter pilot, first American in orbit and beloved (by many, but not all) politician—and Neil Armstrong, aeronautical engineer, professor and first man on the moon. Glenn, Armstrong, Orville and Wilbur Wright and the author, all native Ohioans, one allergic to heights.

The cavalcade of decades and players arrives not so much at a destination but unexpectedly at three related questions. They were perhaps unavoidable after summer 2020's often destructive protests against not only anti-black racism but also against the underlying founding declaration of the American nation itself. Unavoidable also after the Jan. 6, 2021 storming of the U.S. Capitol in rejection of the 2020 election of Joe Biden as president and against constitutional procedure itself. Question One: With political-cultural divisions hardening into intolerance, with homicide rates having surged in cities across the country, and the Capitol itself enclosed for months by razor wire and troops, can digitally dominated, attention deficit Americans maintain, and pass on, freedom? Two: Can they underwrite the opportunity others elsewhere might have to hold or obtain liberty? And three: If not, then the citizens of what other nation might?

And now, said the dog Mr. Peabody to his boy, Sherman, let's climb into the Wayback Machine and travel to the time when …

Chapter One:
Forward Slash

Cheers for Trump. What Was that About?

It was Sept. 8, 2015. Thousands of people had gathered on the west lawn of the U.S. Capitol for a noon rally. Featured among numerous speakers were a hero of the war in Iraq, Sen. Ted Cruz (Texas) and Donald J. Trump, a real estate tycoon and reality television star—or perhaps the other way around—from New York City. The latter two were among the many Republican Party presidential hopefuls for 2016. All the speakers condemned the nuclear weapons deal the Obama administration had arranged with Iran, excoriating it as, at best, temporary restrictions on Tehran but not long-term disarmament.

President Obama, outmaneuvering Republican-led opposition, presented the Joint Comprehensive Plan of Action (Russia, China, Germany, France and the United Kingdom also participated in the talks) as ordinary legislation. It would need a simple majority for ratification. Those opposed insisted it amounted to an international treaty, which would have required a most unlikely two-thirds Senate approval. Instead, the president's supporters neatly flipped the script and made it subject to a resolution of disapproval. At the time of the rally, such a resolution loomed. But Democrats already had enough members committed to blocking it.

I then worked as Washington director of CAMERA, the 65,000-member, Boston-based Committee for Accuracy in Middle East Reporting and Analysis, a news media watchdog. As such I was a minor representative to a series of meetings organized by pro-Israel groups seeking some way to block the Iran deal. They took place in a conference room with glass walls and a lofty view of the U.S. Capitol. But even on sunny days, we saw only long and generally discouraging odds. That was due in no small measure to President Obama's determination to get the JCPOA through and complementary squishiness of the 10 Jewish members of the Senate, Democrats all and none daring to oppose, more than in symbolic gestures, their party's leader.

CAMERA's D.C. office was in the Hall of the States building, a virtual lobbyists' central, two blocks from the Capitol. For security reasons—advocates of fair coverage of Israel occasionally being threatened from the far right, far left and by Islamic supremacists (three mutations of the same virus)—CAMERA did not appear in the building directory. The nameplate on the office door gave no hint as to our presence; U.S. mail went to a post office box. Sure, exercise your First Amendment rights. But watch your back.

Curious to hear the speakers, my colleague Sean Durns and I walked the short distance to the rally. We especially wanted to hear Cruz, whom veteran Harvard University Law School Prof. Alan Dershowitz had called one of his brightest students. Cruz was a leading critic of the Iran deal. Of another one-time student, Dershowitz recalled that Barack Obama also had taken his course.

Trump, like Cruz, was a draw. Not as a serious politician, of course, but a favorite of New York City's tabloids. He was the serial husband of beautiful wives, best-selling ghost-written author and TV celebrity whose signature line, on his show "The Apprentice," was "You're fired!" A number of retired generals and corporate executives who joined the Trump administration early on apparently had not watched much television.

Cruz, a first-term senator and former Texas solicitor-general, and Trump were among 16 Republicans seeking the GOP's 2016 presidential nomination. Of the ambitious Cruz, fellow Republican Sen. Lindsey Graham (S.C.) later would say "if you killed Ted Cruz on the floor of the Senate, no one would convict you." Cruz would bolster Graham's belief by pandering to a defeated President Trump's most rabid supporters in late 2020 and early 2021.

With Trump, historian Daniel Boorstin's classic definition of a celebrity as someone famous for being famous would become flesh, one more such American example. Yet given Obama's political career—seven years in the Illinois state senate, where he was conspicuous for voting "present," two-thirds of one term as a U.S. senator, but election nevertheless to the presidency in 2008 and 2012—why not 16 Republican candidates (or as it would happen, 22 Democrats initially seeking their party's 2020 nomination)? To paraphrase Mao Zedong, let a thousand ambitions bloom.

The Washington Post reported that "hundreds" attended the anti-deal, anti-Obama program, organized by Trump, Cruz, the Tea Party Patriots and the Zionist Organization of America. More accurately, comparing the crowd to another, larger mid-day rally in the same spot in 2002, that one to support Israel during the second Palestinian intifada, I guessed perhaps as many as 10,000 had turned out for Trump, Cruz, et. al. Strangely, many were not typical participants in a Capitol protest. I'd grown up in small Ohio towns and more than a few men in the crowd that day would have looked quite at home at the Henry or Seneca County fairs. Stocky or angular, they were weathered fellows in baseball caps and blue jeans even on a warm, late summer day. Their headgear bore John Deere or Massey-Ferguson logos. I presumed, perhaps having worked inside the Beltway too long, that they—like Trump—were out of place.

Trump was blatantly superficial. "I've been making lots of wonderful deals, great deals, that's what I do. Never ever, ever in my life have I seen any transaction so incompetently negotiated as our deal with Iran. And I mean never."

Details? Apparently, none were necessary. The men in the ball caps cheered.

"We are led by very, very stupid people. Very, very stupid people. We cannot let it continue," Trump declaimed. Again, not only not much vocabulary but no specifics and more cheers.

Under Obama and congressional leadership, America "can't beat anybody," Trump asserted. But "we will have so much winning if I get elected that you may get bored with winning. Believe me!" *The Post* quoted. "You'll never get bored with winning!"

Clownish generalities. Durns and I looked at each other. This man was not to be taken seriously.

Now Cruz, he was substantial, at least to us. He predicted, accurately if indirectly as it turned out, that should the deal pass, the Obama administration would become "the leading financier of radical Islamic terrorism. ... It's worth remembering that if this deal goes through, we know to an absolute certainty that people will die. ... I want to ask every Senate Democrat, 'How will you look in the eyes of the mother or father or sons or daughters of those who are murdered by jihadists, those Americans who are blown up, those Americans who are shot, those Israelis who are murdered" if they vote to send billions of dollars to Iran? In the event, it would be approximately $150 billion directly from Uncle Sam to the ayatollahs, plus more financial succor through loosening of international economic sanctions. For Cruz, tepid applause.

When he called the Obama administration's pact with Iran "an existential threat, and by existential I don't mean a couple of Frenchmen in berets drinking coffee and smoking bad cigarettes," Durns and I were the only ones in the vicinity who laughed.

What *was* that, we asked ourselves after the rally. Not so much about the speakers as about the inverted—to our minds—audience reaction to what they said. Lingering on the Trump- Cruz enthusiasm gap, we decided the rally had been an aberration. We failed to grasp that America's politics, and to no small measure the country itself, had become one big reality TV show, every citizen on camera—in his or her own mind—or at least on cellphone selfie, and the more outré' the uploaded behavior, the higher the ratings.

Who were those men in the jeans and John Deere caps? Part of the middle American throng of forgotten men and forgotten women who would boost the 2016 Republican presidential primaries turnouts by 50 percent, people who disdained a political-cultural establishment—Republican and Democrat—that disdained them. People who in 2020 would cast more votes for President Donald J. Trump, 74 million, than for any other presidential candidate in U.S. history ... except former Vice President Joseph R. Biden, Jr., who that same election collected 81 million. The men in the ball caps that day might well have been bookend harbingers of the reactionary progressives who would flock to Sen. Bernie Sanders (I-Vt., Socialist-Brooklyn) in that year's Democratic primaries and would again in 2020, nearly giving him the nomination, but for the intervention of party elders, both times.

A year and a-half after the anti-Iran deal rally I got a bit part in the national reality TV production. As usual, I was off-camera and anonymous. By then I'd retired from CAMERA and was working part-time for the Jewish Policy Center, a small think tank affiliated with the Republican Jewish Coalition. This was an example of bi-polar bipartisanship, since I'd come to Washington in December, 1980 as a Democrat and press secretary-in-training to Rep.-elect Bob Shamansky (D-Ohio). But as Ronald Reagan, another former Democrat, famously said, "I didn't leave the party; it left me."

Someone from the Trump transition team—the master of glittering generalities having defeated Hillary Clinton, mistress of leaden generalities—had contacted the JPC. The incoming administration wanted our 10 top policy recommendations, and as fast as possible, kept to bullet points on no more than two pages. Transition staffers were making the request of many people and institutions around town.

Suggestions for the president-elect about what to do for the 10 top problems facing the United States, in two pages or less? No problem. Several of us quickly jotted down our thoughts. My draft went like this:

Russia bad. Iran bad. North Korea bad. China very bad. U.S. military too small. National debt too big. Federal government too big. Taxes too high. Social Security, Medicaid and Medicare only for the indigent. Nuclear power plants mandatory in Democratic congressional districts. Success: ten bullet points, barely one page.

For some reason, substitutions for a few of these were made in our final submission. For some reason, the White House never called with a job offer. Probably a lucky break, in retrospect. Never hired, never "You're fired!" Trump had carried his "Apprentice" signature line into the Oval Office, with a vengeance. And, as a conservative-turned-liberal-returned-conservative I began to suspect, per Reagan, that during the Trump years the Republican Party was leaving me too.

Chapter Two:
First Backslash

Cheers for Obama. Who Was That About?

It was May 8, 2008, *Yom Ha'atzmaut*—Israel's Independence Day on the Hebrew calendar. In possession of an invitation from the Israeli Embassy in Washington, D.C., having pre-registered, provided my name, date and place of birth and been vetted by unknown eyes, I joined hundreds of other similarly cleared invitees climbing the steps of the Commerce Department's Mellon Auditorium on Constitution Avenue. In the long foyer we emptied our pockets, passed through the inevitable metal detectors and were scanned by security officers.

On the other side of the detectors lovely young women from the embassy checked us in. There was something about that Mediterranean climate; it even preemptively affected young diaspora Jewish women who, planning to make *aliyah*, worked for the mission. If Sophia Loren in her 20s had been an Israeli, she would have been staffing that registration table.

At last, we could enter the auditorium itself—a large, high-ceilinged, chair-less hall with an over-elevated stage and exasperating acoustics. There we mingled, drank Israeli wine and snacked on hummus and pita, tabbouleh, diced Israeli salad and other *hors d' oeuvres*. Yes, Palestinian Arabs insist Israeli Jews culturally appropriated *their* cuisine, but then they acquired it from the Lebanese, Syrians, et. al. Ultimately, good food belongs to those who eat it. If not, the tomato still would be a barely edible, tiny green thing growing in the Andes Mountains. No ketchup for you!

We caught up with colleagues and contacts we hadn't seen since the previous Yom Ha'atzmaut reception. We met new ones—maybe a military attaché from a post-communist Eastern European country. And we quietly exchanged business cards with a diplomatically agile first secretary from a White House-dependent Arab delegation or two. Washington's transactional sociability at its best.

The American and Israeli national anthems would be sung, the former in English, the latter in Hebrew. An inspirational video highlighting the land, people, religions and accomplishments of Israel would be shown in glorious high-definition successor to widescreen Technicolor. No matter how many times one had made the 11-hour flight from New York's JFK or Newark's Freedom airports to Ben-Gurion outside Tel Aviv, no matter how many times one's luggage arrived two or three days later, the video invariably refreshed one's love affair with Israel. In addition to the ambassador, leading Democratic and Republican members of Congress—always pro-Israel stalwarts—would address the crowd. Often a big name in the current administration would join them. That was the standard, predictable program. But this Thursday night, a rumor buzzed through the hall that a "surprise guest" would make his, or her, appearance. True? And if so, who? Hillary, Barack, Beyoncé? This was a tantalizing departure from the usual.

A little over an hour into the scheduled two-hour event, a beaming Sallai Meridor, the Israeli ambassador and scion of a prominent Herut-Likud Party political family, took the microphone. "Ladies and Gentlemen, please welcome our special guest, Senator Barack Obama!" And then something remarkable happened. A congeries of short, black evening dresses, interspersed with trim, dark suits and ties, rustled to the front of the hall, crowding as close to the stage as possible. It was as if a magnet, suddenly energized, had pulled those 35 years old and younger into one charged mass.

I'd seen this twice before. The first time came on Nov. 22, 1956. Nine years old, I watched from the nose-bleed seats in the cramped old Toledo sports arena as Elvis Presley, making his first national tour, parted the curtains and ecstatic screams erupted; the stampede to the stage would follow. The second came a decade later, on Aug. 14, 1966 in Cleveland's cavernous, 75,000-seat Municipal Stadium [mercifully demolished in 1997], when the Beatles mounted a temporary platform over second base to begin their show. Each time, first for Elvis, then for John, Paul, George and Ringo, thousands of emotionally self-flagellated teen and pre-teen girls hurled themselves toward the objects of their adoration. In Cleveland, four songs into the Beatles' performance, the joyfully distraught females actually overran, lemming-like in their thousands, a line of bulky city policemen. This forced the Fab Four to flee and suspension of the show.

It was a bit more restrained with Obama. A bit. But a similar electricity crackled around the young enthusiasts. If the senator had started singing, sob-like shrieks would have rent the room.

Obama did not need a song. He had them with his appearance, his bearing. He looked, I thought, like a self-made Manchurian Candidate from GQ—*Gentleman's Quarterly*. His suit fit his tall, lean frame perfectly, trim but not tight, the work of a tailor who knew the difference between savvy and showy. When he spoke, the under 35's melted.

No wonder the perpetually befuddled Sen. Joseph Robinette Biden, Jr. (D-Delaware)—miscast presidential hopeful in 1988 and 2008, victor, campaigning from his basement as the moderate anti-Trump, in 2020—had said about Obama in 2007, "I mean, you got the first mainstream African-American who is articulate and bright and clean and a nice-looking guy. I mean, that's a storybook, man." I mean, had Biden been packing all those implicit racial stereotypes, even if reversed, into one revealing sentence, his political career would have been over. I mean, man, as a Republican. As a Democrat, he became Obama's vice-presidential running mate, and eventually would be elected president by a Covid-19 pandemic distraught nation increasingly intent on ripping out its central nervous system and replacing it with Twitter, Facebook, Instagram and their ilk.

The Illinois senator's smile radiated a confident warmth. It was so far from the stretched and frozen, sincerely sanctimonious rictus with which Jimmy Carter unaccountably snared the country—me included—in 1976. Obama's beaming face wordlessly conveyed a message sought with almost religious intensity by so many who believed as an article of their religio-political faith that about the wars in Afghanistan and especially Iraq, "Bush lied and people died!" And the message in its calculated authenticity was: "Yes, I am Barack Obama, the one for which we all have been waiting. We know, you and I—almost as one—that I am a politician.

But more, we know that I am the one who knows all wars must end, who can stop the rise of the oceans, who can reconcile Islam and the (admit it, guilty) West, and provide Affordable Health Care for All. Soon the Nobel Peace Prize committee will surrender its award to me on the basis of … aspirations. If only my benighted when not obstructionist opponents would acknowledge the righteousness of my, which is to say, our, that is, your, desires."

Of course, the senator said nothing at all like that. That was my projection of what the post-adolescents crowding the stage thought they were hearing, at least subliminally. If one had attended a half-a-dozen or more such Yom Ha'atzmaut receptions and listened to a couple dozen senators and representatives, let alone participated in more than 20 annual policy conferences of the American Israel Public Affairs Committee, the big pro-Israel lobby, then one heard Obama utter boilerplate. He favored close U.S.-Israel ties. He referred to shared values, the big democracy and the little democracy. Etc. At least I thought he did, refer to the usual truisms which had the advantage of actually being true, that is.

But nothing new, nothing objectively to support the spell he cast by his mere presence. Obama's effect was like that time Charlton Heston, on his way to an appearance at Ohio State University in the mid-'70s, walked unannounced through Port Columbus International (now John Glenn International, flights to Canada and the Dominican Republic) Airport. I was waiting to interview him for my newspaper, the *Citizen-Journal*, then the Scripps-Howard chain's Columbus morning daily. In sunglasses and a hound's-tooth patterned sport coat, a little shorter than his movie screen height, Heston—without apparent effort and an entourage consisting only of his wife and one assistant—emanated a charisma so tangible it caused the concourse crowd to fall back in awe even before it recognized him.

During the interview, in the ride across town from the airport to Ohio State's Center for Tomorrow—a small hotel-conference venue just west of the Olentangy River—Heston was accommodating. He focused on the session he would lead in the center's cozy auditorium, a showing and subsequent discussion of the 1968 Western *Will Penny*. This was a minor box office film but an effort of which Heston, who starred as an aging, out-of-luck cowboy—was quite proud. As he talked, with a businesslike concentration on film-making and acting, I nearly forgot this was the same man who bestrode movie screens across the country in 1956 as Moses in *The Ten Commandments* and three years later as the lead in *Ben-Hur*, for which he won the Oscar as best actor.

The Obama charisma effect seemed quite similar, at least on those up to a certain age, perhaps up to a certain level of political/celebrity exposure. It reminded me of George Burns' observation: "Sincerity is everything. If you can fake that, you've got it made." No doubt few of the under-35s knew of Burns (nee Nathan Birnbaum) or his 75-year career in vaudeville, radio, television, movies and political science. Too bad.

By crowding the stage, the younger Israeli Independence Day celebrants had opened a rather large space behind them. Toward the back stood a markedly older demographic. Among them, Morris J. Amitay and myself. Speaking of Charlton Heston, there was Morrie Amitay. His career as a junior diplomat, congressional staffer, senior pro-Israel lobbyist and venerable lawyer was flush with incidents. Among them: successfully suing for tens of millions of dollars on behalf of victims of Iranian-funded Palestinian terrorism, backstage diplomacy reaching through Senate leadership into the White House to boost the until-then sluggish U.S. resupply of Israel during the 1973 Yom Kippur War, and one close-call assassination attempt—the bombing of his suburban Maryland home while his children slept in their beds. Now there would have been an entertaining, not to mention illuminating, film. And, like Cruz and Obama, Amitay was yet another Harvard Law alum. A former AIPAC executive director, still head of an important pro-Israel political action committee, Morrie was fuming.

"How could Meridor host Obama but not Hillary [Clinton] and McCain? Congressional support for Israel needs to be bi-partisan and appear bi-partisan! Sallai knows that ...." At the time, former first lady and senator Hillary Clinton and Obama still were fighting for the Democratic Party's 2008 presidential nomination and Sen. John McCain (Ariz.) seemed likely to win the Republican nod. Morrie said the embassy would hear from him. "If they say scheduling problems kept Hillary and

McCain away [that would prove to be the excuse] then they shouldn't have invited Obama."

But that night, the absence of Clinton and McCain seemed to pass largely unnoticed. One left feeling that had either or both materialized, their presence would have registered as an annoyance at best. Such was Obama's star power among the younger pro-Israel crowd (and, as it would prove, among many in the older cohort as well). That encompassing glow, coupled with the implicit promise of a bi-racial president leading a post-racial America, meant Obama's grip on Jewish voters would survive his long relationship with the anti-Jewish, anti-white, anti-American Rev. Jeremiah Wright and his intent, announced early in his administration, to put "daylight between the United States and Israel" and eight years of policies generally doing just that.

Meridor's successor as Israeli ambassador, historian Michael B. Oren, would experience first-hand and document President Obama's abiding animosity—Senator Obama's 2008 boilerplate notwithstanding—to the Jewish state and its uncooperative prime minister, Benjamin Netanyahu. Denial in the face of the otherwise cognitively dissonant was a diaspora Jewish specialty. Hence, for example, the multi-generational adoration of Franklin D. Roosevelt, who did next to nothing to rescue European Jewry during the Holocaust or even attempt to mitigate the Nazi genocide.

Oren's book *Ally: My Journey Across the American Israeli Divide* (Random House, 2015), would become a best-seller, though not very influential among U.S. Jewry. When Obama flashed that smile, American Jewish voters—78 percent in 2008—imagined they basked in its reflected light. Then came four years of unfounded outreach to Iran, siding in "the Arab Spring" against Egyptian President Hosni Mubarak and so creating an opening for the Muslim Brotherhood, allowing his own red line to be violated with impunity in Syria and "leading from behind" in Libya. These all contributed to a Middle East in flames, hundreds of thousands dead, millions of refugees and Israel apparently isolated. Never mind. Such was the electricity Obama sparked at that 2008 Yom Ha'atzmaut celebration and among Jewish voters in general that in 2012 the community's electoral cognitive dissonance emerged barely dented. According to exit polls that year, he still received 72 percent of the Jewish vote.

" 'And now, Sherman,' said Mr. Peabody again, 'this time let us step into the Nearly All the Way Back Machine …'"

Chapter Three:
It All Started with Vietnam

Wallace, Nixon; One Grenade, One Molotov Cocktail

For the Baby Boomer multitude and the legacy and burden, tangibles and intangibles, it lays on its successors—the Generation X'ers, the Millennials and the other pop-sociology cohorts—remember, it all started with Vietnam. Even when it didn't.

One example among many: Long before Trump, prior to Obama, ahead of a close encounter with Richard Nixon, a presidential candidate ran over me. Political stage scenery included war and race riots then as now. The candidate represented a not-insignificant part of the electorate. He possessed a political tuning fork that vibrated advantageously to both frequencies, pro and con, on the war in Indochina. George Corley Wallace, Jr., governor of Alabama, would win 10 million votes, amounting to 13.5 percent of the total, five southern states and 46 electoral votes as the 1968 presidential nominee of his segregationist American Independent Party. He also would teach a journalism student a thing or two about press conferences held by experienced politicians. The summer of 1967, between my college sophomore and junior years, I interned for the Findlay, Ohio *Republican-Courier*. At 19, I drew my first paycheck as a professional journalist, $85 a week (said to be worth more than $600 in 2020 purchasing power, but in my pocket then about like $85 today).

The Republican-Courier (later simply *The Courier*) was a rare small-town morning newspaper, so I worked the 5 p.m. to 1 a.m. shift. This meant, among other things, that I made the return trip from Findlay to Tiffin on straight, flat, semi-trailer crowded U.S. 224 in no more than 30 minutes. I once hit 110 m.p.h. in my turbo-charged Corvair Spyder convertible, just for fun. Assuming the rear-engine Corvair didn't hydroplane on wet pavement or jerk in sidewinds, which it was prone to do (hence Ralph Nader's best-seller, *Unsafe at Any Speed*) I could get home in time to watch the last half-hour of *The Untouchables* reruns. "All right, Nitti! Drop that Tommy gun! Up against the wall!" I *was* 19.

Findlay, then about 25,000 population (now more than 40,000), was one of only two Ohio towns, Marietta on the Ohio River being the other, to vote for Republican presidential candidate Barry Goldwater in 1964. It was home to Marathon Oil Co, then a major producer and distributor, with fields in the United States, Libya and elsewhere. Subsequent mergers and divestitures would see Marathon relocate to its eponymous tower in Houston but leave its refining subsidiary, Marathon Petroleum, in Findlay. The business had started as the Ohio Oil Co. in the late 1800s as part of the petroleum industry's Pennsylvania-Ohio first wave. Hence the Quaker State Oil brand today. In the cornfield behind my parents' home, a short stripper well still pumped occasionally, a tarry, creosote-scented reminder of that long-ago boom, an upsurge of wealth partly responsible for the great old houses lining Main Street south of downtown in Findlay.

The summer of 1967 was the season of the geo-politically seismic Arab-Israeli Six-Day War and in the United States of "the long, hot summer" of race riots in more than 100 cities. Destructively prominent were conflicts in Newark, N.J., and the five-day upheaval in Detroit in which 43 died and more than 300 were wounded. The Motown riots had a minor echo in nearby Toledo.

In short, Findlay that summer was a good time and place for a Wallace campaign stop. During his 1968 run, for example, Wallace's campaign literature would label the 1965 Voting Rights Act "one of the most tragic, most discriminatory pieces of legislation ever enacted" and promise that as president the Alabaman would work for its repeal. The governor denounced the Democratic and Republican parties as mirror-images run by politicians who didn't care about the working man. Wallace simultaneously belittled anti-Vietnam War protesters as sandal-wearing hippies, practically inviting them to end their long-haired woes by lying in front of his limousine, and attracted voters opposed to U.S. involvement in the conflict.

The man who famously stood on the steps of his state's capitol in Montgomery vowing "segregation forever!" flew into Marathon's capacious airport on the west side of town on June 21. His plane might have been an old DC-3. (In 2018, a 50-year *USA Today* retrospective of Wallace's 1968 run said the campaign aircraft possessed "a tendency to stall on landings and take-offs.") Obsolete or not, it deposited him safely onto the tarmac. Just out from under the wings the man often described as a pugnacious bantam stood, jaw and chest characteristically outthrust, to face the press.

Gathered in a tight scrum were camera crews from Toledo television stations, reporters from *The Toledo Blade,* news services, local radio and for some reason, me. Why *The Republican-Courier* dispatched its greenest, most temporary staffer to cover a de facto presidential candidate I never learned. As intern, my regular beat included picking up admissions, births and discharge notices from local hospitals, funeral home death announcements—hence my first glimpse of a dead body—and reporting on the endless chain of summer "homecomings" in the villages scattered across Hancock County outside Findlay. At one I actually witnessed a Stanley Steamer (see: Stanley Motor Carriage Co., 1902 – 1924) puffing through town.

But there I was at Wallace's press conference, determined to ask him a question. No, determined to put a man I regarded as an intolerable bigot on the hotseat. This quickly proved beyond my meager journalistic prowess.

"Governor!" I shouted, along with other newshounds baying for recognition. He turned his head slightly left of the microphones to look directly at me. In unison with his, the heads of three or four uniformed Alabama state troopers—each wearing mirrored sunglasses like those favored by the guards in actor Paul Newman's prison feature *Cool Hand Luke*—also turned. Now they too stared right at me. Or so I felt, it being impossible to tell what was happening behind the silvered reflectors.

"On what constitutional grounds do you oppose federal school desegregation orders?" There, I had him. Or so I imagined, for about a second.

"Young man," Wallace drawled, leaving a space long enough between "young" and "man" to make clear he really meant "sonny boy," "the Constitution doesn't say a thing about education. That's a local and state matter." The governor then proceeded to administer me—and voters who might be reached via the assembled press—a tutorial about the dangers of Washington's overreach to Americans' hard-earned freedoms. Did I think the people of Alabama were any less able to run their own schools than the good people of Ohio? By the time I could reformulate my "not exactly" into a decent follow-up question, the governor was replying to someone else and I, though still standing, had been deflated like a blow-up giant pumpkin the day after Halloween.

Wallace then headed to a rally in McComb, about 10 miles from Findlay. McComb, a village of approximately 1,200 people then, seemed a most unlikely place for a national campaign rally. Yet Wallace drew a crowd of approximately 5,000, which according to *The Lima News* (to natives, Lie'-mah, not Lee'-muh like that place in Peru), interrupted his 42-minute speech with applause 20 times.

The Alabaman campaigned in 1968 under the slogan "Stand Up for America." He used sometimes raucous rallies to garner plenty of free press coverage. Some opponents called him "George Hitler, the Smiling Bigot," but Wallace managed to reach 21 percent popular support in one Gallup poll before his vice presidential running mate, Gen. Curtis LeMay (USAF, Ret.), started musing publicly about the advantages of waging nuclear war on Ho Chi Minh and the North Vietnamese.

Donald Trump's 2016 election as president recalled for some commentators Wallace's effort 48 years earlier. They heard Trump's slogan, "Make America Great Again," as an update of Wallace's "Stand Up for America." They noticed Trump's rallies—usually bigger and more enthusiastic than Democratic candidate Hillary Clinton's. After the latter's shocking loss, shocking to the news media's self-referential cadres, these scriveners recognized similarities between the populist resentment of Washington's dominant liberal elite that ignited Wallace supporters and the angry abandonment felt by Trump backers. These were the voters— Jefferson's sturdy yeomanry among them—disdained by Clinton and her bi-coastal *cognoscenti* as "deplorables," soon to be anathematized as "racists," the all-purpose, secular fundamentalist malediction replacing "anti-Christ!"

But the context for Wallace and Trump, seen both in the 2016 and 2020 Democratic presidential primary campaigns of Sen. Bernie Sanders and the mid-century demagoguery of Sen. Joseph McCarthy (R-Wis.), was laid out by Richard Hofstadter in his famous 1964 *Harper's* magazine essay, "The paranoid style in American politics." Observing the leverage a minority of right-wing extremists derived from Sen. Barry Goldwater's (R-Ariz.) presidential race that year, Hofstadter, a Columbia University professor of American history, wrote:

"I believe there is a style of mind that is far from new and that is not necessarily right-wing. I call it the paranoid style simply because no other word adequately evokes the sense of heated exaggeration, suspiciousness, and conspiratorial fantasy that I have in mind. In using the expression 'paranoid style' I am not speaking in a clinical sense, but borrowing a clinical term for other purposes. ... [T]he idea of the paranoid style as a force in politics would have little contemporary relevance or historical value if it were applied only to men with profoundly disturbed minds. It is the use of paranoid modes of expression by more or less normal people that makes the phenomenon significant.

"Of course this term is pejorative, and it is meant to be; the paranoid style has a greater affinity for bad causes than good. But nothing really prevents a sound program or demand from being advocated in the paranoid style. Style has more to do with the way in which ideas are believed than with the truth or falsity of their content. I am interested here in getting at our political psychology through our political rhetoric. The paranoid style is an old and recurrent phenomenon in our public life which has been frequently linked with movements of suspicious discontent."

Recurrent movements of suspicious discontent, indeed. Influential in the 1960s and early '70s, prominent on the left and right in 2016, they dominated in the months after the police killing of George Floyd in Minneapolis in May, 2020. The resultant demonstrations, riots and removals of not only Confederate statues but also those of Washington, Lincoln, Grant, Theodore Roosevelt and Christopher Columbus exposed a feckless political class bowing to movements of suspicious discontent, movements including not just men in overalls and John Deere caps but also the over-schooled, under-learned woke generation. For the latter, the politics of self-righteousness was their secular fundamentalist substitute religion. Therefore, no sense arguing with them about it; their minds were not only made up but also sanctified. The proper role for dissenters was sacrificial.

Richard Nixon, from Scorn to Pity

Former Vice President Richard M. Nixon was campaigning for the Republican presidential nomination in 1968 with a promise to end the Vietnam War. *The Sandusky Register*, for which I was a 20-year-old intern the summer after my encounter with Gov. Wallace, sent me to cover Nixon's campaign stop in Cleveland. Since the Erie County Commissioners' weren't meeting that day and there'd been no fatal car crashes yet, no runaway stagecoach rides (it happened that summer, injuries but no fatalities) at Cedar Point Amusement Park—Roller Coaster Capital of the World—I was free. Nixon's itinerary included a noon-time address in Public Square in front of the Terminal Tower, which dominated the city's skyline before Cleveland's post-1990 revival. Prior to his speech Nixon held a press conference in a nearby hotel.

I took my seat, along with a handful of actual, post-college reporters, in a small meeting room and waited for Nixon to enter. I realized with a start I was sitting next to Herbert Kaplow, a veteran NBC and later ABC TV News correspondent. When he was 22, Kaplow began his journalism career by reporting on the Nuremberg War Crimes trials. I didn't know that at the time, but the thickly-browed, serious faced and deep-voiced Kaplow was such a presence I thought about changing my seat. Then Nixon walked in.

My visceral dislike of the man had taken root about the time of my bar mitzvah in 1960, when he had the audacity to challenge John F. Kennedy for the White House. When I heard a radio news cut of the former vice president declaring to the press, after his 1962 loss to Pat Brown in the California governor's race, "you won't have Nixon to kick around anymore," my adolescent mind believed it and my heart felt relief. Yet here he was, six years later, standing at a podium eight or 10 feet away, again seeking the presidency. And within 30 minutes, visceral dislike turned, if not to sympathy, then pity.

Nixon answered the questions put to him; he'd been through this kind of thing countless times as representative, senator and vice president. But then why was he so nervous? He shifted frequently from one foot to the other. His hands clenched and unclenched the sides of the podium. Sweat stood out on his upper lip and his forehead. The five o'clock shadow, with which editorial cartoonists took such delight, seemed to darken visibly along his jaw. In the next 50 years I would not see a public man or woman so visibly uncomfortable in his or her own skin. Why, no matter how qualified he might have felt himself to be in experience, study and interest, did Nixon put himself through such personal torture?

Whatever the reason, it would not matter. Republicans were wary of New York Gov. Nelson Rockefeller—not only an East Coast moderate but one who'd divorced and remarried!—who challenged Nixon in the primaries. Democrats at their Chicago convention that summer had their own problems. There were reasons to feel uneasy with likely nominee Hubert H. Humphrey. A former senator from Minnesota, Humphrey was Lyndon Johnson's vice president and thereby tainted. He bore the stigmata of Vietnam, urban riots, the assassinations of Martin Luther King, Jr. and Robert F. Kennedy and the challenge by Wallace—though the Alabaman would draw votes from both Humphrey and Nixon. Ominously, youth protesters and berserk police rioted outside the Democratic convention that summer. The fates against Humphrey, it would be Richard Milhous Nixon who took the presidential oath in January.

Among other things, Nixon announced his plan to "Vietnamize" the conflict, drawing down America's approximately 550,000 troops in Indochina and replacing them with South Vietnamese soldiers. This seemed to ignore the fact that Saigon (capital of South Vietnam and the name of Ho Chi Minh City before the American retreat) already fielded more than 850,000 troops from a population of less than 20 million and its forces had suffered many times more casualties than the Americans. Politics and policy regardless, fighting raged with GIs battling North Vietnamese regulars and the post-Tet Offensive remnants of the South's Viet Cong when I reported for basic training at Ft. Jackson, South Carolina, early in 1970.

I had not been drafted and certainly had not enlisted. I was more fortunate, less brave and less resigned. Immediately upon graduating from Ohio University and losing my 2-S student draft deferment, I inscribed my name on waiting lists at several National Guard and Army Reserve units. County draft boards still sent eligible young men notices, but virtually no Guard or Reserve companies were being activated for overseas duty.

Not that I opposed the war. While in high school, I'd argued with my friend Ron Zartman's father: The mighty United States could defeat a third-rate country like North Vietnam in short order; we only had to decide that's what we wanted to do. He, a Korean War veteran, scoffed. "It would take half-a-million men," he stated, dismissing my teenaged certainty.

It was 1964. There were 23,000 Americans in South Vietnam. Two hundred and sixteen had been killed that year; South Vietnamese forces had lost 7,500. Mr. Zartman exaggerated wildly, I was sure. Besides, I suspected Americans would not tolerate sending 500,000 troops. We'd have to win well before that. "Bomb them back to the Stone Age," the saying went, if Ho Chi Minh and his communists didn't wise up, give in and accept LBJ's offer to electrify the Mekong River Valley with a southeast Asian New Deal-like version of the Tennessee Valley Authority. Talk about the pit-falls of mirror-imaging.

A year later, as a college freshman, I confidently predicted victory to some classmates. "LBJ [President Lyndon B. Johnson] will never allow the fighting to be a campaign issue in the 1966 congressional elections." That the United States would permit communists—successors to the Nazis in totalitarian evil—to triumph was inconceivable. At least to me. Yet by the end of '66, the United States had deployed 200,000 GIs to South Vietnam. More than 3,300 died that year.

"Domino theory" and "blood-bath" warnings ultimately would prove true in defeat. Laos and Cambodia fell along with South Vietnam. The Cambodian Khmer Rouge's auto-genocide murdered 1.5 million or more of the country's seven million people; hundreds of thousands of South Vietnamese, many fleeing "boat people" among them, also would perish. But President Johnson never had a strategy for victory he could articulate to the American public, not even with Mr. Zartman's half-million American troops in Indochina.

By the time Nixon defeated Humphrey, none of my male friends or I wanted to chance being the last Americans to die in a war supposedly in the process of being "Vietnamized." So, when the Seneca County draft board notified me to report for my pre-induction physical in September, 1969 I saw the last grains of sands in my personal hour-glass slipping away. The notice read, "You shall report to the Army induction physical station high in Erieview Plaza in downtown Cleveland. You will then march in your underwear, along with scores of other likely draftees, from examining doctor to examining doctor, in full view of office workers in adjacent towers, and be approved as 1-A, fit for combat despite your bad ear and near-sightedness. Your country's reached the point at which it needs even you, boy." That's not exactly what it said, but it should have.

A few days later, Capt. Donald Cook, commander of the 223rd Tire Repair Company, 83rd ARCOM (U.S. Army Reserve Command), Fremont, Ohio—my parents' occasional bridge partner—let my father and mother know there were several openings in his unit and my name had risen to the top of the list. On Oct. 4, 1969 at Camp Perry—home since 1907 to the National Pistol and Rifle Championships—on Lake Erie, I took the oath to uphold the Constitution and defend the United States of America. God, so help me. For the next six years I would be a reservist. I had traded two years of active duty and almost certain deployment to Vietnam as a draftee for nine weeks of basic training, nine weeks of AIT (advanced individual training, which would turn out to be changing tires in the motor pool at Ft. Rucker, Alabama), and five and-a-half more years with two weeks of annual camp, and monthly weekend or one-night-a-week drills. My hour-glass had been refilled.

The 223rd was one of two tire repair companies in the entire U.S. military. One was active duty, one—Capt. Cook's—reserve. We had a full complement of mobile tire repair equipment. In theory, the 223rd could arrive on the battlefield, during or just after fighting, section and repair damaged jeep and truck tires, tank and half-track treads, vulcanizing as necessary, and get those caissons rolling again, just like in the official U.S. Army song. In theory.

In practice, we exercised our deuce and a-half trucks (2 ½ ton, stiff clutch, stiffer manual shift brutes) by driving around Sandusky County. In my two years with the 223rd, before being transferred to 83rd ARCOM headquarters in Columbus, I never saw anyone in the company open the trailers and actually use our tire repair equipment. My MOS, military occupational specialty, confirmed by the Ft. Rucker motor pool, was 57-C-20, tire repairman. That meant, in military fashion, that I worked as a de facto clerk-typist.

I'd been lucky, as I had been in 1962. Then late for summer school touch-typing class—Mom, a secretarial school alumna, had farsightedly insisted—I skidded my Sears' MoPed through a red light in front of an oncoming truck. The brick pavement near Napoleon Senior High was wet, the momentum-powered truck piled high with tomatoes headed for the nearby Campbell Soup plant. The truck's horn blared, my heart leaped into my throat and…downshifting from second to first (the only two gears) and braking, I slid past its on-coming front bumper, somehow keeping the MoPed more or less vertical.

Lucky, as I would be in March, 1973. After a late-winter snow storm, heading back to Columbus following a surprise birthday party for my father in Tiffin, to which we'd returned, I skidded my insurance auction '71 Buick Skylark Grand Sport—350-cubic inch V-8 engine, four-barrel carburetor, resonating dual exhausts and factory chrome wheels, 11.5 miles per gallon—off U.S. 23 north of Marion, Ohio. The four-lane, divided highway had been cleared and I was passing a slower-moving car to the right. Suddenly, the plowed portion narrowed to one lane and, instead of pavement, the Buick now was riding on hard-packed snow. And then it started sliding, left and right, gently at first but quickly with greater force. Foot off the accelerator, doing about 50 miles per hour, I fought the steering wheel.

I had a choice: The car alongside was smaller than my hefty Buick. I could try to steer back toward the single cleared lane, probably striking the other car side-on-side, superior momentum in my favor. In the paradoxical slow-motion of adrenaline-fueled crisis, my life, or at least part of what there had been of it, did flash before my eyes. It was a surprising quick-clip parade of familiar faces. Nostalgic, as if they were saying goodbye.

I was steering left, not right, and off the highway toward the median. So, this is how I am going to die, I thought with a calm, probably shock-like, clarity. Then the big machine settled softly into a deep, snow-filled ditch, like a baby into a thick blanket. Uninjured, I stared at the steering wheel, almost laughing in nervous relief, my heart—the crisis over—starting to pound. I rolled down the driver's side window, crawled out into the snow and stumbled up the ditch to the highway. Eventually— after half-a-dozen passing cars ignored my scarecrow-like flapping—I waved down a tow truck. The Benzedrine-fueled driver, with straggling hair and red eyes, the plastic No-Doz vial on his dashboard nearly empty, smiled.

"Climb in. I'll hook you up. Been towin' for nearly 20 hours. Never made so much money!"

I didn't think much about my draft-dodging good fortune until early in the 1980s. In Washington, D.C. I had become friends with a Vietnam War veteran who then worked at the American Legion headquarters. He'd been lucky, too, more consequentially. When asked, he told a few stories about his infantryman experiences, about the buddy who survived grievous wounds, about another who, though lightly injured, died. "Maybe from fright, or lack of will." I understood that others suffered, and some died, in my place. Also, that I could not, honestly, claim moral standing because I had not fought in a futile, or foolish, let alone "imperialist" war. I still thought we should have fought, just smarter. Provide air cover for a massive South Vietnamese invasion of the North. Why play on only our half of the field? But for pure, stupid luck, there was that one live grenade in basic training.

It was late February, 1970, President Nixon was still "Vietnamizing" and more than a year away from the Cambodian incursion, and we, the 160 members of Ft. Jackson's basic training company D-9-2 (Company D, 9th Battalion, Second Brigade) were nearing the end of our cycle. The reservists and national guardsmen in the outfit, who did not have Vietnam ahead of us, felt increasingly if egocentrically light-hearted. One of our last hurdles was the grenade throw.

It turned out I had to unlearn everything I knew about tossing grenades. I had studied the subject thoroughly as a child in the 1950s. Who hadn't watched as John Wayne yanked the pin from a pineapple-shaped, mustard jar-sized grenade—maybe with teeth clamped onto the pin as he fired his M-1 carbine with a single hand—and with his free palm lobbed the little bomb over a wall and into the Jap machinegun nest? Or Nazi bunker? Or Red Chinese trench? I certainly had, repeatedly.

Seen and imitated in the field between our house and the Maumee River in Napoleon, after spring plowing but before the crop—in soil-saving rotation of soybeans, corn and wheat—was up. Twice we found arrowheads, left by Stone Age people who'd preceded the first French and then more numerous German settlers a century and a-half earlier. With friends I reenacted what we'd seen in *The Sands of Iwo Jima* and countless other Hollywood sagas. Clods of dried dirt made perfect grenade substitutes. We gathered a couple at a time, ran at the enemy, stopped and, in Wayne-like pose, leaned back and stiff-armed a clod in a slow, lazy arc aimed at the feet of another combatant who, a few rows away, similarly fired at us. The clods would hit the ground and burst into satisfying little puffs of dust.

Two days of drills with dummy, World War II-style pineapple grenades preceded the real thing. We were informed that our M-67 fragmentation grenades did not look anything like the antique, square-shrapnel practice pineapples. Instead, I was disappointed to learn, the M-67 resembled a baseball-sized round can, with a pin holding the fuse lever in place. Once the pin was pulled and the grenade thrown, lever releasing with the toss, one would have four seconds to take cover before serrated razor-wire coiled about the explosive core blasted a five-meter killing radius.

During drills our sergeant-instructors repeatedly bellowed, "Do not 'John Wayne' it! Do not lob your grenade! Twist and pull pin. Then throw like football. Got it?" Not "like a football" but "like football." No article necessary. "Got it?!"

"Yes, sergeant."

"I said, 'Got it?!'"

"Yes, sergeant!"

This routine proved effective with the other 159 members of Company D-9-2. Of course, the drills made no lasting impression on someone imprinted with heroic images of World War II as conveyed by Republic Pictures, Warner Brothers and the other movie studios and who therefore had lobbed dirt clods along the Maumee River. Which is to say, two days of grenade practice made no impression on me.

The morning of the live grenade toss dawned damp and chilly. We marched from our company area, which still featured World War II-era two-story, wooden, fire-trap barracks, through Ft. Jackson's plentiful southern pines to the grenade range. A watch tower from which several officers observed the proceedings dominated the site. A sawdust-covered pit flanked by long wooden walls and fronted with a high, earthen barrier lay in front of the tower. Near the bottom of the pit were two grenade sumps, long pipes cut diagonally into the ground. Should a trainee drop his grenade, a safety officer had two or three seconds to shovel it barehanded into a sump before the inevitable blast.

At the range we were ordered to stand single-file outside a gate of sorts under the tower. A mist-like rain continued to settle on our inexplicably non-water repellant field jackets. One at a time, trainees were called through the gate into the pit. One at a time, the rest of us in line not only heard but also felt the powerful concussion as a grenade exploded on the other side of the earthen barrier.

"Rozenman!"

I started. Once again, as in first grade arithmetic, 10th grade Latin, or that hide-'n-seek game with Kathy M.'s younger sister, Suzie, my mind was elsewhere.

"Rozenman!!" I donned the heavy flak vest someone handed me and darted through the gate. In the pit, which gently sloped like a wide funnel toward its center, I found the two range safety officers. They were both young sergeants in steel pot helmets and flak vests. I remember thinking even then, "How much extra hazardous duty pay must these guys get?"

The routine was to hurry each trainee through his one live toss. This was to ensure he acted on instinct, on what had been borne home in the previous days' drills. Not to think was not to hesitate. Not to hesitate was not to err. At least, that was the theory, and it worked, most of the time.

One of the sergeants handed me a little cardboard cylinder. "Got it?!" he screamed.

"Got it!" Not that I was confident I had the thing. In fact, in the chilly mist it felt a little slippery. But I understood I wasn't supposed to mention that. Still, did he have to shout?

"Lift the lid!"

There's a lid? Somehow, I'd missed that memo. Fumbling a bit, I pried off the top of the cannister and removed the grenade.

"Got it?!"

"Yes." One of those times when "yes" meant "I have no idea." I held the grenade, this dull, metal ball of death, in my right hand, a hand big enough to throw a fastball, but not a split-fingered fastball. The grenade seemed split-fingered size.

"Twist and pull pin!"

With my left hand, I did. The pin slipped out effortlessly. My right hand still hugged the fuse handle to the body of the grenade.

"Now throw like football!"

And with all those long-ago years of training stored deep in my little hippocampus in unknowing anticipation of this moment, I leaned back and, in my best John Wayne imitation, lobbed the thing toward the earthen wall and the Jap machinegun nest dug in just on the other side.

Both range safety officers leaped on me, the three of us landing, in our helmets and flak jackets, at the bottom of the pit. "Ka-boom!!" The grenade, barely clearing the dirt mound, blasted itself to lethal bits a few yards away. The concussion tore the air almost before I heard the explosion. The atmosphere rushed back together, two invisible but felt shock waves smacking each other even before the sound of the blast, and my body seemed to shake from the inside out.

Then, silence, for a second. Followed by the long blare of a klaxon. "Cease all training! Cease all training. Rozenman! Report to the tower, immediately!"

I raced up the two or three flights of steps to the top of the tower. There I found a handful of regular Army personnel, sergeants, lieutenants and a captain, waiting for me. Have you ever been chewed out and deserved it? Chewed out thoroughly, up one side and down the other, by more than one person, more than one authority figure, for something you'd just done completely and dangerously wrong, and knew right then you deserved what you were getting? And not been particularly bothered?

That was my experience in the tower. Because the more they berated me, the longer it went on, the more I began to suspect they were releasing steam, more relieved I hadn't killed the safety officers than incensed at my bungling, demonstrating to the company standing silently in file below just how grave a matter my failure had been. The more they shouted, the more I realized I was not going to be punished further. I understood that, most importantly, I would not hear the dreaded verdict, "Recycle," which would have meant that—like a high school delinquent who'd flunked sophomore year—I'd have to repeat basic training.

Finally, they dismissed me. Back on the ground, I heard fellow trainees mutter "Good job, you screw-up," and other less complimentary remarks. Some just stared, as if they'd never seen such a sorry imitation of a soldier. But as we marched back to company area, I felt relieved, even happy. Basic training was almost over, and I knew absolutely no one ever was going to give me another live grenade. It could not have crossed my mind that far in the future on a bright summer day in the Gaza Strip I would be handed a Molotov cocktail.

But long before that, in fact in the coming few weeks, we would observe Hell Night in Transient Company, revise the Army alphabet, and feel a tremor called the Kent State University shootings.

Chapter Four:
Back in the Real World, So to Speak

Apology, Request, and Death on Campus

In March, 1970 those in charge at Ft. Rucker, Alabama—the U.S. Army's sprawling helicopter training installation—did not trouble themselves much about reservists and guardsmen passing through before being returned to their home units. They had bigger problems to avoid. Those of us who'd arrived after a bus journey from Ft. Jackson through South Carolina, across Georgia and down into southeast Alabama's "Wiregrass Country" were lodged in Transient Company's barracks. The building was home to those ready for deployment overseas, short-timers about to be discharged, other regular army enlisted men between assignments and those pending court martial on charges serious enough for trial but not for confinement in the guardhouse. And wayfaring reservists and guardsmen.

Ft. Rucker housing was decades ahead of Ft. Jackson's rickety basic training barracks. In one of the latter the first night, while we were still in reception station, the ancient furnace had shuddered to a halt and the indoor temperature quickly plummeted to match that outside on an early January night, somewhere around 40 degrees Fahrenheit. We emptied our newly-issued duffle bags, including four sets of fatigue shirts and pants, field jackets, underwear and socks onto our bunks and burrowed under, trainees trying to get warm beneath heaps of olive drab.

At Ft. Rucker, the barracks were two-story, red brick, with fluorescent lights along the hallways, each room a bay with a window and four single beds—not bunks—and double-doored vertical metal lockers instead of hardened cardboard footlockers. The buildings could have passed for dormitories at an overcrowded state university. But the population in Transient Company that spring by no means resembled a dorm full of undergraduates.

Reeling from the sudden onset of food poisoning or intestinal flu one night, I made repeated trips from my bed, down the first-floor hall to the latrine, and back again. On the third or fourth cramp-induced journey, I had to step past two black troops standing in the corridor. Odd that they should be there after lights out, I thought. More peculiar was that they lived on the second floor, not the first. I didn't know their names but recognized them. The first was very tall, wiry, with an almost purplish-black complexion, dangling arms and a strangely-shaped, pinched face marked by deep-set, even beady eyes. I would have said he was ugly-looking, but my parents had made it clear in no uncertain terms, years earlier, that I was never to call anyone ugly. One took note of facts, but did not always need to shout them. The second soldier was shorter, of average build and a milk chocolate complexion.

I was wearing briefs and a T-shirt. Like much else about the Army, aesthetically speaking, I hated the olive-drab boxer shorts we'd been issued in reception station at Ft. Jackson. Go into battle in boxer shorts? Unsupported combat? Seriously?

As I hurried by I heard the tall one say, "Nice ass." Intent on getting to the toilet, I didn't register his remark.

A couple minutes later, once more wiping myself, I saw that strange, ugly face, beady eyes seeming to glow red, looming high over the stall door. Looking down at me from his impossible elevation, he snarled, "Don't say a word!"

Ft. Rucker in those days, perhaps like the rest of the frayed, unpopular, draftee-filled U.S. Army in its Vietnam-bred miasma, seemed fraught with racial, that is, black-white, tension. We'd no sooner arrived than we heard the story, passed among the lower ranks, of another nearby barracks in which the black soldiers recently had thrown out their white compatriots' belongings and declared the building "for blacks only." More officially, we'd been cautioned by our sergeants to avoid crossing the big, open area near the base bowling alley and PX by ourselves on pay-day weekends, especially at night. Apparently, there'd been some robberies; we automatically assumed a racial aspect.

Assumptions aside, one afternoon after working in the motor pool, I'd gone upstairs in the Transient Company looking for an acquaintance. I asked a couple of black soldiers if they'd seen him. "Is he a cracker, like you?" one said. Seeing my blank stare—a cracker? I'd grown up in semi-rural Ohio, and a cracker was something one crumbled into one's tomato soup—the other said, "You know, a pig. A white pig."

So, I wasn't completely surprised that the pinched face on top of the elongated neck was glaring down at me. But when he reached a long arm over the stall door to unlock it, I leaned forward, still on the stool, and relocked it. "Why don't you talk to me?!" he growled.

"You just said not to talk to you."

Oops, mistake. Trying to reason with the unreasonable.

"I told you don't say a word! Now, talk to me!"

This was getting annoying. I was frightened but also really put off. My guts temporarily quiet, all I wanted to do was crawl back into bed and try to get an hour or two of sleep. By now I also was dehydrated and feeling shaky. Who the hell was he to be standing there, in my way? I was frightened and angry. A thought, which never had occurred to me before in my entire life, entered my mind with cold clarity: if I had a gun, I'd shoot him. Such was the seamless, two-headed emotion called humiliation-revenge.

Once more the long arm came down and unlocked the stall door. Again, I slid the ineffectual little bolt back into place. He rattled the door, snarled something I couldn't make out, and then his friend had his arms around the taller man. "C'mon, let's get out of here," he said, dragging the first away. They were gone, but Hell Night in Transient Company was just getting started.

No sooner had I pulled the blankets up to my shoulders—it was April in Alabama but now as the diarrhea tapered off I had chills—when the man in the bed opposite mine rolled off his mattress onto the floor. He'd been tossing and turning, muttering. He also reeked of liquor. Too drunk to break his fall, he hit the floor tiles hard.

"Fuck!" he shouted.

"Shut the fuck up!" snapped one of our other two roommates on the other side of the bay.

I jammed the pillow across my eyes and ears and tried to sleep. But a minute or two later the drunk sat down hard on my bed. This furtive country boy, a hillbilly greaser who looked a few years older than the usual draftee and managed to wear his slick dark hair as long as he could get away with, was a new addition to our bay. He was awaiting a court-martial on a statutory rape charge. Worse, he was an enlisted man and she an officer's daughter.

In the meantime, he tried to slide his hand under my blankets and squirm in with me. Weak as I felt, I swung my right arm against the side of his rib cage and over he went, again. This time he got his hands under the rest of his body, but he still hit the floor hard.

"Fuck!" he swore.

"Shut up, I told you!" came the voice from the other side of the room.

I watched as the drunk crawled around the floor, picked himself up and fell back into his own bed. Soon he was snoring, loudly and regularly. And I thought with certainty, if I had that gun, I'd shoot him too. Maybe only in the leg, though. Thus comforted, I finally fell asleep.

The next day I felt nearly normal. Whatever illnesses I'd experienced—physical and atmospheric—seemed to have passed. Near the main entrance to the Transient Co. barrack, the tall black soldier's friend stopped me. "About last night," he said, "he wanted me to tell you he's sorry. He was stoned, you know?"

Like so many others in those days. Like that was ever an excuse.

A week or two later, I unaccountably had a free hour in the middle of a workday. So, I was sitting in the day room, a sort of combination study hall/arts-and-crafts lounge, reading. In the midst of its sprawling territory, which included a trimmed 18-hole golf course for officers and a hardpan nine-hole adventure for the enlisted, each of which I'd managed to play once—"Don't hunt for balls in the rough, there's cotton-mouths"—Ft. Rucker offered a library, housed in a tiny cottage, for enlisted men. Women too, I suppose, but there were only a few women on active duty in non-commissioned ranks then. So few as to make virtually no difference, especially not to short-time reservists and guardsmen.

At the library I had checked out, permanently as it would eventuate, a few books. Among them were Sherwood Anderson's *Winesburg, Ohio*, with its cast of small-town grotesqueries who would have been quite at home in Transient Company and anthropologist Lionel Tiger's *Men in Groups*. The Joint Chiefs probably should have been reading the latter and perhaps did when developing the more successful, racially integrated all-volunteer service that would roll over Saddam Hussein's reputed million-man army in Kuwait and Iraq in 1991. In any case, whoever ordered for the little enlisted library at Ft. Rucker meant to improve the military mind. Which mind in the day room worked like this:

The entry of a sergeant interrupted my reading concentration. Casting an eye about the three or four soldiers perusing books and magazines or doing hobby work, he announced, "I need someone to make stencils of the alphabet. All 24 letters."

I started to rise and open my mouth. I was a second away from informing him that the alphabet, as we had acquired it from the Romans, succeeding the ancient Phoenicians and Hebrews with their earlier versions, contained 26 letters. But then my military mind kicked in. Never contradict a superior. Never. Especially not in front of others and certainly not unless one's position was about to be overrun, probably by angry men using another alphabet altogether. I clamped my jaws together and sank back into my chair. Let another unfortunate decide whether to omit "q" and "x" or "k" and "v".

Tuesday, May 5, 1970. My release from active duty dawned. In civilian clothes again at last, lugging a duffle-bag crammed with olive drab and those inflexible, feet-killing black combat boots—probably designed by the same mastermind with friends highly placed in acquisitions who came up with the water-absorbent field jacket—I caught a taxi at the main gate. We headed for Dothan Regional Airport 25 miles away. I was leaving Transient Co. behind, but not quite yet the company mentality.

On the front seat, between the cabbie and myself, was an open cigar box. In it were the essentials: cash from fares, a flask of whiskey, and a small revolver. The drive passed quickly if a bit erratically as far as the white centerline was concerned. And whatever good old nonsense the driver uttered, I agreed. Did I know there were catfish smarter than some people? Yes, I most certainly did. And pigs with damned fine memories? Uh huh. And so on for the next 35 or 40 minutes. Where was the Grand Ole Opry's Minnie Pearl when I really needed her?

Inside the small terminal I bought a copy of the *Dothan Eagle* and scanned the front page. My jaw dropped. In heavy black letters, a headline insisted "Ohio National Guard Kills Four at Kent State University." My brain swirled. No, that had not happened, could not happen. Maybe the day before in some alternate universe, but not in this one. Yet it had.

On the flight out of Atlanta's Hartsfield International to Columbus, I happened to sit next to a youngish salesman for Noxell, the parent corporation of Noxzema skin cream and Cover Girl cosmetics. We struck up a conversation. He said he'd served in Vietnam some years earlier. I told him I was on my way home from basic and AIT. He said it was too bad, what happened at Kent State, but he didn't seem sympathetic toward the students. Hippies, draft-dodgers. I said—in the purity of hypotheticals—I thought if my unit was ever ordered to fire on protesting students, maybe some older Reservists might, but my friends and I would refuse. Our conversation ground to a halt.

I caught another taxi, this one to the garage near campus to which my father recently had moved my car, the '67 Camaro that had survived the return trip from Dixie to the Buckeye State by way of friends on Long Island and in Pittsburgh the previous, extended Labor Day holiday. A block from my apartment on Chittenden Avenue east of the Ohio State University law school building, something odd happened. I ran into a military checkpoint. Given the barriers in the intersection, troops in battledress with helmets and rifles, I could have been at Checkpoint Charlie on the demarcation line between East and West Berlin, in downtown Washington, D.C. after the riots and fires following the April 4, 1968 assassination of Rev. Martin Luther King, Jr. or any other intersection riven by calculation and passion.

"What are you doing here?" one of the soldiers asked.

"I live here," I said. Pointing to the small, gravel parking lot off the alley just south of Chittenden, I said, "I need to park my car there."

"Only authorized personnel can pass," he said. "Let me see your driver's license."

That would not help. It showed my parents address in Tiffin, Ohio not mine in Columbus. I'd never updated it when I'd been at college. Ohio University in Athens was only a temporary address, not my place of residence for voting, and since the license had not expired, neither had I renewed it for Columbus. And in 1970, paper drivers' licenses did not carry pictures anyway. I could have been anyone.

"This doesn't say Columbus," the soldier said.

"Look," I said, lifting my baseball cap-style fatigue hat to reveal my nearly-shaved head, "I'm a reservist, just getting back from active duty." No male student or campus-area hanger-on wore hair like mine unless he were military.

He looked at me and smiled. Probably a National Guardsman mobilized for riot control. After Nixon's late-April Cambodian incursion, colleges across the country had erupted in protests. These intensified following the Kent State killings. Most of Ohio's big state universities were about to be closed for the rest of the academic year, final exams be damned. OSU would be shut by request of Gov. James A. Rhodes the next day.

The rumor around Columbus was that after city police and Franklin County sheriff's deputies, augmented by Ohio State Highway Patrol officers, had been unable to quell disturbances on and around the university, having used all the tear gas in central Ohio, the Guard had to be called out. At the time, doubt persisted as to whether the state university system including Ohio University, Miami, Bowling Green State, Kent State and Toledo would reopen in autumn. (It would, and uneventfully, but that spring, tense with uncertainty, one could have gotten even money betting to the contrary.)

"Go ahead," he said, waving me through. "But stay away from 15th and High," he added, referring to the intersection near the main campus gate and adjacent stores and bars. "I hear there's still tear gas there."

An hour later I was reclining on the roof above the front porch, having climbed out our second-floor living room window. Like many of the old duplexes near the university, ours had been further chopped up for student housing, with two smaller apartments on the first floor, two larger ones on the second and third levels. Leaning against the old, brown bricks, enjoying the sun, I saw on the roof of an adjacent porch a long-haired, long-limbed young man and a girl in cut-off blue jeans and a tie-dyed T-shirt. They were sharing a marijuana joint and making out. Marijuana possession could still get you seriously jailed in those days, but what really was unusual was their face paint. Both had made themselves up like Indian braves about to hit the warpath. They looked like extras from a touring company version of the musical "Hair." Nixon's Vietnamization of the war might not have been going well, but Vietnamization of the campuses seemed to be proceeding just fine.

Chapter Five:
Protest Marches, Adjective and Verb

"I Ain't Marching Anymore." Au Revoir, Phil Ochs

It was Oct. 21, 1967 and an estimated 80,000 to 100,000 people, mostly college students, had answered the call of the National Mobilization Committee to End the War in Vietnam. We gathered on the Mall in front of the Lincoln Memorial, jamming the areas along the length of the Reflecting Pool and under its adjacent trees.

A handful of us from Ohio University's student newspaper, *The O.U. Post,* were there. We told ourselves we were going more as observers than participants, to cover the biggest anti-war protest to date. I didn't realize I was the only one who meant it. The experience became an early if then only vaguely comprehended lesson in what during the Kennedy administration already was called "managed" or "slanted" news, one that would take years of reiterated examples to sink in.

This was two decades before erosion of journalism's self-proclaimed barrier between news and opinion made itself undeniable. The professional trauma of reporting dispassionately the civil rights movement at home and the war in Vietnam abroad accelerated the trend. So did Tom Wolfe's 1965 best-selling *Kandy-Kolored, Streamlined Tangerine-Flake Baby.* Its seductive promise that journalists' flights of self-expression could transcend the mere reporter's craft for the heights of best-selling literature—not to mention convey "the underlying truth" instead of just the necessary facts—began to seduce many scriveners. The press—which televised, on cable and digitized on computer screens became The Media—began to believe it not only was streamlined and tangerine-flaked but also as important as the news it covered, if not more so. One need only spend five minutes with today's *New York Times, Atlantic* magazine or National Public Radio, let alone cable's CNN and online relative newbies like Vox or Salon to realize how thoroughly such self-regard transformed and diminished the press. In classic Gresham's Law ("bad money drives out good") fashion, "fake news"—more accurately yet less obviously news forgeries—had become a chronic problem long before Donald Trump started wielding the term as a protective shield.

My objection to the Vietnam war was that the United States hadn't already won it, not that American soldiers my age were halfway around the world fighting communists, indigenous peoples or both in Indochina. Which meant, I would find on our return to Athens, that my *O.U. Post* colleagues would print their own march endorsements-as-reports but spike my less-than-enthusiastic commentary. Cancel-culture, a half-century early. Not that they hadn't gladly taken advantage of my offer to drive us all to Washington and back. In my four-speed manual transmission, 150-cubic inch, 150 horsepower rear "pancake" engine, turbo-charged 1964 Corvair Spyder convertible, no less. As noted, Chevrolet's Corvairs, unbalanced with the trunk in front and engine in back, were prone to hydroplane on slick surfaces and erratic in sidewinds. But on dry roads in calm weather, they could corner like sports cars.

Wanting to be in the protest but not of it, I wore muted plaid slacks instead of my usual blue jeans, plus a buttoned-down shirt and V-neck sweater. Thus overdressed, I sat with my schoolmates on the ground for hours listening to speakers including novelist Norman Mailer (his 1979 best-seller, the "true crime novel" *Executioner's Song*, perhaps would epitomize journalism as fiction, or maybe the other way around), poet Robert Lowell and America's pediatrician, Dr. Benjamin Spock. Spock, having told our parent's generation to "relax" when it came to child-rearing, was—his babies now at least in adolescence—a prominent anti-war campaigner.

The speakers were leavened by entertainment headliners including folk-pop singers Peter, Paul and Mary, rhythm and blues stars Sam and Dave and anti-war folk balladeer Phil Ochs. Whatever they said, Mailer, Lowell and Spock made no impression on me. But I still recall Peter, Paul and Mary's crystalline harmony coming through live, and outdoors at that. The mental snapshot of Sam and Dave working through their soulful, insistent hit, "Hold On, I'm Comin'" remains unfaded. In fact, as far as I was concerned, it proved the high-point of the protest. What the erotic beat and lyrical innuendo protested, I couldn't say and didn't care.

We squatted or stood for hours without, as far as could be seen, concession stands, or shelter from the skies. But my girlfriend of that weekend, an O.U. transfer student from Syracuse University, somehow managed to find her Orangeman ex-. He was hanging by his knees, red-eyed and upside down, from a branch in a tree along the Reflecting Pool. "LSD," she explained.

Periodically the chant "Hey, hey, LBJ, how many kids did you kill today?" rippled through the crowd. Near me a couple debated whether President Lyndon Baines Johnson should be impeached, "like that other President Johnson."

"Andrew Johnson was impeached, but not convicted," I interjected.

"What?" they both said.

"He wasn't convicted. He got to stay as president."

"That makes no sense," the boy said. "We know he was impeached."

Right. It was time to levitate the Pentagon.

As the speeches and music drew to a close, an estimated 35,000 or more of the crowd that had stretched eastward from the Lincoln Memorial began walking to nearby Memorial Bridge to cross the Potomac River and reach the Pentagon. With 620,000 square feet it is still the world's biggest office building. That fall afternoon it was headquarters of a U.S. military that became more fascist and imperialist the closer one got to a draft notice.

The bridge forced a nearly immediate bottleneck, so the protest march became, to paraphrase *The Washington Post's* Oct. 17, 2019 50-year retrospective, more of a protest "shuffle." By late afternoon tens of thousands, most but by no means all college students, had reached the Pentagon grounds and the great, five-sided structure. It opened in 1943, in the midst of World War II, having taken less than a year and a half to build, no environmental impact statement required. The Pentagon looked like a gigantic paper weight that, metaphysically at least, kept Arlington and the rest of the adjacent northern Virginia suburbs from flying off into space.

This was important since Abbie Hoffman and Jerry Rubin, co-founders of something they called the Youth International Party (political "Yippies," as [barely] distinguished from sex-drugs-and-rock 'n roll hippies) had promised to levitate the Pentagon. The Yippies were a small part of the National Mobilization Committee's coalition behind that day's demonstrations, but perhaps the most headline worthy. In fact, headlines, in print but more actually in people's heads, was the point of the Yippies.

Rubin's observation that people remember what they see on television and in movies, not what they hear, closely paralleled communications theorist Marshall McLuhan's oft-repeated assertion that "the medium is the message." Said Rubin: "…[T]elevision is a non-verbal instrument! The way to understand TV is to shut off the sound. No one remembers any words they hear; the mind is a technicolor movie of images, not words." A half-century later, in the bubble-world of 24-hour, seven-day-a-week televised talking heads, incessant, repetitious words at least must be drilled home with incessant, repetitious images. So too with online advertising and especially so with running-to-keep-up print media; the hardcopy *Washington Post* under Trump derangement syndrome, for example, became very much a newsprint version of CNN's bottom-of-the-screen crawl.

That Hoffman and Rubin earlier had promised to levitate the Pentagon had official Washington, and even some other march organizers, on edge. The pair forecast an "exorcism to cast out evil spirits." " … We will dye the Potomac red, burn the cherry trees, panhandle embassies, attack with water pistols, marbles, bubble gum wrappers, bazookas, girls will run naked and piss on the Pentagon walls, sorcerers, swamis, witches, voodoo, warlocks, medicine men and speed freaks will hurl their magic at the faded brown walls," Hoffman pledged. Actually, the walls were gray, but magically speaking, that wouldn't matter.

To make sure levitation did not take place, military police, federal marshals and thousands of troops from the Army's 82nd Airborne Division surrounded the Pentagon. An iconic *Washington Star* news photograph from the afternoon's hurled magic showed a long-haired young man, wearing a thick turtle-neck sweater, sticking a flower in the barrel of a soldier's rifle. Another, somehow less iconic photo, distributed by Associated Press, portrayed a young man in sunglasses and a dark jacket screaming at military police. "Flower power!" sounded so much nicer than "Scream power!"

After an hour or so at the Pentagon, toward the back of the thick and what seemed to be unorganized crowd, unable to see what was happening in front but with the headquarters of American militarism still firmly earthbound, no naked girls to be seen dashing about, I'd had enough. Hungry and feeling the chill of evening coming on, I suggested to one of my *O.U. Post* colleagues—I think it was Bill Sievert, but after 50-plus years won't attest to the fact—we go find a restaurant.

This turned out to be almost as easily done as said. Heading south, the most open direction out of the crowd, we somehow managed to cross roads that eventually would become I-395, on which decades later I would spend countless hours in crush-hour commuting to and from the District of Columbia. Thank God for recorded books. On the other side, still not far from the Pentagon and protest, we stumbled upon a Hot Shoppe. It was a veritable oasis of hamburgers, French fries and hot coffee! Start the revolution without us!

The Hot Shoppes were a Washington, D.C.-based chain of drive-in restaurants. What would become a network and then a great deal more began in the late 1920s. William Marriott, a young Mormon from Utah, decided to open an A & W Root Beer franchise in the city. Unless one's last name is Hilton, the rest, as they say, is history.

Speaking of history, Abbie Hoffman, arrested in 1973 on drug charges, hid under the name Barry Freed until he served a short prison term in the early '80s. Aged 55, he committed suicide in 1989. Ochs, the anti-war folk singer who dropped out of Ohio State University in his senior year when passed over for editorship of the student newspaper, *The Lantern*, and who later described his song-writing as journalism, killed himself in 1976 at age 35. Rubin and Hoffman were two of those tried as "the Chicago Seven" in 1968 on charges stemming from disruptions at that year's Democratic National Convention. Rubin disrupted, and partially discredited, both the trial and U.S. House Un-American Activities

Committee hearings, at one of which he appeared in Revolutionary War costume. "Nothing is more American than revolution," he testified, practicing guerrilla theater jujitsu on committee members. In 1980, Rubin—who famously warned against trusting anyone over 30—became a stockbroker with the firm of John Muir & Co. Never quite conventional, he declared he could raise consciousness more effectively from the inside than outside. Turns out that in a world in which post-World War II capitalism lifted hundreds of millions of people out of subsistence poverty nothing was more revolutionary than a healthy balance sheet. Hence, the pre-capitalist reaction of the progressive left. Rubin died in 1994, several weeks after being struck by a car while trying to cross Wilshire Boulevard near his Los Angeles penthouse. He was 56.

By the time the siege of the Pentagon unraveled the morning after the march, with the firing of tear gas, arrests of approximately 700 protesters, and several dozen beatings administered with rifle butts, our Ohio University contingent was long gone. We headed west on U.S. 50 from Arlington toward Athens, Ohio, 270 miles distant. En route we made an unscheduled stop in Triadelphia, West Virginia.

There, having been snared along with two other vehicles simultaneously in a crossroad speed trap, hurtling along at 35 miles per hour in a 25-mile zone in my Spyder, turbo-charger rumbling on the downshifts, I found myself in traffic court. On Sunday afternoon. Triadelphia, West Virginia judicial motto: "Take a number. Next!" The magistrate was a reasonable man. He said I could plead not guilty, in which case I would spend the next two days in jail awaiting trial on Tuesday morning, or I could plead guilty and pay the fine, which I remember as $50 ($390 in 2020's purchasing power). My colleagues and I pooled our resources, paid the ransom and left Triadelphia. Slowly.

The United States Marine Corps was founded in 1775, predating the Declaration of Independence by nearly a year, the Constitution by 12 and the Pentagon by a mere 167. My wife, Melinda, retired from the Corps as an officer after 20 years on active duty—Intelligence and Latin America Foreign Area Officer. The *Cleveland Jewish News* once headlined a feature on this local lady under the headline "Nice Jewish Girl a Marine Officer." Despite my own less than illustrious military career—six years rocketing to the rank of Specialist 4th Class (equivalent to corporal but without command authority over privates) in the U.S. Army Reserves— we attended the Marine Corps' annual birthday ball at the Washington, D.C. Hilton in November of 2018, in black gown and heels (her) and rented tuxedo (me). We felt the pride of service, camaraderie, patriotism, memories of those not there, an intangible yet rocklike warmth But it's not necessary to go to a Marine Corps birthday celebration to get the feeling that pervaded the Hilton that evening, its big, oval ballroom packed with all ranks from private to general, men and women, all races.. Any summer Tuesday evening in Washington will do.

If you've never seen the U.S. Marine Corps silent drill at sundown—the "Sunset Parade"—do so. I've taken my daughters twice, as children and young women. The ordered pomp, at once impressive yet understated, the solemn bugle sound of Taps, the breath-taking precision of the Marines as they march, inspect, then twirl their bayoneted carbines to one another without a word, will move any American heart. Any *American* heart, descendant from the Mayflower or newly-naturalized. Whether you watch it performed at the Iwo Jima Memorial next to Arlington National Cemetery, or in front of the Lincoln Memorial, that large building in the background will be the Pentagon. Still there after all these years, unlevitated in 1967, restored from smoking ruin in 2001.

So, it did all start before Vietnam. Before Korea. Just after Japan surrendered. And it has continued through the fall of Saigon, destruction of the Twin Towers, into Iraq and Afghanistan, perhaps on to battles for Taiwan et. al. still to come. Benjamin Franklin was right. Not just a Defense Department, but a republic, if despite our chronic myopia, we can keep it.

May Day: Workers of the World, March!

For May 1, 1980 Israel's Histradut trade union confederation, various kibbutz movements and other left-of-center and socialist organizations had planned their annual march and rally in Tel Aviv. A few days before, Monia Avrahami, the *menahel* (director) of Kibbutz Ma'agan Michael's *ulpan*, a Hebrew language work-study program then common on many of Israel's collective farm-and-factory villages, told participants to get ready. We would be bused to Tel Aviv, about 60 miles south down the main Mediterranean coast road, to join marchers recruited from all over the New Jersey-sized country.

The opposition Labor Party, its Histadrut union affiliate and other organizers wanted a big turnout. In 1977, Israel's center-right, non-socialist Likud Party and its allies had, after 29 years of futility since the Jewish state's founding in 1948, actually won an election. This political upheaval had certified the country's standing as a genuine two-party, or rather two-bloc democracy instead of a semi-permanent majority bloc-minority parties oligarchy. Labor and its partners, who long had disdained the Herut Party-led elements that became Likud and its leader, the prickly Jewish nationalist Menchem Begin, thought '77 an aberration and hoped for a big May Day demonstration to reinforce their view.

"And wear white, shirts for the men, blouses for the women," Avrahmi had instructed. Ulpan volunteers, mostly but not entirely young Jews, hailed from the United States, United Kingdom, France, Argentina, West Germany, South Africa, Rhodesia (in its fading, pre-Zimbabwe incarnation), Denmark and, as unhappy refugees, Iran. There was even one stocky, red-headed Jewish boy from Finland, or maybe it was Norway—Scandinavians look so much alike—who already was a veteran of the Finnish, or Norwegian, coastal defense artillery. Imagine the fun at drills. Ka-boom! Another fishing boat sunk!

In the run-up to May Day, Ma'agan Michael was decked out in flags. The blue-and-white Israeli flag, Star of David prominent in its center, decorated the kibbutz. But on pole after pole, it was paired with the red banner, gold hammer-and-sickle emblazoned at the upper left, of the Soviet Union. This was not just nearly half a century after Stalin's show trials had consigned many of his early Bolshevik colleagues—Jews prominent among them—to death by a bullet in the back of the head in the sub-basements of Moscow's Lubyanka Prison or in the frozen wastes of Siberia, but while the Soviet Union still armed Israel's Arab enemies. And certainly, by then the material benefits of capitalism over Marx and Lenin's "scientific socialism" were undeniable. Not that Soviet Premier Nikita Khrushchev didn't try to deny them during his 1959 "kitchen debate" with Vice President Richard Nixon in a model American home on exhibition in Moscow's Sokolniki Park.

"The Jew who is not political is a fool," someone once cautioned. Yes, and the Jew whose politics are suicidal is also a fool. There continue to be many such, not a few running deep-pocketed, well-endowed Jewish non-profit organizations. They insist on imaging that everyone else is, or certainly would be if only properly instructed, like their own theoretical best selves. That being the case, and in the contrarian spirit of the muted plaid trousers I wore to the march on the Pentagon, I chose a blue shirt.

"I should not allow you on this bus!" Avrahami said, glaring at me. Ordinarily an amiable fellow, who some years later went on to manage a professional dance troupe in Haifa, Avrahmi was not pleased. Wanting to go to the march but not wishing to imply support for anything tainted Commie red, I replied, "It's free choice, isn't it? Besides, my white shirt's dirty." Avrahami relented, shrugged and said, "Get on."

An estimated 100,000 people—2.5 percent of the country's four million population then—marched along one of Tel Aviv's broader north-south boulevards and gathered in *Kikar HaMalechay Yisrael* (Kings of Israel Square). This was a large plaza around city hall, a gray, concrete slab of mid-century modern office building in the center of town. May Day, as the annual workers' holiday, began in the United States in the 1800s. But after adoption by European Marxists and other leftists in the late part of the century, it was supplanted in America by Labor Day, the first Monday after the first Tuesday in September. U.S. workers, their labor leaders recognized, were more interested in getting ahead than getting together in European-style proletarian solidarity. Senator Bernie Sanders lay unimaginable decades in the future.

May 1, 1980 in Israel was pleasant, more like late June in the States, and my long-sleeved dress shirt and blue jeans proved too warm. But unlike at the concessions-free '67 march on the Pentagon, participants in Tel Aviv could wander across Ibn Gabirol Boulevard on one side or Frischmann Street on another to grab a cold Coke or Kinley Orange (a thirst-quenching legacy of British Mandate times) and falafel-stuffed pita sandwich and enjoy them in the shade of an awning or large umbrella. Which, since the speeches denouncing Begin's allegedly fascist government and praising Israel's apparently oppressed workers were in Hebrew, I did.

The march was one of the biggest in Israeli history up to that time. The 350,000 turn-out in 1983, in protest of the extension of Israel's war against the Palestine Liberation Organization in Lebanon, during which a grenade would be thrown, killing one marcher, set the record. What struck me most that May Day was the ease with which I could recognize plain clothes police. Lounging in doorways, leaning against parked cars, almost always smoking, trying to look casual in their own white, or checked shirts and jeans or slacks, they somehow stood out from similarly attired men all around them. Maybe it was their typically stocky builds that gave them away. Or the sunglasses. Or walkie-talkies. Or nearly unchanging stares— felt if not seen from behind the glasses. Brothers in attitude if not much else to Gov. George Wallace's Alabama state troopers who had stared at me 13 years earlier.

I would see such men again at Lag b'Omer celebrations in 2000. Lag b'Omer is the minor holiday on the 33rd day of the seven weeks between Passover and Shavuot, between the Israelites' freedom from Egyptian slavery and Moses' receipt of the Ten Commandments on Mount Sinai, the point of that freedom. The seven weeks are a time of mourning but on Lag b'Omer festive activities, including marriages, are permitted. The Lag b'Omer plainclothes men, however, were not Israeli or America security operatives, but rather Tunisians, upholding the rule of strongman Zine el-Abidine Ben Ali. Ben Ali's color portraits hung everywhere, even in small shops. The plainclothes men were protecting holiday celebrations on the island of Djerba. About 1,500 Jews, the current generations of a community that believed it dated to biblical times, were joined by hundreds of former Tunisian Jews visiting from Israel or France.

As editor of B'nai B'rith's *International Jewish Monthly*, I'd taken advantage of a Tunisian government invitation to cover the festivities. The presence of the numerous and intentionally obvious security police at a large Jewish celebration in the midst of a much larger Arab population, albeit one ruled by a Western-leaning dictator—was reassuring. So were Ben Ali's photographs. Someone definitely was in charge here, even if he was someone who could never win an election in America. Well, not without a leftward adjustment in his vocabulary and the inevitable long, explanatory piece, headlined something like "Building a People's Democracy: Mr. Jefferson, Meet Mr. Ben Ali" in *The New Yorker*.

In 2002, a suicide bomber would drive a natural gas tanker rigged with explosives to the door of a venerated Djerba synagogue. Al-Qaeda claimed responsibility for the blast, which killed 19, mostly European tourists, and wounded more than 30. In 2011, one of the "Arab Spring" revolts overthrew Ben Ali. Nothing gold can stay, Robert Frost told us. Not brass, either.

"Let My People Go!"

Sunday, Dec. 6, 1987. I picked up Don and Deborah Cymrot, fellow members of Congregation Olam Tikvah, a large Conservative synagogue in Washington, D.C.'s northern Virginia suburbs, and drove to the Vienna Metro station. We took an Orange line train to McPherson Square and walked toward Constitution Avenue. We were about to join what would prove to be the largest assemblage of Jews in U.S. history.

Organizers such as the National Council for Soviet Jewry and United Jewish Appeal charities called the day "Freedom Sunday." A march and rally were planned to urge the Soviet Union to end its long attempt at forced assimilation—even Hebrew teaching was banned, emigration to Israel denied the country's several million Jews. Kremlin leader Mikhail Gorbachev was in town, scheduled to meet President Ronald Reagan in the White House the next day. Participants wanted to make sure our issue was on their agenda. Like Moses and Aaron speaking to Pharaoh, we would make a demand of Gorbachev: "Let our people go!"

Estimates of the crowd reached as high as 250,000 people. Many were local, but many more were bused in from greater New York City. We marched east on Constitution toward the U.S. Capitol, banners flying. The procession hummed with a sense of exhilaration

The crowd spilled back from Capitol Hill west along the Mall. Several giant television screens—a relatively new feature for large-turnout events—had been set up. That made it possible for us to see the speakers on the temporary stage far in front, including *refusenik* heroes Natan Sharansky and Yosef Mendelevitch, as more than mere specks. Also addressing the crowd in person were Speaker of the House James Wright (D-Texas) and Senate Minority Leader Bob Dole (R-Kansas). Providing a musical interlude were, shades of the 1967 March on the Pentagon, Peter, Paul and Mary. Vice President George H. W. Bush appeared via the jumbo television screens.

I walked through the multitude toward Washington Monument in the middle distance, then turned and circled back. Even an agoraphobic—if a Jew or philosemite—would have felt the buoyant vibrations. They did not arise so much from what was said by each speaker as that it was said at all, in public, not far from the White House, site of the next day's summit meeting, and before such a great, supportive crowd. *"Let my people go!"*

From 13,000 in 1988 to 24,000 the next year, then 200,000 in 1990, 176,000 in '91, a prolonged tide of Soviet Jewish immigration flooded into the Jewish state. It receded into the range of 20,000 annual arrivals only in 2004. More than one million new citizens helped boost Israel's population from 4.2 million in 1987 to 6.2 million in 2004, supercharging the economy and completing the Jewish state's transformation from second- to first-world country. In retrospect, a modern, miraculous exodus to the land of renewed promise.

Back on the Orange Line, headed home as individuals once more, no longer anonymous particles in a unique mass, the Cymrots and I felt a sense of satisfaction. We'd taken ourselves to the right place at the right time, even if we had not had to go far. That day, we'd contributed our mite to a cause greater than ourselves.

History may have no right and wrong side, contrary to the clichés of contemporary politicians and journalists. One of the first historians, Thucydides, put it bluntly: "The strong do what they can and the weak suffer what they must." Rather than a right and wrong side, an arc bending toward justice, so long as inherently imperfect human beings breathe, feel, think and act, history's pendulum both swings and spirals, at times forward, at times backward—as in Afghanistan more or less since the 1979 Soviet invasion, the former Yugoslavia in the 1990s' Balkan wars, Rwanda during the 1995 genocide, the Congo repeatedly for decades and Syria in the 2011 – 2020 civil war. Millions slaughtered, millions wounded, millions more made homeless. The arc of history often resembles a broken corkscrew. And, humans being what they are, the breaks at times seem enlarged by the very attempts to mend them.

So it was that on the same day as the march, Dec. 6, 1987 an Israeli Jew was stabbed to death shopping in the Gaza Strip. The next day, an Israeli truck in the Strip killed four Palestinian Arabs in a traffic accident. Gaza was then still under Israeli control, the Israel Defense Forces having ousted Egyptian occupation troops in the 1967 Six-Day War. About 5,000 Jews had built small communities in Gaza, living amidst approximately 600,000 Arabs in a territory roughly the size of a small county in the eastern United States. On December 8, after the truck accident, riots erupted in what would become the first Palestinian *intifada* ("shaking off"). An Islamic fundamentalist organization, an offshoot of Egypt's Muslim Brotherhood that would become known as Hamas (Palestinian Islamic Resistance Movement), spread rumors about the truck accident alleging a Zionist conspiracy.

From '87 to the Oslo Accords in September, 1993 intermittent violence, mostly but not always directed at troops, would cost approximately 160 Israeli lives, 100 civilians and 60 members of the military; 1,100 Arabs killed by Israeli forces, and another 800-plus deaths at the hands of other Palestinian Arabs in a score-settling *intrafada*. Incessantly renewed images from the first intifada of armed, gas-mask wearing Israeli soldiers chasing rock-throwing Palestinian youths through Gaza's narrow alleys would flip the Jewish state onto the defensive diplomatically and in public opinion throughout much of the West. Of the *intrafada*, barely a news media peep and so hardly a consciousness-raising blip.

Eight years after the rally for Soviet Jewry, at the same place on the Mall, the western slope of Capitol Hill looking toward Washington Monument, Nation of Islam leader Louis Farrakhan, the United States highest profile antisemite, would gather—take your pick—400,000 people, the National Park Service estimate; 837,000, a Boston University-ABC Television approximation; or more than one million, claimed by Minister Farrakhan and others. Local chapters of the National Association for the Advancement of Colored People and other established civil rights organizations joined him in organizing the Million Man March. Well-known speakers included African American civil rights icon Rosa Parks, author Maya Angelou, mayors Marion Barry and Kurt Schmoke, of Washington, D.C. and Baltimore, respectively, and the Rev. Jesse Jackson.

Farrakhan delivered a stemwinder. He riffed on George Washington's status as a slave owner and his membership in the Masons—the Nation of Islam leader's Masonic conspiracy theory at times presaged the 2004 movie *National Treasure.* A box office smash, part thriller, part historical mash-up, the plot posited a Masonic map pointing to unimaginable riches coded into the back of the Declaration of Independence. The alleged hidden hand of devilish Masons, of course, has been a recurrent obsession of American political paranoids since the 1820s.

The Nation of Islam leader claimed a role as divinely ordained prophet, asserting that his vast audience "came not at the call of Louis Farrakhan, but you have gathered here at the call of God. … And although the call was made through me, many have tried to distance the beauty of this idea from the person through whom the idea and the call was made." Farrakhan rebuked those who scorned him as a prophet, if not all of his message. Those rebuked included President Bill Clinton.

The minister said his criticisms of America's deep-seated flaws were those of a doctor come to prescribe healing. He warned that "white supremacy" hurt whites as well as blacks. And then Farrakhan returned to "the secret of the Masonic order." That esoteric knowledge concerns "a master builder that was hit in the head. The secret of the Masonic Order is a master that ruffians roughed up. … These racists hit him in his head and carried him on a westerly course and buried him in the north country, in a shallow grave. Many tried to raise him up but they didn't have the master grip. It would take a master to come after him."

Whatever. A Nation of Islam founding belief is that white people resulted from a failed experiment 6,600 years ago on the island of Patmos by the black scientist Yakub (the biblical Jacob). Facts, in this case chronological ones, are troublesome things—a big reason why "narrative" and "lived experience" are currently popular, as opposed to Kipling's "six honest serving men," who, what, when, where, why and how. Jacob (Ya'akov in Hebrew)—individual or archetype—must have lived, according to his world as described in Hebrew scriptures, early in the first half of the second millennium B.C.E., more like 3,600 years ago. That is, not the Nation of Islam's 6,600.

Throughout his career, Farrakhan has reiterated a favorite theme, that of "the Satanic Jews [who] control everything and mostly everybody." In 1984, he said, "the Jews don't like Farrakhan, so they call me Hitler. Well, that's a good name. Hitler was a very great man." He added he wasn't "proud of Hitler's evil against the Jewish people, but that's a matter of reckon," of calling to account.

Three years after the Million Man March he claimed that "the Jews have been so bad at politics that they lost half their population in the Holocaust. They thought they could trust in Hitler, and they helped him get the Third Reich on the road." This "the Jews helped Hitler" fantasy parallels Farrakhan's career-long falsehood that Jews led the African slave trade. But that commerce in human beings feature key roles played by dominant African tribes and Arab traders. It predated, and in some cases post-dated, the European-directed "triangular trade" across the Atlantic Ocean to the New World.

A few noted black leaders, including Rep. John Lewis (D-Ga.) and Mary Frances Berry, chair of the U.S. Commission on Civil Rights, boycotted Farrakhan's Million Man March. Lewis called it Farrakhan's attempt to "resegregate America." In that sense, a harbinger of the Black Lives Matter organization assertions post-George Floyd and underlying "critical race theory." Nevertheless, despite the minister's consistent hostility to Jews, homosexuals, inter-racial marriage and the Nation of Islam's belief whites were unevolved "potential humans" and "sinful by nature," the march was billed as a promotion of renewal and empowerment among black men. It mostly was reported that way by uncritical news media.

I'd considered driving in from the suburbs to cover the march in person. After identifying myself as editor of the *Washington Jewish Week*, I would ask participants questions along the lines of "since we know Farrakhan's a race-baiting demagogue, and even he admits indirect responsibility for rhetoric contributing to the assassination of Malcolm X, what are you doing here?" I decided to go to a driving range and hit a bucket of golf balls instead.

This was not the first time I had lazily if fortunately over-ruled myself when it came to the Nation of Islam. In the summer of 1969, right after college graduation, putting distance between myself and letters from my draft board in Ohio, as noted above, I worked at Outta Sight in Atlanta, Ga. Outta Sight was a men's clothing store run by Mike Ivers, a neighbor and friend of my aunt, Margaret Kloville, one of my father's sisters. Mike gave me a job and Aunt Marge let me sleep in a spare bedroom while desultory correspondence between the draft board, my parent's home in Tiffin, then to me in Atlanta and back, let time pass while I waited for an opening in a National Guard or Army Reserve unit.

The men Outta Sight catered to were of two types: African Americans from neighborhoods near its downtown Atlanta location— around the corner from the store was a metal lamp-post bearing a small plaque that noted Margaret Mitchell had lived nearby while writing *Gone With the Wind*—and old Jewish men from Miami who happened to be passing through. The customer ratio was, at the least, nine-to-one locals to out-of-towners.

We sold bright slacks—their colors of almost Day-Glo iridescence—synthetic knit golf shirts, also vividly colored—and, especially for our July 4th sale (in Atlanta that summer days of 90-degree temperatures and 90 percent relative humidity followed in oppressive routine)—alpaca wool, rainbow-colored, Italian cardigan sweaters. Twenty-five dollars wholesale, $50 dollars retail (roughly $300-plus today). We couldn't keep them in stock.

Several times that summer I'd noticed a young man, dressed impeccably in a sharp black suit, white shirt and dark tie, selling newspapers up and down the sidewalk in front of the store. He was short, with close-cropped hair and sunglasses. He hawked *Muhammad Speaks*, the official publication of the Nation of Islam. Though the Nation's membership was small, the paper's readership was larger.

Jaymo, Outta Sight's manager, also glimpsed the *Muhammad Speaks* salesman. Jaymo was a slender, well-organized man of café-au-lait complexion and cool demeanor. I'd had it in mind to buy a paper, or try to. I'd never seen the salesman offer a copy to a white person. As a journalism major, and having worked two summer internships on small dailies, I was curious about *Muhammad Speaks*. That summer I periodically picked up copies of *The Great Speckled Bird*, Atlanta's serio-frothy "underground" weekly. But by the time I had a free moment, the *Muhammad Speaks* hawker had disappeared up the street.

Jaymo shook his head. "Black Muslims. Nothing but trouble."

A week later the short, square-shoulder salesman was back, attired as he had been before. But this time he'd stationed himself directly in our recessed doorway, in shade back from the sidewalk sunlight. Any potential customer who attempted to enter would have to sidestep him first.

I was about to go out and ask him to move when Mike Ivers called me to the storeroom. "Put these in the cases by the front door," he said, pointing to boxes full of red, orange, yellow, black, green and blue Ban-Lon-like golf shirts. (Ban-Lon, a sort of crimped nylon knit then widely popular, was a strange fabric for sportswear; it didn't breathe like cotton.)

By the time I got back to the front door, the *Muhammad Speaks* vendor was gone. Driving back to Aunt Marge's after work that night and listening to the radio, I heard a short report on local news:

"A guard at the central post office downtown is in critical condition with gunshot wounds at Grady Memorial Hospital. Police say he was shot after telling a newspaper seller to stop bothering customers and move on. A suspect is in custody." The suspect was our salesman.

The second time the Nation of Islam entered my work life was the first time I got a hint of its antisemitic conspiracy theorizing. It was 1977, give or take a year, and I was sitting in Columbus Mayor Tom Moody's office with two other men. One was Jerry Gafford, the mayor's chief of staff. The other was Major Kemo, a leader of Cleveland's Fruit of Islam.

Gafford, who later would work as senior vice president for corporate affairs for Lazarus and Federated Department Stores, was both a no-nonsense expediter and Moody's approachable righthand man.

I was filling in for the *Citizen-Journal's* regular City Hall reporter, the inimitable Jerry Condo. Condo came straight from Central Casting, the inveterately skeptical but somehow never cynical newspaperman with nearly manic energy and unbending determination never to be scooped by the rival *Columbus Dispatch*, let alone the radio and television tag-alongs. When, decades later I saw a re-staging of *The Front Page*, Ben Hecht and

Charles MacArthur's crazed 1928 comedy about star reporter Hildy Johnson's frantic efforts to keep secret a scoop that literally just dropped in on him in the person of an escaped killer, I knew I'd seen Johnson before. Only then his name was Jerry Condo.

Major Kemo was of a different cut, neither Gafford- nor Condo-like. He said he wanted Columbus to fund a project similar to that his Fruit of Islam conducted in Cleveland. The Fruit of Islam is the security arm of the Nation of Islam, its paramilitary-trained members assigned to protect the Nation's mosques across the United States. Farrakhan, as the movement's leader, commands the Fruit of Islam.

The project Major Kemo pitched to Gafford was, he said, designed to improve life in black inner-city neighborhoods. It aimed to instill pride in African American men, who then would set good examples for local youth. The effort also would help counter illegal drug use, promote black-owned businesses and conduct neighborhood clean-ups. The major said it had achieved measurable success in Cleveland.

Kemo had not objected to my presence as a reporter. Gafford listened and asked questions. We were wrapping up when Gafford inquired, "Have there been any objections to your work in Cleveland?" "Only from B'nai B'rith types," Kemo said. "But that could be expected."

B'nai B'rith types? Like my parents? What the hell was he talking about? I was speechless.

"What did he mean, B'nai B'rith types?" I asked Gafford afterward. The mayor's chief of staff didn't know but said he would check with counterparts in Cleveland about the major and his program. I don't remember if the Fruit of Islam won the contract it was after in Columbus, but if it didn't, Sam and Mollie Rozenman weren't to blame. And 20 years later, when by one quirk after another, I found myself working at B'nai B'rith International headquarters in Washington, D.C., I never heard anyone mention the Fruit of Islam, not even when Farrakhan's followers occasionally turned up outside what was to them the headquarters of the international Zionist conspiracy, to condemn, via bullhorn and placards, us conspirators within.

June, 2018 and Farrakhan was still instructing his followers about the evils of Jews and Judaism. During a three-hour sermon at his Chicago mosque headquarters the Nation of Islam leader warned against "Satanic Jews who have infected the whole world with poison and deceit." According to the Jewish Telegraphic Agency, "Farrakhan also claimed that contemporary Jews are responsible for promoting child molestation, misogyny, police brutality and sexual assault, among other social ills. In addition, he asserted that contemporary Judaism is nothing but a 'system of tricks and lies' which Jews study in order to learn how to 'dominate' non-Jews."

Two months later a widely-circulated news photograph showed four men seated on the altar at singer Aretha Franklin's funeral. Facing 4,000 mourner-celebrants were Rev. Jesse Jackson; Rev. Al Sharpton—who helped incite the antisemitic and deadly 1991 Crown Heights riots and 1995 Freddy's Fashion Mart killings but went on to host an MSNBC-TV program, advise President Obama and deliver widely-publicized eulogies at the funerals of Trayvon Martin, George Floyd, Daunte Wright and other blacks killed by police or security guards—former President Bill Clinton and Nation of Islam Minister Louis Farrakhan.

Two months after that, in October, 2018 a man who sounded like a pale Farrakhan posted on social media that Jews were the spawn of Satan and intent on destroying white America. He then massacred 11 worshippers at the Tree of Life synagogue in Pittsburgh.

History's relentless ebb and flow—is it an arc humans bend toward justice or that broken corkscrew we use repeatedly to pull up meanness and sorrow? Or both, simultaneously? If both, then the direction of movement must depend on the relative strength and motivation of Viktor Frankl's two post-Holocaust "races." Frankl, the young Austrian psychiatrist who survived Nazi death camps and went on to write the best-selling *Man's Search for Meaning*, asserted that the only meaningful human division separating races is that dividing the decent "race" from its opposite.

Chapter Six:
Celebrity Journalism. Stop the Presses!

Andy Warhol, Elvis Clinton and More

"Andy Warhol's at the Pace Gallery for the opening of his new exhibit," City Editor Bill Keesee said. "Eva Glimcher's set up an interview. Go over and see what you can get." It was March, 1978. Glimcher had opened a Pace location in Columbus after launching galleries in Boston and New York and later would be credited with expanding central Ohio's previously dry art interests to contemporary works and trends.

The assignment didn't thrill me. I might not have known art, but I knew I'd always thought Warhol a *poseur*. Yes, he was perhaps the best-known American, maybe best-known international pop artist. Brilliantly commercial, a more efficient and productive than competent draftsman, according to Dominic Green's April 18-19, 2020 *Wall Street Journal* review of *Warhol*, Blake Gopnik's 961 page (!?) biography, Andy Warhol was an inspired popular culture conceptualizer. He seemed to exemplify— as did the often-married, occasionally starring actress Gabor sisters, Zsa Zsa, Eva and Magda—historian Daniel Boorstin's observation that celebrities were people famous for being famous. Like Donald Trump. The Kardashians—Kim, Khloe and Kourtney et. al. more recently filled the same role, for which Rep. Alexandra Ocasio Cortez (D-N.Y.), *cum laude* graduate in international relations and economics from Boston University, 2011 and thereby walking indictment of B.U. in particular if not higher education in general, also contends.

Even more to the point, Andy Warhol epitomized his own honest observation that in the 20th century (post-Marcel Duchamp's and sophisticated *fin de siècle* Paris' displacement of high-brow with low-brow after rolling right through middle-brow) "art was whatever you could get away with." And not only art but also, as it would emerge, in much of politics, journalism, even, via mortgage-backed derivatives, finance.

What Warhol was getting away with at Pace/Columbus was a series of large, Day-Glow portraits of current sports stars. The artist took Polaroid snapshots of baseball pitcher Tom Seaver, tennis star Chris Evert, boxer Muhammad Ali and other top athletes—already known commodities able to sell themselves—stenciled and silk-screened them poster-sized, overlaid with slashes of color. I liked the bright results, all action, zest and fame, but not at $15,000 each. (That would be about $60,000 in 2020 dollars).

The Pace, on East Broad Street just east of downtown, was close enough to the *Citizen-Journal's* newsroom on the mezzanine at 34 S. Third Street on Statehouse Square, in the old *Columbus Dispatch* building, to walk to. I found Warhol at the curb, in a large bus that had been converted into a luxurious motor home. One of the Pace staffers—perhaps Eva Glimcher herself but on this memory fails—had to remind the artist why I was there. He didn't seem the least interested in being interviewed. He proceeded to demonstrate his disinterest with one- and two-word grunts, occasionally varied with a three- or four-word reply, to my increasingly agonized questions.

Ten or 15 minutes of this left me convinced Warhol was not only a phony but an arrogant S.O.B. to boot. My exclusive with the great artiste was turning into the most futile interview I'd ever attempted. Much more of it and I would have to return to Keesee with nothing but, for the first time in four years at the daily, a confession of total failure.

Warhol was seated at the RV's version of a kitchen table. He'd barely turned his head to look at me. Desperate, I took a copy of that day's *C-J* that I happened to be carrying, plopped it on the table in front of him, and asked, "If you edited my paper, what changes would you make?"

Bingo! He was suddenly interested. His hands stretched over the paper, his eyes intent on the copy as he leafed through the pages.

"Well, for the first thing," he said, finally taking notice of my miserable presence and looking at me, "I'd put the comics on the front page." That became the lede of the short feature I managed to eke out. "If Andy Warhol ran this newspaper, you'd be reading the comics on page one." We'd also run the pictures bigger, much bigger. And bury the hard news of world and national disasters in smaller type inside, as it deserved. Something like that.

The *Citizen-Journal* got a story, Pace Gallery its publicity, and Warhol continued in the stratosphere of worldwide celebrity without visible means of support, at least that I could see.

He definitely was right, though, about art being whatever one could get away with, and I would find he was right too that "in the future everyone will be famous for 15 minutes." Evanescently famous if, in my case, misspelled. A few years later, in Washington working as Rep. Shamansky's press secretary, my erroneous 15 minutes arrived. Bob was the only Democrat to represent Ohio's 12th district, then the eastern half of Columbus and Franklin County, plus Delaware and parts of Morrow counties to the north and northeast, between 1958 and the present, and then just for two years. In those long years there was only so much Democracy the 12th district could stand.

Shamansky's two most publicized legislative initiatives, neither successful, were proposals for a federally-funded competition and prize for the first 100-miles-per-gallon automobile and an end to the subsidy to tobacco farmers. *TIME* magazine stopped in one day to interview Bob about one or the other efforts. In those pre-Internet days, *TIME, Newsweek, The New York Times, Washington Post*, and ABC, CBS and NBC evening news shows were the seven sisters of the American news media. If one of them reported on something, it became certified news. Other national, regional and local outlets might well follow. For a *TIME* reporter to interview a freshman congressman seemed a big deal. At least to the freshman congressman's staff.

The reporter even included a quote from me in his article. As Rosenmann, I think, not Rozenman. I got my 15 minutes. Misspelled. Warhol was right. And wrong.

Golfing for Dollars: A Most Unlikely Sixsome

Jack Nicklaus, probably history's best golfer before Tiger Woods burst onto the scene, grew up in Upper Arlington, an affluent suburb of Columbus. His father operated a pair of drug stores. The story is told that in winter young Jack would clear two spaces of snow, scores if not hundreds of yards apart, and then spend endless hours hitting golf balls from one clearing into the other. Nicklaus and Tom Weiskopf, winner of the 1973 Open (the legendary British, not the upstart U.S. Open) played on the same Ohio State University golf team in the early '60s. Off the course in the early to mid-'70s, Weiskopf was a mail clerk in the U.S. Army's 83 ARCOM headquarters at Ft. Hayes in Columbus. My cousin, Ron Shankman, an excellent amateur golfer with several holes-in-one to his credit, and I, a lifetime non-excellent duffer with no such godly shots, served in the same headquarters unit. Ron was a finance clerk and I, as mentioned, a non-commissioned public information officer.

After roll call at some Monday night drills, Weiskopf—the day before on television playing in a PGA tournament, 16 of which he won—would head upstairs to the commanding general's office. I believed it was to impart putting tips. I snapped and developed a couple "grip-and-grin" handshake photos for 83rd ARCOM publicity in which commanding officers would congratulate the lowly mail clerk on his recent lucrative showings.

In 1976, Nicklaus launched his Memorial Tournament at Muirfield Village Golf Club in Dublin, then a one- or two-stoplight village eight or 10 miles distant from downtown Columbus. Dublin, in part due to publicity surrounding the Memorial Tournament, eventually would grow to a good-sized suburban city with three public high schools, office buildings and shopping malls. In 1977, the city desk at the *Citizen-Journal* sent me to cover the Memorial's preliminary pro-am event, specifically the sixsome that was to include the host, Nicklaus, fellow PGA touring pro Roger Maltbie (eventually winner of that year's Memorial), and former President Gerald Ford, comedians Bob Hope and Jackie Gleason, and singer Glen Campbell.

It was a hot, humid Wednesday just before Memorial Day weekend. Ford, center on the University of Michigan's 1932 and 1933 national championship football teams, was still athletically long and lean as he addressed his ball on the tee, if not always accurate off it. The same could not be said for the rotund Gleason, whose short, jerky swing looked like an illustration of everything not to do with a golf club, unless maybe you were trying to kill a gopher.

But most memorable, in the humidity and crush of spectators around the first tee, was Campbell. The self-proclaimed "Rhinestone Cowboy" whose hits also included "Wichita Lineman," "Gentle on My Mind" and "By the Time I Get to Phoenix" and whose variety show ran on CBS Television from 1968 through 1972, was wearing cowboy boot golf shoes. That is, high, medium brown and intricately worked cowboy boots, polished to a rich gleam, with metal spikes. This was long before courses forced players to switch to soft plastic spikes that are gentle on their greens. Golf boots, on a day when one sweated standing still in the shade.

"I'm a rhinestone cowboy/Getting cards and letter from people I don't even know/And offers comin' over the phone ..."

A grand time was had by all, tramping around the rolling, verdant course, bursting in nature's rich green everywhere one looked. After the round, Ford, less than a year out of the White House, held a press conference. "No political questions," the moderator admonished.

My hand up and he called on me early.

"Mr. President, what do you think about President Carter's attempt to call a Middle East peace conference with the Soviet Union?" Okay, it's been more than 40 years so I'm not sure that was my exact question, but it was something along those lines. I hadn't made the first of my 20 trips to Israel, was not yet involved with organized Jewish community life, but had started reading Jewish and Israeli history. I knew Carter's reported desire to get the Kremlin to co-chair a reconvened Geneva conference bringing together Israel, Egypt, Syria, Jordan and the rest was a bad idea. Why exhume a diplomatic Rube Goldberg contraption with too many parts that hadn't worked before?

Ford, looking exasperated, turned to the moderator, silently asking "can you toss this jerk out of here?" The moderator glared at me, then turned to another reporter and said, quite firmly, "Next question."

I took that as a no-comment from Ford.

Later, interviewing Bob Hope went more smoothly, so long as I ignored the fact he never looked at me. This wasn't the Andy Warhol cold shoulder, however. Hope was amiable from the start and patiently let me exhaust all my questions. He just never took his eyes off the golf tournament on television in his motel room.

Bob Hope (Leslie Townes Hope), born in England in 1903, moved with his family to Cleveland in 1908. He reached show business stardom, which lasted nearly 80 years, as a stand-up comedian, actor, singer and author. He, Bing Crosby—*the* American male singer before Frank Sinatra, before Elvis Presley and maybe more versatile than either of them—and the glamourous Dorothy Lamour co-starred in the wacky "On the Road to …" movies. Hope, eventually Sir Bob Hope, K.B.E., made more than 50 U.S.O. tours to entertain U.S. military abroad from World War II through the first Persian Gulf War. "It's great to be back in Korea," he told one audience of G.I.s before South Korea's great leap forward. "You've made so many improvements. Last time I was here, the roads were only mud. Now there's a white line running down the middle of the mud…"

In addition to films and Broadway, Hope starred on radio and television. He hosted the Academy Awards 19 times, more than any other performer. And, among many other things, he appeared at the Ohio State Fair 15 times, five times more than Johnny Cash, 10 times ahead of Kool & The Gang, and surpassed later only by The Oak Ridge Boys. At times a part owner of baseball's Cleveland Indians and football's Los Angeles Rams, possessor of a 3-1 record as a professional boxer before seeking a slightly less punishing line of work, he was for much of the 20th century, as he might have put it in his self-deprecating stage manner, unavoidable. Author Richard Zoglin called his 2014 biography simply *Hope: Entertainer of the Century.*

Of all his wide-ranging sports interests, Hope's first love was golf. From the 1960s on he was a major force behind the Bob Hope Desert Classic on the PGA tour, and over the course of his career a putter became an omnipresent prop during stage performances and television shows. A 1973 White House photograph shows Hope putting a golf ball across the Oval Office carpet toward an ashtray "cup" held by President Nixon. So it was that I found Hope, a man worth hundreds of millions of dollars, by himself, sitting at the foot of the bed in his room at a mid-priced, family-style motel at Morse Road and I-71. He was resting between shows at the Ohio State Fairgrounds a few miles south. The city desk had arranged the interview and given me the room number. I just took the stairs to the second floor, walked down the hall, looked through an open room door and there was Bob Hope, holding a putter and staring intently at the TV.

To be polite, I knocked on the door frame.

"C'mon in," Hope said, not taking his eyes off the golf tournament. "Pull up a chair."

I did. It was a sort of triangular interview, me looking at Hope, him with his eyes on the television, me periodically glancing at the screen to see what so fascinated him. But it was friendly enough, and Hope, who had another show to do back at the fairgrounds a little later, didn't rush me.

He was in his mid-70s then but still quite active. "I've read you're one of the busiest people in Hollywood," I said. "Who sets your schedule?"

"I guess you could say I'm the perpetrator of my own schedule," Hope replied. That schedule sounded like a long-running whirlwind, as he described it. And that became my lede: "Bob Hope perpetrates his own schedule."

When I left, I asked if he wanted me to close the door.

"No, don't bother. I'll get it," he said, still watching the golf tournament.

The world could have walked in on Hope and so long as it didn't disturb his golf viewing, he wouldn't have minded.

"Here She Comes, Miss America!"

Andy Warhol was infuriating, Gerald Ford annoying, Bob Hope interesting, but Miss America 1963, Jacquelyn Mayer, was more than beautiful. She was still striking, polite and focused when I interviewed her in the late '70s, even after the massive stroke that almost killed her at age 28.

It's no longer so—something *is* lost when something's gained, as the lyric has it—but as late as the early 1980s, when there were still only three major television networks, the annual Miss America pageant from Atlantic City, N.J., was must-see-TV. Through the 1970s, more than 20 million households were glued to their sets for the breathless announcement and, amidst tears of joy, coronation. Tens of millions waited for the moment. That was the moment following the end of the bathing suit competition—the bathing suits were one-piece stretch undergarments attached with double-sided adhesive tape to gorgeous young women wearing high heels—and after the talent and interview portions. "And what would *you* do to bring about world peace?" By 2018 the *intelligentsia* would await breathlessly the answer, not from a beauty in high heels but rather 15-year-old child of the Corn People Greta Tintin Eleonora Ernman Thunberg, Swedish schoolgirl and secular environmental Joan of Arc. Something was lost …. But not that moment, instead the one when perennial master of ceremonies Bert Parks would croon, "Here she comes, Miss America …"

When Jackie Mayer, 20, a pretty, bright-eyed brunette from Sandusky, took the crown, a ripple of pride crossed northwestern Ohio. Sandusky was only 35 miles from Tiffin, and Mayer only five years older than I was. Many Buckeyes felt we knew her, almost. Or someone like her. The summer of 1968, when I'd worked as an intern at the *Sandusky Register*, I sometimes drove on the part of Ohio Rt. 2 renamed Jackie Mayer Highway. Once I reported on summer school at Sandusky High, metaphorically following her footsteps.

But in fact, there weren't many like Jacqueline Mayer. She had dropped out of Northwestern University after one year to join Fred Warring and His Pennsylvanians—one of the last touring big bands—as a singer. She hoped for a career in show business. Still, the problem with winning the Miss America title was its built-in obsolescence. There'd been a new Miss America each year since 16-year-old Margaret Gorman, "Miss Washington, D.C." took the title in 1921, so the winner's reign, and usually her fame, were necessarily fleeting.

Yet Jackie Mayer returned to the headlines, briefly, in 1970. After Thanksgiving dinner with her family, she suffered the cerebral blockage that nearly killed her. She would have to persevere through seven years of rehabilitation, from relearning how to walk and talk to functioning almost as she had in her suddenly long-ago time as Miss America. Near the end of that long rehab, Mayer—married to John Townsend and, before the stroke, mother of two children—was in Columbus. She had begun a new career, using her personal experience to work with medical professionals, patients and families, eventually serving as spokeswoman on strokes for the American Heart Association and National Stroke Association.

The *Citizen-Journal* city desk scheduled an interview, so on a bright, chilly spring day I sat by the pool in an otherwise unoccupied courtyard of a well-appointed motel in suburban Worthington, waiting for Miss America. After a bit, a door opened and she walked toward me, alone, a hesitation or trace of uncertainty still in her movements. She sat down and we started to talk.

There was also at times a catch in her voice, maybe lingering slippage between brain and vocal cords. But any feeling of concern on my part quickly dissipated. Looking at her, if I didn't see the glamorous 20-year-old, I definitely saw a beautiful, dark-haired woman in her mid-30s. In fact, my lede would be something like "Jackie Mayer has a quiet beauty that doesn't fade."

More than beauty, she had grace. And not just polished manners, but a kind of gravitas much spoken of yet little enough encountered. I felt—unlike with Warhol, Ford, George Wallace among others, but a bit like with Heston—that I was in the presence of someone really worth listening to. Her husband was a horse-racing executive and they lived on a 50-acre farm near Pittsburgh. She said she felt called to use her experience to help teach and inspire others. Her answers to my questions were neither self-promotional nor matter-of-fact, but rather almost searching. As she explained how riding was part of her physical therapy, I began to understand that no one activity or set of activities amounted to rehabilitation for Jacqueline Mayer. For her, the underlying prescription was determination. In every activity, big or small, day-to-day, Miss America for a year had learned life-long perseverance.

"He'll be Back!"

The May 8, 2020 print edition of *The Wall Street Journal* included a feature headlined "Chess Is King Amid the Pandemic." It reported that during lock-downs in the face of the COVID-19 plague, people across the globe had turned to competing against each other in online chess. "'We've just been exploding,' said Daniel Rensch, the chief chess officer of Chess.com. 'It's been crazy.'" And that was before the fall's much-watched "Queen's Gambit" television mini-series.

A large color photograph of a cigar-chopping fellow, his craggy faced framed by a bristle of gray whiskers along the jaw, illustrated *The Journal's* feature. The old man, in what looked like a designer version of a high school letter jacket, ostensibly was playing chess against his pet donkey. The man was former Mr. World, Mr. Universe, seven-time Mr. Olympia, Hollywood's *Conan the Barbarian* and *The Terminator*, two-term governor of California, Arnold Schwarzenegger.

Playing distant opponents, including old friends on other continents, "is how the former governor of California is spending quarantine," the article said. "And he isn't alone. His pandemic chess habit is shared by a growing crowd" of athletes and politicians. In the photograph, over Schwarzenegger's right shoulder, can be seen a statuette of an impossibly perfect, or rather hyper-perfect, male figure, flexing bulging biceps, a superstructure chest spreading V-like in near defiance of the human genome above sculpted abdominal muscles. The awe-inspiring torso tops a narrow waist, the whole anchored by trunk-like thighs. It's Arnold, just as photographers caught him in his first-place Mr. Olympia run, from 1970 through 1975, from ages 23 to 29. (He would come out of retirement from professional body-building to take the title again in 1981 at an elderly 35, just to prove he could.)

The 32-year-old Schwarzenegger who walked off the elevator onto the mezzanine floor of the old *Columbus Dispatch* building on Jan. 18, 1978 was an instantly recognizable yet third version of the Mr. Everything of the late 1960s and first half of the 1970s, and of the senior citizen in *The Wall Street Journal's* 2020 picture. If memory serves, that day in 1978 he was wearing gray slacks and a burgundy turtle-neck sweater. But even in street clothes instead of posing briefs, and three years into his first body-building retirement, the expansive chest and plane of shoulders scoffing at both gravity and mere mortal musculature were unmistakable. I rose from my desk in the *Citizen-Journal* newsroom and walked over to shake his hand.

"It's good to see you again," I said. "We can talk in the conference room."

This was a little rectangle enclosed on three sides by glass and furnished in sturdy gray Steelcase, selected in the standard Scripps-

Howard Newspaper Co. option: That is to say, like our Plymouth press cars, bottom-of-the-catalogue serviceable. So, Schwarzenegger and I sat on armless chairs with thin vinyl cushions around a small table and left the room's balky metal shutters open.

I had interviewed him the first time a year earlier, when he arrived in Columbus to promote the annual Mr. World competition he and Jim Lorimer, the mayor of suburban Worthington and himself a power-lifter, were running. Power lifters are the grunting, barrel-chested men who hoist prodigious amounts of weight—former deputy secretary of state Richard Armitage, bench press personal best of 330 pounds among them. Power-lifters are not body-builders; the latter are the men and sometimes women who hoist prodigious amounts of weight to become hugely-muscled yet finely chiseled Greek god hyper-images.

Schwarzenegger at first came across as a bit more formal than Bob Hope, but Hope had nearly half a century on him in the celebrity game. Yet even at that initial interview, "the Austrian Oak's" ambition, confidence and charisma were palpable. As with the auditorium in Deerfield Beach, Fla. years later when Bill Clinton entered, our workaday newsroom seemed almost to vibrate at Schwarzenegger's presence.

Schwarzenegger's charisma was joined at the hip with a determination to succeed that was naked yet not quite megalomaniacal. As he indicated at the time and made clear later, his laser-like focus on becoming the world's top body-builder had been less a goal in itself than a step, albeit big, enroute to becoming wealthy and famous in the world at large. Still, if more reserved than Hope, he was in no way brusque. By our second interview in 1978, he was conversational. He talked about his hopes for the long-mooted *Conan the Barbarian* film project, plans for a mail-order vitamin and supplements business and desire—no, intention— to make an even larger mark outside body building, beyond even acting. *Conan*, a violent wizards-and-warriors fantasy eventually released in 1982 starred Schwarzenegger as the avenging Conan, James Earl Jones as the murderous Thulsa Doom (great name for a villain, better name for a heavy metal rock band) and became an international success.

Launched as Mr. World, relaunched as Conan, Schwarzenegger, who emigrated on his own from Austria at 15, made his mark. Unlike so many entertainment and political celebrities of the past half-century, Schwarzenegger was not merely famous for being famous, he forced his way into the spotlight and remained there, through a self-willed fusion of abilities, determination, desire and vision.

He did not always succeed; the defeat in 2005 by California voters of his Propositions 76 and 77, two years into the eight years of his governorship, left him politically emasculated.

Prop. 76 would have given California's chief executive "power to unilaterally cut spending when revenues did not meet projections," *The New York Times* reported. Prop. 77 was "a redistricting plan designed to break the hammerlock Democrats have had for a decade on the California legislature and its congressional delegation." Republican Schwarzenegger lost despite having "staked his time, his prestige and several million dollars of his personal fortune on the ballot campaign that he said was needed to fix a dysfunctional political system."

His party affiliation was due, he had famously explained, to the fact that when he arrived in the States from the United Kingdom in 1968 at 20 years of age, the people who sounded like they were speaking to his immigrant's aspirations—freedom to succeed under a limited, non-interfering government—were Republicans and those who sounded like the socialists he'd left behind in Europe were Democrats.

Then there was his affair with a housekeeper that led to the birth of a son and, eventually, his divorce by Maria Shriver. Maria Shriver was the daughter of Eunice Kennedy Shriver and Sargent Shriver, Jr. Eunice Shriver was a sister of President John F. Kennedy and Sens. Robert and Ted Kennedy and founder of the Special Olympics. Sargent Shriver helped create the Peace Corps, was ambassador to France and Democratic presidential nominee Sen. George McGovern's vice-presidential running mate in 1972. In other words, the teenaged emigrant had married into one branch of America's de facto political royalty (the Bush family—Prescott, George H.W., George W. and Florida Governor Jeb—being another). And lusted his way out.

If daunted, then still unbowed, Schwarzenegger left the governor's mansion in Sacramento in 2011 and immediately returned, profitably, to movies, television and video games. It's been observed and confirmed repeatedly, that F. Scott Fitzgerald's observation "there are no second acts in American lives" was wrong. This is the land of do-overs. By 2020, Schwarzenegger was into at least Act IV.

As we finished the interview in '78, he gave me an autographed a copy of the copiously illustrated 1977 Simon & Schuster release, *Arnold: The Education of a Body Builder*, which he'd co-written with Douglas Kent Hall. It's been on my bookshelves ever since, and after 1979 next to my autographed copy of *My Life*, Moshe Dayan's autobiography.

Three Men in a Picture

In horse racing, you'd call it a trifecta plus the daily double. What were the odds on being a non-Israeli to interview all three generals in the iconic 1967 Six-Day War photograph *and* ghost-writer for both President George W. Bush and Sen. Hillary Clinton?

One of the most well-known pictures of the 1967 Six-Day War shows a trio of Israeli generals, in combat fatigues, walking triumphantly into Jerusalem's Old City. Like parts of eastern Jerusalem, the Old City with Judaism's most sacred site at which Jews are permitted to pray, the Western Wall, had been occupied by Jordan for 19 years. Up until a few hours before the photograph was snapped.

Two of the three men are instantly recognizable. In the center, patch over his left eye, is Defense Minister Moshe Dayan. To Dayan's left is Chief of Staff Yitzhak Rabin. To the defense minister's right walks a short if solidly-built man. Instead of a helmet, like those worn by Dayan and Rabin, this fellow wears a baseball cap-style fatigue hat. The anonymous officer is Uzi Narkiss, overall commander of the first Jewish soldiers to control a unified Jerusalem in 1,897 years. Andy Warhol notwithstanding, what should have been the 15 minutes of fame in Narkiss' strong 27-year military career passed with barely an asterisk. To his subordinate, Gen. Motta Gur, went history's nod for the stunning radio message, "The Temple Mount is in our hands."

Yet the way quantum fate works, Narkiss, not Dayan or Rabin or even Gur would become the person who most stimulated my interest in Israel and restimulated my interest in Judaism. In 1975 or '76 he was in town to speak for the Columbus Jewish Federation. Retired from the military, he then worked as a senior civilian official at the Jewish Agency and World Zionist Organization, assisting with absorption of Jewish immigrants from around the world. On the dubious assumption that as a Jewish news reporter—other Jews worked on the sports and business pages, but not on the general newsroom staff—I would be adequately prepared, my editors at the *Citizen-Journal* sent me to the Federation's office to interview Narkiss.

We met in a small conference room that doubled or tripled as library and storage space. Small and middle aged, at first sight Narkiss was not inspiring. I would not have been surprised to find him sitting behind a cluttered counter in a dusty shop repairing watches. Though I had begun, in a desultory way, to read about modern Israeli history, I knew nothing about Narkiss not in the Federation's press release announcing his talk or discernable from the famous photograph. But when he spoke, quietly, almost matter-of-factly, a thrill shot through me. So, there was another way to be Jewish, other than that of my never quite—to me, anyway— fully American grandfathers with their lingering accents, inescapable memories and massive disinterest in baseball, and other than that of my parents, aunts and uncles with their assimilated, small-town Midwestern Jewishness, simultaneously organic yet vestigial. There was another way, a more positive, assertive way and this man talking to me, a man born in Jerusalem, who fought and triumphed in Jerusalem, and years later would die in Jerusalem, his city and the new-old capital of the Jews, embodied it.

Dayan was another story. He spoke in Columbus late in 1979. Narkiss had appeared at a local synagogue. Dayan, by then both an easily identified celebrity and gaunt from the cancer that would kill him a little less than two years later, filled the main floor of the grandly refurbished, 2,800-seat Ohio Theater on Statehouse Square downtown and properly listed as a National Historic Landmark. I covered his talk for the Ohio Scripps-Howard state bureau, which served the *Citizen-Journal, Cleveland Press* and *Cincinnati Post*. Dayan was not giving a post-speech interview, so I unprofessionally handed one of his aides my paperback copy of his autobiography, *Story of My Life*, which I'd brought along with my notebook and microcassette tape, and asked if the general would autograph it. The aide looked dubious.

"Tell him I'm moving to Kibbutz Ma'agan Michael next month." The aide took the book and disappeared backstage. He quickly reappeared, handing the paperback to me. On the inside of the front cover was Dayan's scrawled English signature, big and legible: M. Dayan, with the "n" extending in a bold stroke back under the whole.

Rabin's signature appears at the bottom of a thank-you note. As publications editor at the Jewish Institute for National Security Affairs, I wrote the first monograph on U.S.-Israel strategic cooperation, "United States-Israel Strategic Cooperation: Conversations and Comments." Published in 1989, it included interviews with Menachem "Mendy" Meron (Maj. Gen., Ret.) director-general of Israel's Ministry of Defense from 1983 through 1986; U.S. Ambassador to Israel (1977–1985) Samuel Lewis; Maj. Gen. Amos Yaron, Israel's defense attaché in Washington (1986-1989); Pentagon officials and portions of Rabin's Nathan Golden Lecture on Middle East Security for JINSA.

We sent copies to all those cited in the monograph as well as to other U.S. and Israeli diplomats, military officials, members of Congress, think tank staffers and the press. Sometime later I received an appreciative note from Rabin, on his stationery as defense minister. Other outfits would produce longer, more detailed examinations of U.S.-Israel strategic cooperation later but Rabin's message meant we'd gotten off on the right foot.

Don't Have "60 Minutes" to Explain Yourself

"Mike Wallace is on the phone and he sounds angry," a colleague said as she transferred the call.

It was 1991 or '92 and I was managing editor of the *Miami Jewish Tribune*. We'd just published an editorial urging a local synagogue to rescind its decision to honor Wallace.

Wallace, of course, was the star inquisitor of CBS-Television's highly-rated "60 Minutes" news magazine program. He died at 93 in 2012. A 2019 documentary, "Mike Wallace Is Here," cited him as inspiration for modern sharp-edged (if often two-dimensional) television interviewers.

"Why," demanded the veteran correspondent and multiple Emmy winner, "did you write that editorial?"

This was surreal. Unlike "60 Minutes," the *Tribune*, and our sister weeklies in Ft. Lauderdale and West Palm Beach were little known outside south Florida. Still, Mike (Myron Leon) Wallace had seen our editorial, been provoked to call and wanted an answer.

Overcoming my surprise, I gave him one: His reputation as a fearless investigator did not hold up when it came to coverage of Jews and Israel. As we'd argued in the paper:

In a "60 Minutes" segment in 1975, Wallace asserted—despite overwhelming evidence to the contrary—that "today, life for Syria's Jews is better than it was in years past."

A 1982 Wallace report on Israel spotlighted one critic and deleted the views of two supporters.

In a 1984 segment, Wallace erroneously claimed that Israel, Jordan and Lebanon once were part of what "historians call Greater Syria." He asserted that Israeli possession of the Golan Heights "affronts Syrian dignity" without noting that Israel won the territory in a 1967 war of self-defense and kept it in another such conflict in 1973. Syrian dictator and Soviet ally Hafez al-Assad wanted only as sympathetic a hearing in Washington as Jerusalem got, Wallace told viewers.

He replied to harsh criticism of the 1984 segment from *Near East Report*, the newsletter of the American Israel Public Affairs Committee. "Let me assure you," the correspondent told *NER*, "I am proud of my Jewish heritage. I am a supporter of a free, strong and independent Israel."

Perhaps, but three years later, "60 Minutes" aired a segment in which Wallace looked beyond the 400,000 Soviet Jews who'd received invitations to emigrate to Israel. "Nonetheless," he insisted, "the fact remains that one and a-half million Soviets identified as Jews apparently live more or less satisfying lives" in the U.S.S.R. "And theirs has been a story largely untold." Largely untold because it was largely untrue.

In this report, Wallace did not challenge the obviously false claim by Samuel Zivs, the Jewish deputy leader of the official Anti-Zionist Committee, that only a few Jewish malcontents wanted to emigrate. Nor did Wallace tell viewers of Ziv's 20 years as Soviet spokesman on "the Jewish question." And the investigative journalist never mentioned government crackdowns on Jews, Jewish ritual and study.

In 1988, "60 Minutes" and Wallace took on Israel's U.S. supporters, AIPAC in particular. In a segment charging that pro-Israel political action committees "had given $6 million this year to a variety of candidates"—the actual amount was about $2.7 million for the previous 18 months—Wallace claimed "there are many who charge that AIPAC, with its sights set only on Israel, is just too demanding of U.S. politicians." He didn't say that campaign donations by pro-Israel PACs paled in comparison to those on behalf of labor unions or corporations.

The Conference of Presidents of Major Jewish Organizations described the segment as "filled with distortions, innuendoes and inaccuracies."

Having worked on *NER* before going to the *Tribune*, I was familiar with Wallace's coverage of Jews and Israel. Hence the editorial. As I remember, the phone call ended in quiet disagreement. Ignoring the editorial, the synagogue staged its fund-raising tribute to him.

The "Mike Wallace Is Here" documentary included what one reviewer called a "stormy" interview with Menachem Begin. Wallace presses the Israeli prime minister on any difference between Palestine Liberation Organization leader Yasser Arafat and himself as head of the pre-state Irgun, which the British condemned as a terrorist group.

Wallace's false equivalence exposes either prejudice or confusion. The actual link would have connected the British, who used force to prevent Jews from entering Mandatory Palestine instead of assisting them, which they were obligated to do under the League of Nations/United Nations' Palestine Mandate, and the PLO, which used terror to drive Jews from Israel.

Wallace later described himself as "an American reporter, a Jew who believes in going after facts on the ground as Daniel Pearl [the *Wall Street Journal* correspondent beheaded by al-Qaeda in Pakistan in 2002] did, and reporting them accurately, let the chips fall where they may."

As I wrote for a commentary distributed in 2019 by the Jewish News Syndicate: not always.

Elvis Jefferson Clinton in Florida

"The Clinton campaign called. We can have an exclusive interview with him, but we'll have to meet him at Beth Emeth synagogue in Del Ray, and ride with him to Century Village in Deerfield Beach."

Days before Florida's 1992 Super Tuesday presidential primary, Arkansas Gov. Bill Clinton and Massachusetts Sen. Paul Tsongas seemed to be, if not the last men standing, the two leading contenders for the Democratic Party's presidential nomination, with Clinton ahead of Tsongas. By then Senators Bob Kerrey of Nebraska and Tom Harkin of Iowa had dropped out, leaving former California Governor Jerry Brown trailing the two front-runners. Now, as managing editor of the weekly *Miami Jewish Tribune, Broward* (Ft. Lauderdale) *Jewish World* and *Palm Beach* (Boca Raton, West Palm Beach and Palm Beach) *Jewish World*, I was going to interview Clinton. We'd get a campaign scoop not only ahead of the rival *South Florida Jewish Journal* but even the *Miami Herald* and Ft. Lauderdale *Sun-Sentinel*.

I reached Beth Emeth (Hebrew for House of Truth) in time to hear Clinton finish talking to an overflow crowd. A campaign staffer then led me through more people milling about the parking lot to a dark blue Chrysler sedan. Clinton quickly arrived, accompanied only by Dee Dee Myers, his pert blonde spokeswoman. She'd already had extensive experience working on Democratic campaigns since graduating from college in the early 1980s, and would, on Clinton's inauguration, become the first woman and second-youngest White House press secretary.

Sandwiched between Clinton and Myers in the back of the Chrysler, I started working through the nine or 10 questions I'd scribbled into my reporter's notebook, taping with a microcassette recorder as we rolled the 10 or 12 miles south on I-95 to Deerfield Beach, a police car in the lead.

The candidate said President George H. W. Bush and Secretary of State James A. Baker were undermining chances for Arab-Israeli peace by pressuring Israel but not demanding anything of the other side. Referring to the 1991 Madrid Conference that brought together Israel and Arab states, including bitterly hostile Syria, in the illusory "end-of-history" window opened by Saddam's defeat, the Soviet Union's collapse and

America's temporary status as sole superpower, Clinton said he "had the impression, when these peace talks opened, that we really had a shot at an agreement between the Israelis and Palestinians. Even if nothing else happened, that would have been an historic moment. But I think that all these external moves by the United States may have so muddied the atmosphere that even that may be less likely."

In particular, the question of Israeli settlements in the disputed West Bank and Gaza Strip and Syrian Golan Heights should have been left for direct negotiations between the Jewish state and Arab countries, Clinton said. "If the United States keeps trying to decide the issue," increasing pressure on Israel apart from Arab-Israeli talks, "then the Arabs may wonder what they have to give away—or whether they have to give anything away." If the Bush administration was going to lean on Israel, why not also demand the Arabs abandon their economic boycott, promote democracy in their own countries or seek genuine accommodation with the Israelis? "The only way to get an agreement is if everybody's got something to give, and something to get," he asserted.

Clinton also prodded Bush to counter the Jew-baiting of his Republican primary challenger, columnist Patrick Buchanan. A day or two earlier outside Atlanta, Buchanan nettled Jewish hecklers by asserting that his rally was "of Americans, by Americans and for the good old USA."

After Iraqi leader Saddam Hussein ordered his military to seize Kuwait in 1990, but before the first Persian Gulf War in 1991 in which a U.S.-led coalition routed Hussein's occupation army, destroying much of it, Buchanan infamously declared on television that "there are only two groups that are beating the drums for war in the Middle East—the Israeli Defense Ministry and its amen corner in the United States." In a follow-up newspaper column, he wrote " 'the civilized world must win this fight,' the editors thunder. But, if it comes to war, it will not be the 'civilized world' humping up that bloody road to Baghdad, it will be American kids, with names like McAllister, Murphy, Gonzales, and Leroy Brown." As for Congress, Buchanan had labeled Capitol Hill "Israeli-occupied territory." In this he wasn't far from neo-Nazis who claimed America was run by the Z.O.G.—Zionist occupied government—a charge found pre-Internet on obscure broadsheets like *The Spotlight* but in the digital age and post al-Qaeda's Sept. 11, 2001 attacks, just a click away on any computer screen.

"The president should speak out against antisemitism wherever it occurs, and especially when it occurs in his own back yard, in his own party," Clinton told me. Further, Bush "should avoid doing anything in a way which stokes the antisemitic fires that are always at least smoldering embers in corners of virtually every nation in the world." The governor referred to Bush's earlier battle with congressional backers of loan guarantees to support Israel's absorption of a wave of Soviet Jewish immigrants. He said "if the president had wanted to support a delay in approval of loan guarantees last fall—even though Israel already had agreed to one delay—he could have done it under circumstances that would not have inflamed the latent antisemitism in the United States."

In the loan guarantee fight, Bush had referred to himself as "one lonely man on the telephone against all those big, rich Jewish lobbyists." This was in part an allusion to several thousand delegates—rich, poor or middling Jews and non-Jews—on Capitol Hill for AIPAC's annual members' congressional visits. Yet this was the same Bush who had played a significant role in the rescue and migration to Israel of thousands of oppressed Ethiopian Jews.

Clinton said Iraq had to be prevented from acquiring nuclear weapons and pressed to comply with all United Nations resolutions requiring disclosure and destruction of any weapons of mass destruction and their means of production. "We have to do whatever it takes to make sure Iraq complies with the rules," the candidate added. He disagreed with those who claimed that after the end of the Cold War, Israel no longer was a strategic asset to the United States. Citing the possible spread of nuclear weapons to Iraq, Iran and other Middle Eastern countries, the candidate said, "I'd sure hate to think what it would be like to deal with all those other countries with no Israel there."

Spoken like a man who would have opposed President Obama's 2015 Iran deal, a man who could not have won the Democratic presidential nomination in 2020. But if hindsight is golden, so was Bill Clinton at his next stop, the sprawling Century Village retirement community in Deerfield Beach. The candidate was to address a large auditorium filled with Century Village residents, and representatives of local and national news media were on hand. As we waited, I heard other reporters asking, "When do we see Elvis?" This was the first time I'd heard Clinton identified with the greatest rock n' roll star, the man who famously flashed from truck driver to worldwide celebrity—screaming, shrieking, fainting girls and young women in his wake, boys and men aping his hair and dress—in less than two years. The equivalence was apt.

When Clinton strode onto the stage at the retirement community, excitement crackled throughout the auditorium. If a giant version of your junior high school science class van de Graaff static electricity generator had been set up in a center aisle, the spark-like charisma Clinton exuded would have melted it. People in the audience seemed to be tingling. Watching their reaction as Clinton just smiled—that warm, all-encompassing beam that let each person present understand they were the one and only one he was speaking to—I was simultaneously rapt, amused and apprehensive. Like Viktor Frankenstein with his esoteric and occult scientific knowledge, one could do great good, or ill, with such charisma. And at Bill Clinton's level, not only in an old black-and-white "B" thriller.

His speech hit some of the points made during our interview, but also included domestic topics. On expanding the federal government's involvement with medical insurance, for example, he seemed to be for it. Before driving back to Miami, I called my editor, Buddy Korn, Jr. "Save some space on the front page," I said needlessly, as if the *Miami Jewish Tribune* regularly interviewed presidential candidates. "I've got some great stuff."

Although I been reporting on candidates and elected officials off-and-on since George Wallace in 1967 and Nixon in '68, helped draft a couple of speeches for Ohio Gov. Rhodes in my first writing and editing job out of college—Information Writer I in the Ohio Department of Development—speeches as near as I could tell never actually delivered—and worked as press secretary for U.S. Rep. Bob Shamansky, I'd never run into a campaigner so captivating as Clinton. I should have known better, but irresistible charm is irresistible, at least temporarily.

The article I wrote, some of which is quoted above, appeared in our Miami, Broward and Palm Beach papers and was distributed nationally and overseas by the Jewish Telegraphic Agency. Clinton won most of the southern Super Tuesday primaries, doing well among blacks and Hispanics and edging Tsongas with Jewish voters, according to exist polls reported by the general press.

Yet there was a warning signal in my notes from Clinton in Del Ray and Deerfield beaches. What I thought I heard the governor say about Israel and antisemitism, for example, was not quite what I found scrawled in my notebook. Running the tape recorder for clarification, I found that Clinton's affirmations had been artfully phrased, each with a loophole obvious on second hearing. That is, plain when miles away and safely outside his charismatic radiation field. Yes, pro-Israel ... as firmly as possible, as conditions warrant. Definitely, ready to expose anti-Jewish bigots ... especially in someone else's party. It would all depend on what the meaning of "is" is, as the nation later would learn during the Monica Lewinsky impeachment scandal. William Jefferson Elvis Clinton, slick indeed.

I mentioned my belated realization years later at a small party in suburban Washington. Another guest, it happened, was Jerry Oppenheimer, author of numerous celebrity tell-all biographies. Oppenheimer was writing a book about Bill and Hillary Clinton. His manuscript would become *State of a Union: Inside the Complex Marriage of Bill and Hillary Clinton* (HarperCollins, 2000), a best-seller until battered by a hostile *New York Times* review. Always good to be with the in-crowd, and protected by it.

My remark about Clinton's mastery of verbal gymnastics appeared in *State of a Union*, a bit contorted. For example, the status of the *Tribune* and sister editions—our combined print run in the early '90s had been nearly 100,000 copies—was erroneously reduced to "a small weekly." I was tempted to write HarperCollins, demanding corrections in subsequent editions. But maybe one day the big publishing house might be interested in a manuscript of mine and, who knows, perhaps option it to the movies. Even after I discovered he was a fictional character, Walter Mitty was one of my early heroes, along with Cleveland Indians' slugger Rocky Colavito and Barry Goldwater, who didn't play for the Indians but whose Republican Party similarly struggled to break even. So, I decided against insisting on rectification by HarperCollins. But not to repeat my 1992 vote for Clinton. It would be Dole, U.S. Senator Robert Joseph Dole (R-Kansas) of all people, in 1996. Once lost, journalistic virginity requires embarrassing and often unsuccessful contortions to regain.

Chapter Seven:
The First President Bush

You Call This Politics?

George H. W. Bush was running for president, the first time. It was 1979 and the former congressman, former U.S. ambassador to China and former CIA director was in Columbus for a fund-raiser and press breakfast. Bush was being squired about by long-time Ohio GOP donor Gordon R. Zacks.

"Gordy" Zacks ran the family's RG Barry Corp., founded by Florence Melton, her husband Aaron Zacks and Harry Streim in 1947. Melton grew up poor in Philadelphia, invented the first washable, foam-soled slippers, and the rest—including bath-robes, shoulder pads for suit and sports coat jackets, and handbags—was profitable history. Eventually, she would start the Florence Melton School of Adult Jewish Learning in conjunction with Jerusalem's Hebrew University. The project would become the largest of its sort in North America, England, Australia, South Africa and Israel. Florence Melton also endowed Ohio State University's Melton Center for Jewish Studies.

When Gordon's brother Barry (hence, the RG Barry name) decided to go out as a solo act, he started the Max & Erma's restaurant chain, a Columbus-based upgrade of the T.G.I. Friday's franchise. Gordy Zacks would become an informal advisor to George H.W. Bush and national finance committee co-chairman for his second, successful presidential campaign in 1987-1988.

The press breakfast was being held in the downtown Christopher Inn. The Christopher was an interesting place, if apparently not quite interesting enough. A circular structure 12 or 14 stories high, the hotel opened in 1963 on East Broad Street, three blocks from the State House. It closely resembled Los Angeles' Capitol Records building, completed eight years earlier. Both, as often remarked, looked like stacks of disturbingly large concrete 45 rpm records, the Christopher perhaps unintentionally. Regardless, hearing the Bob Allen Trio's melodious jazz in the downstairs poolside cocktail lounge was a must for Buckeyes out on the town in those days when there wasn't nearly as much town to be out on. In one of those cases of all-too-common cosmic injustice, the School Employees Retirement System demolished the Christopher in 1988 to make way for its new headquarters about which, whatever else can be said, it does not look like a stack of giant records or boast an indoor pool-side bar.

I kept thrusting my arm up during the coffee-and-rolls press breakfast, and Bush kept calling on other reporters. As the event broke up, I squeezed into a knot of people around the presidential hopeful. I maneuvered until facing him and asked my question. "Do you think the Clark amendment should be repealed so we can help the anti-communist rebels in Angola?"

Sen. Dick Clark (D-Iowa) had sponsored an amendment to the 1976 U.S. Arms Export Control Act that prevented U.S. weapons going to any non-governmental military or paramilitary in Angola. Several rebel groups had cooperated in fighting to oust the Portuguese from their large African colony. They then battled each other in Angola's civil war, which became one of the biggest Cold War proxy fights between the United States and Soviet Union. Influential American conservatives pushed for aid to UNITA, the National Union for the Total Independence of Angola; the Kremlin armed the MLPA, the Popular Movement for the Liberation of Angola. But even after congressional passage of the amendment—another reaction to, or extension of our failure in Vietnam—Bush, as CIA director, refused to confirm that Washington had stopped helping UNITA.

Bush looked down at me quizzically. Peculiar question, he might have been thinking, especially here in Columbus. This young reporter must be an odd bird. Whatever, he took the fatherly approach. Almost whispering, as if taking me into his confidence, he said, "Look, there aren't the votes to repeal the Clark amendment. Anyway, those UNITA guys don't stand a chance."

At that moment, I decided I didn't want to see George H. W. Bush in the White House. So unimaginative, so conventional. A decade later, shortly after Iraq's 1990 invasion of Kuwait, British Prime Minister Margaret Thatcher famously cautioned Bush, then president, "George, don't go wobbly on us." The admonition's context has been disputed, but then-defense secretary, later vice president Dick Cheney's denial aside, not Thatcher's use of it. She's got that right, I thought in 1990, recalling my coffee and Danish with George at the Christopher.

As for UNITA, it eventually would be defeated militarily and outmaneuvered politically in Angola by the ruling MPLA. But by then, the Soviet Union itself would be gone, to the surprise and, at first, professional regret—the world would be too unstable now, they feared—of more than a few Western policy makers. Among the non-celebrants were denizens of an entire academic discipline called "Sovietologists" and a chunk of Washington's post-World War II "wise men," George H. W. Bush temporarily among them.

Chapter Eight:
We're Off to See the Dictator!

For the Moment, We're Not in Kansas Anymore

In April, 1944, Dinko Ljubomir Sakic, then 22, received a promotion. He was elevated from assistant commandant to commandant of Jasenovac concentration camp in Yugoslavia. His wife, Nada, was half-sister of the previous camp commander and Sakic himself known as a "fanatic" supporter of Ante Pavelic, leader of World War II Croatia's pro-Nazi *Ustashe* regime. It *is* who you know. Networking matters.

Estimates of the Serbs, Jews, Roma and others murdered at Jasenovac—"the Auschwitz of the Balkans"—vary greatly, from 35,000 to 200,000 or more. The camp, 62 miles from Zagreb, was not a German-style industrialized killing factory. It lacked gas chambers and crematoria. Instead, victims were slain the old-fashioned ways—beaten, stabbed, shot, strangled, blow-torched or drowned in the adjacent Sava River.

A former inmate recalled Sakic arrogantly striding through Jasenovac in a well-pressed uniform and polished boots, "like a fashion plate." A photograph from those days confirms the image. The well-dressed commandant occasionally tortured and killed prisoners himself, sometimes shooting them in the head with his pistol.

With the Allied victory in 1945 and collapse of *Ustashe* rule, Sakic and his wife fled the Balkans, first to Franco's Spain, then—like countless Nazis and Nazi allies—decamped to the land of the *pampas*, steaks and the tango, Juan Peron's Argentina…

… The original "Mission Impossible" ran on CBS Television from 1966-1973. A sequel series lasted from 1988 through 1990, and Tom Cruise headlined a later, successful movie franchise. "Mission Impossible's" first one-hour programs typically featured star Peter Graves (brother of James Arness, U.S. Marshal Matt Dillon in television's venerable "Gunsmoke") and his Impossible Missions Force. In each episode the team of secret agents, which favored deception, manipulation, even blackmail over slug-fests and shoot-outs, undertook improbable assignments from an anonymous secretary of an unidentified U.S. spy agency. The missions usually targeted an enemy dictator or crime outfit. And always with the sobering proviso that if Mr. Phelps (Graves' IMF name) or other team members failed, were captured or killed, "the secretary will disavow any knowledge of your mission." IMF, Impossible Missions Force, was not to be confused with the International Monetary Fund. Or maybe the fund was just an elaborate cover.

Anyway, as undergraduates, my roommates, neighbors and I watched religiously. "Mission Impossible" featured intricate—for network television—plots with their covert skullduggery, shadowy back alleys and tension-building music by composer Lalo Schiffrin. The show provided an exquisite counter-point to my Accounting 101 and History of American Journalism classes. To make clear to domestic viewers that the action was taking place not really at the Desilu Studios in Hollywood but rather in whatever sinister foreign locale Phelps and his people had infiltrated that particular week, the word "police" on law enforcement vehicles was rendered variously as "polize," "polisia," "poleic" or other simulacrum.

So, when I received a phone call in Zagreb, Croatia early in March, 1998 informing me that "you will be picked up tomorrow morning by a limousine from the presidential palace. Be on time," "Mission Impossible" theme music began playing in my head and my deodorant began to fail. The meeting between our three-man B'nai B'rith delegation—of which I as press spokesman and editor of *International Jewish Monthly* magazine (banner notwithstanding, *IJM* was a bi-monthly then) was the most junior—and Croatian President Franjo Tudjman was on. We were in Zagreb to witness the opening of the last war crimes trial of a major World War II-era concentration camp commander, Dinko Sakic. Tudjman had invited B'nai B'rith's immediate past president Tommy Baer, a Richmond, Va. lawyer, and George Specter, the organization's associate director for public policy, to be official observers at the trial. B'nai B'rith not only had helped located Sakic but also assisted in the search for evidence.

President Tudjman was, to put it mildly, of some historical significance. He fought as a young partisan during World War II against both Yugoslav's royalists and Italian and German occupiers. After Yugoslavia's brutal civil war, Tudjman rose through the military, becoming the country's youngest major-general in 1960. He then earned a doctorate in history and began emphasizing—in contradiction to Yugoslav leader Josip Broz Tito and Tito's Communist Party—Croat nationalism.

Tudjman downplayed the murderous nature of the World War II *Ustashe* regime. The Communist Party expelled him in 1967 and jailed him once in the 1970s and again in the '80s. In his 1989 work, *Wastelands of Historical Reality*, he minimized Croatia's wartime fascism. Tudjman also favored the lower end of death estimates for Jasenovac.

Years before, Specter had called *Wastelands* "clearly a work of antisemitism cloaked in scholarly terms that sought to portray Jews as villains throughout history."

Tito died in 1980 and, without his strongman rule, Yugoslavia began to fragment. It, like the Soviet Union and East Germany, among others, turned out to have been a state but not a nation. Created as the Kingdom of Serbs, Croats and Slovenes by the World War I Allies, its pre-1920s constituent parts—the Austro-Hungarian Empire's Serbia, Croatia, Slovenia, Bosnia-Herzegovina, Montenegro and Kosovo—reemerged post-Tito in combative diversity. Croatia, about the size of West Virginia, had a population of roughly five million people. In 1989, Tudjman formed the Croatian Democratic Union Party, and ruled as Croatia's authoritarian president from 1990 until his death in December, 1999.

In 1994, seeking improved relations with the United States, Tudjman apologized to B'nai B'rith for "the hurtfulness of certain portions" of *Wasteland* "and the misunderstandings they have caused." Perhaps in the belief that the road to Washington ran through his country's remnant Jewish community and thence to Jerusalem, Tudjman had established good relations with Croatian Jews and with Israel—having previously referred to Israelis as "Judeo-Nazis." Approximately 5,000 of the country's 20,000 Jews—whose ancestors first arrived in the third century C.E. under the Roman Empire's European Union-like free travel rules—had survived the Holocaust. By the mid-'90s, the community numbered 2,500 (now 1,500). A sanitized version of *Wasteland*, titled *Impasse*, appeared. Even so, Holocaust survivor, author and Nobel Peace Prize winner Elie Wiesel objected strenuously to the invitation to Tudjman to join other world leaders in Washington for 1993's opening of the U.S. Holocaust Memorial Museum.

Sakic lived openly in an Argentine coastal town and was involved with the Croatian émigré (or *Ustashe* refugee) community. During the 1990s he gave several interviews. He claimed alternately that during his seven-month rule of Jasenovac, guards were forbidden to harm prisoners and that inmates who died fell to malnutrition or disease and, on the other hand, if he had it to do over, he would change nothing but wished more Serbs would have perished and in any case, he slept "like a baby." B'nai B'rith's Spectre was among those whose pressure on Croatia, Argentina and the United States helped turn Sakic from a nearly-forgotten World War II footnote into a diplomatic liability for Zagreb and Buenos Aires.

So, there we were at the new Zagreb Sheraton (built with German investment)—Spectre, Baer and I. With different schedules that day, we would arrive separately at the presidential palace. On a high hill with a commanding view of the city, the palace—not a residence but rather working headquarters of the chief executive—had been Tito's when he visited Zagreb during Yugoslavia's heyday. Opened in 1964, it was a clean-lined, mid-century modern structure, a large white rectangle crowning the peak of Pantovcak forest park.

Even before the limousine arrived, the day opened memorably. Tudjman had fought the 1992-1995 Balkan wars by successfully ousting Serbian forces from Serb-majority portions of Croatia—"ethnically cleansing" several hundred thousand Serbs and by taking a Croat-populated piece of Bosnia-Herzegovina. Though combat had not touched the capital, Zagreb, with its little squares, hodge-podge of 19th and early 20th century buildings and picturesque if a bit rundown central city streets reminded one of a small, somewhat shabby Paris. Especially as the outer ring of communist-era gray apartment blocks, in their dormitory-prison blend of structural concrete sadness, reflected the French capital's unhappy outer *banlieues*.

The Sheraton, though, was perhaps a sign of post-war progress as well as Germany's desire to gain commercial-diplomatic influence in the Balkans. I decided to take advantage of the health club, with its good-sized indoor pool, before breakfast. The club catered both to hotel guests and locals, downtown workers or residents. I jumped into a free lane and began swimming.

To my left, a lithe young woman. I looked twice to be certain. Yes, she wore only the bottom of her bikini. To my right, another lithe young woman. They weren't twins but could have been sisters. This one also wore only a bikini bottom, and in her case just barely—not so much a double *entendre* as simple description. Each female was demonstrably breast-stroking, and as I freestyled ahead, the young lady on my right pulled her bottom halfway down on her well-rounded glutes. After 30 minutes, I climbed out, goggles fogged. Office working women, or just working women? Local bathing custom or universal signal? No time to inquire.

Breakfast in the hotel's linen-table clothed restaurant came, like lunch and dinner, soaked in butter. But the raspberry tea was wonderful, tasting fresh-picked. At ten minutes to nine, I was on the sidewalk in front of the Sheraton. Five minutes later a shiny black sedan—a Mercedes or BMW if memory serves—pulled to the curb. Inside were two men, the driver, square-jawed, square-shoulder and with a noticeable paunch, and his wingman, square-jawed, square-shoulder and with a noticeable paunch. Both wore brown leather jackets. Both smoked cigarettes. They could have been brothers.

The wingman got out, came around the back of the car, opened the curbside rear door, and, saying nothing, made a slight bow. I got in. If I was being taken for a ride, a la "Mission Impossible," at least it was in a classy car.

The sedan moved unimpeded, it seemed, through downtown and then smartly up the winding road to the presidential palace. Conversation was held to the minimum.

"Nice day, yes?" the wingman said.

"Yes, very nice," I answered.

Actually, it was, sunny with just a hint of early spring chill. Evergreens in Pantovcek park provided color and at some bends in the road sections of the city below came into view. After 15 minutes or so we rolled through a gate and halted before a small reception facility. Baer and Spectre were waiting. So was an honor guard, 10 or 20 men in big hats and uniforms of too much red and too much gold. The outfits looked like something Ru Paul might have designed after seeing the Beefeaters at Buckingham Palace.

Several men in dark business suits escorted us up a short walk to the presidential palace. We entered the lobby, finished in white marble and featuring a winding, open staircase to the second floor. Up we went and, accompanied by a foreign ministry official, an interpreter and a representative of the Croatian Jewish community, we were ushered into Tudjman's office.

I'd been told that the Croatian president was suffering from cancer, but the man behind the desk appeared healthy enough. Perhaps that was due to bulking-up caused by steroid-induced fluid retention. Regardless, he acted fully engaged during our conversation.

Baer and Spectre raised our agenda items. These included the importance of the Sakic trial and the Croatian government ensuring that no evidence was suppressed, no minimization let alone white-washing of the accused's crimes. Our delegation encouraged Tudjman to continue strengthening his country's ties to Israel. And the delegation cautioned against any tendency—Tudjman, as noted, had helped foster the trend—of downplaying the Ustashe's Nazi leanings to exalt Croatian nationalism. I took notes.

The Croatian leader, rarely if ever described as amiable, listened, nodded and made replies ranging from affirmative to non-committal. The only disruptive moment came when Baer finally had enough from the Tudjman toady impersonating a court Jew. Middle-aged and sleek, the man periodically interrupted the discussion by pointing at the president and interjecting "this guy here has done so much for our Jewish community" or "this guy here has done so much for Israel." His act should have embarrassed him; it annoyed us. After his third outburst, Baer wheeled on him and said, "First, your president is not 'this guy,' and second, we don't need you to tell us about his credentials." From then on, the fellow was silent.

After the meeting we rode back down the hill to the city center. Bright sun glittered off all sorts of buildings, residential and commercial, large and small. Tudjman, we decided, held his cards close to his vest, always thinking about how to play the one marked "better ties with Washington," without sacrificing domestic political advantage. The next year, "the father of post-Yugoslav Croatia" would die at 77 from what *The Guardian* (U.K.) reported as "stomach cancer and surgical complications."

We did meet real leaders of Croatia's small Jewish community during our four days in Zagreb, including the president of B'nai B'rith in Croatia, Dr. Dragan Stern—who fought as an anti-fascist partisan in World War II—and publisher Slavko Goldstein, Tudjman's unsuccessful opponent in the 1991 president election. One night after dinner we alighted from a cab in front of an old, four- or five-story apartment building near the center of town. The exterior looked like routine maintenance had been routinely deferred, but inside the structure told a somewhat different story. In a high-ceiling apartment, with frosted glass double-doors separating a sizeable parlor from the rooms beyond, we met with five or six people, men and women. They were doctors, lawyers, professors, people who had managed to survive fascists, communists and now, returned from exiles external or internal, imposed or chosen, moved in the shifting space between authoritarian nationalists and would-be democrats.

The apartment, with its old-fashion chandelier, china and framed black-and-white photographs in glass cases, and its high-backed furniture could have been a stage set: "Interior, well-appointed town home, central or eastern Europe, 1925." If there was no money, or intention, for contemporary upgrades, there was just enough to maintain a sort of recollected elegance.

Our hosts and hostesses reflected the room, or vice versa. Over tea and coffee, sugar cookies and another dry sweet I didn't recognize we discussed Croatian politics, the position of the Jews, attitude of the government, the possibility of a more democratic future. In an understated but thorough manner, these people who knew from experience more than most of life's incessant challenges, periodic dangers and occasional rewards, briefed us on the way things really worked in their country. No court Jews here. Back at the Sheraton, I felt as if I'd been in and out of a time machine. The machine's inhabitants were people forced by the 20th century to bear the heavy past while living in a jittery present in anticipation of a motile future.

Before Sakic's trial opened, we had trooped over to the U.S. embassy to meet Ambassador William Dale Montgomery. The embassy occupied an old, good-sized building that look like it previously had been the in-city residence of a well-to-do and long-gone family. The building covered virtually its entire corner lot, edging up to the sidewalks and just steps from the streets. Embassy guards, the customary U.S. Marines with their scrupulously polite, steely-eyed demeanor, manned a small booth at the side door used as the entrance for routine business.

Concrete Jersey-wall style barriers shielded the building from the two facing streets. Five months later Egyptian Islamic Jihad would use truck bombs almost simultaneously to level the American embassies in Tanzania and Kenya, murdering more than 200 people, including 12 Americans and wounding more than 4,000. The attacks by EIJ raised the profiles of an ideologically, and later organizationally, related group called al-Qaeda, led by an Islamic fanatic recluse named Osama bin-Laden.

In February, 1998, a month before our visit to the embassy in Zagreb, bin-Laden had issued his *fatwa*, a ruling on a point of Islamic religious law. It declared that "to kill the Americans and their allies— civilians and military—is an individual duty for every Muslim who can do it in any country in which it is possible...." I don't remember whether Amb. Montgomery mentioned bin-Laden or al-Qaeda in his briefing, but he made clear the State Department wanted U.S. embassies to strengthen security precautions. Bureaucracies moving bureaucratically, it would be five years before his charming but street-side building would be abandoned in favor of a modern, character-less but defensible location. Meanwhile, he and his staff were on alert.

One side of the embassy faced a park-like square. Across it diagonally sat the courthouse in which Sakic was about to stand trial. The building looked vaguely like courthouses in small county seats across New England and Midwest America, meant to be imposing but more commonly just official and staid. The morning the trial opened, the courtroom in which Sakic, after a 53-year-delay, faced justice was jammed. Our delegation had seats some rows back, but because the chamber was arranged in a sort of "L," we could see the accused by glancing about 45 degrees to our right.

At 22, overseeing the brutality that was Jasenovac, authorizing the deaths of thousands, imperiously killing some himself, Dinko Sakic was known as "the Beast of the Balkans." Now, at 77, he sat slumped or perhaps nonchalantly, it was hard to tell. The defense would claim he was in ill-health, but the well-fed man with a ruddy complexion, in a light blue suit and open-collared white shirt, appeared viable enough to us.

The opening formalities did not take long. I found the Serbo-Croatian-to-English translation hard to follow. In any case, the proceedings seemed formal and respectable, though a bit brief. Then court adjourned for the day with instructions to return the next morning.

Most of the crowd had dispersed by the time we exited. But an odd scene was taking place on the steps at a side entrance to the courthouse. There, a stocky older woman, her hair in a scarf, berated Ephraim Zuroff, one of the Simon Wiesenthal Center's chief Nazi hunters. Looking like someone sent from central casting to play a 19th century peasant, she gesticulated, she shouted, she boxed Zuroff on an upper step between herself and the courthouse.

Taken aback, we watched for a bit. Then Zuroff extricated himself—perhaps the woman was running out of steam—and we left. What had she been shouting? The usual, we found out later: That Sakic was a Croat hero, an anti-communist. It was the trial that was a crime. And it was all because of the Jews and their lies.

Quite so, madam. Isn't it always?

The next morning we found the trial still recessed. Sakic, we were informed, had been hospitalized with high blood pressure. He would survive, to be sentenced to 20 years imprisonment—the longest sentence then allowed under Croatian law for crimes against civilians committed during World War II. Hearing the verdict, Sakic would applaud sarcastically. His cell included a computer, on which to write his memoirs, and a television. Sakic visited his wife, then in a home for the elderly, twice monthly. He died at 86 in 2008.

Sakic, the old woman, the vulnerable U.S. embassy, bin-Laden, Tudjman's old-new revisionism. The dots to the 21st century were all there. But at the time, they seemed like individual incidents. Portents, yes, like the faxes that arrived periodically on the machine outside my office at B'nai B'rith in the late '90s from al-Muhajiroun, one of the deranged and deadly serious radical Islamic groups then sheltering in London. Occasionally citing the wisdom of Imam bin-Laden, the communiques warned that the end of the Crusader and Zionist West was imminent, and Allah would bless our slaughter.

Ayatollah Ruhollah Khomeini's takeover of Iran in 1979 and the seizure of Mecca's Grand Mosque the same year, the assassination of Egyptian President Anwar as-Sadat in 1981 and bombing of the U.S. embassy and Marine barracks in Lebanon in 1983 should have established Islamic extremism's lethal sincerity. Still, not understanding how London had become, as Melanie Phillips would title her 2006 best-seller, *Londonistan*, I took al-Muhajiroun's faxes primarily as comic relief. A little over-reach there, guys? Your bin-Laden isn't even a clergyman. He has no authority to instruct any Muslim on his or her duty, right?

On my 54th birthday, Sept. 11, 2001, at 8:46 a.m., American Airlines' flight 11 crashed into the north tower of New York City's World Trade Center. At 9:02 a.m., United Airlines' flight 175 smashed the trade center's south tower. A few minutes later I was in Executive Vice President Daniel S. Mariaschin's office at B'nai B'rith headquarters in Washington with several other staffers, watching a newscast from New York. No one said much; the images seemed too surreal for words.

"We're evacuating the building. Everyone must leave now. The Pentagon's been hit." A security guard was motioning everyone toward the elevators. We lingered long enough to look out the western-facing window in Mariaschin's seventh floor office. Over rooftops of downtown D.C., we could see a thick column of dark smoke rising to the southwest. At 9:37 a.m. American Airlines' flight 77 had driven, a raging fireball, through three of the Pentagon's five Russian doll-like corridor rings.

I hurried back to my office, grabbed my briefcase and left. No time now to check the fax machine. No need, either, since today's message—and that for the next two decades, at least—was written on the wind.

No one knew what other targets might be hit next, so the federal government ordered a complete closure. "Essential" as well as "non-essential" employees—and all non-governmental workers on the federal schedule, had to evacuate. This meant, as in every weather-related early departure, that city streets were jammed. Literally, not virtually. I watched as automobiles took three light changes to clear the intersection in front of the B'nai B'rith building at 17th Street and Rhode Island Avenue, N.W.

The giant snarl recalled traffic during the 1981 snowstorm that brought an Air Florida jetliner crashing onto the 14th Street Bridge, the three-span collective carrying I-395 across the Potomac River between the District of Columbia and northern Virginia. It struck five or ten minutes after Lynda Murray (later James) and I had crossed the bridge that day, after leaving our non-essential work in Rep. Bob Shamansky's office. We were creeping through slush and more new snow, just beyond the Pentagon—I-395 then was more parking lot than expressway—when we heard, not far behind us, a tremendous boom. That's odd, we told each other, a huge thunder-clap in the midst of a blizzard. Normality bias, psychologists note, is the first thing that slows reaction time in dangerous circumstances. It's the first, typical "this-can't-be-happening" response of denial—that sound like a gunshot must have been a firecracker—that induces semi-paralysis and gets you killed.

The 18-mile trip, which usually took 45 minutes, lasted four hours. Vehicles that ran out of gas, or simply lost traction on the slightest grades, were abandoned along or on the roads. There were, and after all still are, only a few bridges funneling traffic in and out of D.C. across the Potomac. Bottlenecks are rush-hour routine. In 2001, really savvy terrorists would have blasted one of the bridges too. Instead of preparing to invade Afghanistan and topple the Taliban government hosting bin-Laden and al-Qaeda, a permanently gridlocked vehicular Washington would have been on its knees, suing for peace.

After 9/11, federal, state and local governments in the region worked to improve emergency evacuation. They met. They planned. They designated better snow emergency routes. Then struck the afternoon rush-hour "Carmaggedon Storm" of Jan. 26, 2011. It took me three and a-half hours to get home. By then a veteran D.C.-area driver, I knew the pitiful alternate routes. I circled my Honda, manual transmission, front-wheel drive, on congested, slippery roads far into the suburbs beyond my usual exit. I never came to a complete stop, swirling as necessary between drivers in distress, flowing through yield and stop signs. For neighbors who didn't, or whose alternates became impassable, drive-time reached five or six hours, sometimes more. Finally home, the real work began, shoveling out parking spaces.

Memo to Washington, D.C. Area Council of Governments: There is no workable emergency evacuation plan. Terrorists or storms, there are too many people, too many cars, too few highways, too few bridges and not enough subways and trains. And all your jurisdictions refuse to build more. But as long as we don't tell the terrorists and discount weather repetitions, we pretend to win.

W., Hillary and a Specter

Many non-Israelis covered Moshe Dayan, Yitzhak Rabin and Uzi Narkiss over the years. But few, if any others, also served as ghost-writers to both Republican President George W. Bush and Democratic Senator Hillary Clinton (N.Y.), and within a few months for the pair.

It was spring in 2001. I was still working as acting communications director for B'nai B'rith International, the worldwide Jewish human rights, humanitarian and educational organization—founded in Sinsheimer's Tavern on New York's Lower East Side in 1843. This founding fact communications directors before and after me also noted fondly and frequently. We often said "café" instead of tavern, but when Sinsheimer's was serving cold mugs of beer, trendy cafes on the Lower East Side were still more than a century into the future. Taverns, on the other hand, most definitely were part of the immigrant scene.

"The White House just called. The office of minority liaison, that is," someone in Executive V.P. Mariaschin's office informed me. "They want a short statement—six or seven sentences—congratulating the American Jewish community on Passover. Can you do it?"

"Sure. When do they want it?"

"Now."

"But Passover's not for a couple of weeks," I pointed out.

"Lots of people in the White House will have to sign off on whatever we give them."

When I worked on the Hill, I had learned that passing legislation was "like pushing wet noodles." So, this would be another such exercise. I saw revisions of a five-sentence throw-away stretching out to the horizon, or at least until we opened the door for the Prophet Elijah during the Seder.

I wrote three paragraphs in which the president congratulated American Jewry on the occasion of Passover, the first recorded holiday in human history linking freedom of religion and freedom of a people, a commemoration that would inspire people everywhere and echo famously in African-American spirituals. Mariaschin's office forwarded it to the White House. I'd nearly forgotten the little exercise when, a few weeks later, a big, stiff, cream-colored envelope arrived, to my attention, from the Oval Office. Inside were several copies of the proclamation, barely changed from my draft, the president's signature in its distinctive bold if disjointed vertical scrawl at the bottom.

Viola, I was a White House ghost-writer!

Not long after, a similar request landed in my in-box. A real, physical in-box, on top of the out box. It would be my last such. What with e-mail already overrunning the work day, I used the in-box mostly to accumulate junk mail—press releases from other non-profits, requests for book reviews in *International Jewish Monthly* from publishers big and small, copies of Jewish weeklies from around the country—many too underfunded and dreary to more than skim—and the occasional letters accusing B'nai B'rith of suppressing a) the white man's leadership in Western civilization, b) the Afro-centric roots of Western civilization, or c) knowledge of the Judeo-Communist sabotage of Western civilization. To such correspondents, if time permitted, which it rarely did, I used the legendary reply attributed to Sen. Stephen M. Young (D-Ohio), whose *Washington Post* obituary would note his "pithy language": "Dear Mr. So-and-So: Just to let you know, some asshole has been writing to me and signing your name. Sincerely, ..."

But this was different, just a few words on a piece of B'nai B'rith note paper: "We need to write a 90-second script Senator Clinton can tape for a video greeting to a Jewish women's convention. Better if it's 60 seconds." We meant me.

Why us? I asked, also meaning me. Jewish Women International (the former B'nai B'rith Sisterhood auxiliary, now quite independent and increasingly left-leaning) had its own communication people.

Don't know, the answer came back, but Clinton's people asked us. It can't hurt to do them a favor. So, I drafted some boilerplate in which the senator expressed her appreciation for JWI's unstinting service both to the Jewish people and humanity in general and forecast that, in the Jewish phrase, it only would continue to go from strength to strength.

Unlike the souvenir copies of President Bush's Passover proclamation, I heard nothing from Senator Clinton's office. *Bupkis*, as they say in Yiddish, absolutely nothing. However, someone at B'nai B'rith did see the video as shown at the conference. "She read it like she'd never seen it before. Wooden."

Sometimes a ghost-writer's invisibility, not to mention distance, is a good thing.

Mrs. Clinton was much better as contending Democratic presidential candidate at AIPAC's March, 2016 policy conference in Washington. When I started as assistant editor of the organization's *Near East Report* early in 1984, AIPAC had an annual budget of around $4 million, a staff of roughly 50, no regional offices, and drew a couple thousand pro-Israel activists to its annual policy conference. By the time I left, as editor of *NER* in late 1988, the budget had doubled, staff grown to around 80, an office opened in Jerusalem, an autonomous, eventually free-standing think tank called the Washington Institute for Near East Policy spun off and policy conferences drawing 4,000 or 5,000 people threatened to outgrow Washington's biggest convention hotels. Proportionately, at least, it was an unheard-of success. Rate of growth, and imputed if not always actual influence, though not absolute numbers, outstripped that of most lobbies, even the really big ones like the American Dairy Farmers or National Education Association, let alone specialized foreign policy interest groups.

So it was that by the presidential election year of 2016, Hillary Clinton addressed AIPAC's annual session in the 20,000-seat Verizon Center (now the Capital One Arena), home to the National Basketball Association's Washington Wizards and National Hockey League's Capitals. A few rows had been closed, but the center basically was at capacity. Former senator, and by now former secretary of state, not to mention former First Lady, Clinton delivered a very good, if not outstanding pro-Israel speech. From many rows up, I doffed my ghost-writer's hat several times to whoever had drafted this particular gem.

Hillary Clinton was, to me, much like Richard Nixon. I'd never liked her, as far back as her First Lady of Arkansas days. She seemed to ooze insincerity and naked ambition at the same time. Gov. Bill Clinton's 1992 campaign pitch that voters could get "two-for-one," the putatively brightest political couple in the United States, with one ballot, brought me up short. I might want him, but I definitely didn't want her.

Inherent hostility aside, I was surprised at how good the speech and Mrs. Clinton's delivery were. Nothing wooden this time; the words hit all the necessary themes, her manner—speaking essentially in the round from the arena floor to a throng of close to 20,000 around and above her—warm, engaging, almost personal. And she looked good, even in the pantsuit outfit—red jacket, black slacks—smiling broadly under neatly trimmed, markedly blonde hair. She waved and the audience loved her, even before she spoke. Republican candidates Trump, Sen. Ted Cruz (Texas) and Ohio Gov. John Kasich would not receive such an embrace no matter what they said. This was the evil ice queen who'd left a trail of broken lives and bankruptcies from Little Rock to Washington, D.C.? Even for someone like myself, who knew from the inside how such events and speeches were fabricated, this was a stellar show.

So good, in fact, that the left-wing news site *Slate* headlined its commentary, "Hillary Clinton's AIPAC Speech Was a Symphony of Craven, Delusional Pandering; Clinton had an opportunity to show some political courage. She decided to alienate the left instead." This anti-Israel thumb-sucker was written by Michelle Goldberg. The piece included the common but erroneous assertion that Jewish settlements in the disputed territories violated international law—they accord with the 1920 San

Remo Treaty, 1922 League of Nations (later United Nations) Mandate for Palestine and more. It referred to "the hawkish elements of the Israel lobby"—as if AIPAC did not include and was not often was led by Democrats. It ignored the Arab nationalist-Sunni Islamist supremacy fueling the Palestinian conflict with Israel. And it presumed that Clinton's primary challenger, Sen. Bernie Sanders (I-Vt.)—a robo-left Israel critic who would campaign for the anti-Zionist, antisemitic British Labor Party leader Jeremy Sanders in 2017 and again in 2019—knew better than she did. Goldberg went on to become a *New York Times* columnist. Clerisies always co-opt loyal novitiates.

So, no matter how good the speech, how well delivered, there was Not that I would vote for Hillary Clinton. There was her nodding, back in the '90s, as Suha Arafat slandered Israel, her unwonted role as Israeli Prime Minister Benjamin Netanyahu's hectoring hall monitor while Obama's secretary of state, and her eager and unelected attempt to foist "Hillarycare" onto a country already hamstrung by government bureaucratization of medical insurance. Not to mention the paper trail that followed her all the way back to Little Rock and the Whitewater real estate affair and the Rose law firm billing records mystery, a trail that would make her illegal use of unsecured e-mail and destruction of 30,000 messages as secretary of state an unsurprising though formally felonious future development.

So, no matter how good the speech, how well delivered, there was nothing Hillary Clinton could do to win my vote. Not even being the alternative to Donald J. Trump. Not that he could get my ballot either. Please. It would be the first time since I began voting in presidential elections in 1968 that the correct answer to the question, Democrat or Republican, would be neither. My disdain for Nixon eventually dissolved into something close to pity, as noted above. But for Hillary Clinton and Donald Trump, a deep concern—not for either of them, both simultaneously superfluous and dangerous personalities—but for an America in which either could ascend the greasy pole of politics all the way, or nearly, to the top.

Chapter Nine:
Conflicted on the Mediterranean

Speaking of Tear Gas, Welcome to Gaza City

I met Lenny Davis at the Erez Checkpoint on the armistice line between Israel and the Gaza Strip early one morning in the summer of 1988. The first Palestinian *intifada*—uprising—was half-a-year old and Lenny, a friend, mentor and first director of the American Israel Public Affairs Committee's Jerusalem office, had arranged a couple of interviews for me with officials in Israel's civil-military administration in Gaza. I edited *Near East Report*, the weekly newsletter on U.S. Middle East policy published in affiliation with AIPAC, the big pro-Israel lobby. Lenny had worked for AIPAC in Washington before making *aliyah*. He would come to know nearly everyone a journalist, academic or politician ought to know in Israel. In the New Jersey-sized country, with about four million Jews then, one could—with persistence—develop such a network. As Lenny Ben-David, he returned to Washington from 1996 to 1999 as deputy chief of mission in the Israeli embassy during Benjamin Netanyahu's initial term as prime minister.

Israel was still improvising its response to the first intifada, perhaps underestimating Palestinian rejectionism, or at least Palestine Liberation Organization duplicity in its long game of talk-shoot-disrupt. So, our escort from the checkpoint over the few miles to civil-military headquarters in Gaza City turned out to be two little Japanese-built rent-a-jeeps, one with the Hertz or Avis logo clearly visible, one with a .50 caliber machinegun mounted in back. Off we went, Lenny and me in my rented Subaru sandwiched between the mini-jeeps, each of them carrying three uniformed Israeli soldiers.

Most of the route our little convoy took traversed a built-up area crowded with four- and five-story masonry buildings, businesses at street level, apartments above, facing a main road. The gritty, dun- and gray-colored areas suggested a shabbier version of older South Florida along the coast from Ft. Lauderdale to Miami. But then, so did some stretches of Israel south of Tel Aviv, lower working-class places but without the refugee camps. Israel's *mahbarot*—tent and tin-hut camps for the 600,000 who went to the Jewish state out of the 800,000-plus Jews expelled from Arab lands—were no longer needed by the late 1950s. But by 1988, the camps in Gaza to which several hundred thousand of the 472,000 – 650,000 Arabs displaced by the 1948-'49 war (original estimates varied widely) had fled were permanent neighborhoods. More tightly packed and frequently with alleys instead of streets, they otherwise resembled adjacent Gaza districts.

Human activity did not distract us much from the physical environment. We had arrived on a general strike day. Streets were nearly deserted; most of the Strip's 590,000 people (1.8 million today, on about 140 square miles, two and-a-half times larger than Washington, D.C.) were indoors. It was quiet. Too quiet.

The civil-military administration for the Strip used an old Taggart fort in Gaza City that the Israelis took from the occupying Egyptians in the 1967 Six-Day War. The latter had inherited it from Great Britain during Israel's 1948 War of Independence. Egypt, four other Arab countries and Palestinian Arab "irregulars" attacked after the British abandoned their League of Nations/United Nations Palestine Mandate.

Great Britain had built a number of the Taggarts as police stations across Mandatory Palestine during the 1936-1939 Arab Revolt. The forts were concrete, two-story, double-winged buildings hinged on a three- or four-story central tower. The revolt featured massacres of Jews and attacks against the British. It led London virtually to halt Jewish immigration into Palestine   in an anxious attempt to appease the Arabs and keep its Suez Canal route open to Persian Gulf oil fields and India. This just as war with Germany loomed, just as Europe's Jews most needed the refuge in British Mandatory Palestine that London in 1920 had promised the League of Nations it would oversee. But illegal Arab migration into the Mandate continued.

We first saw the brigadier general in charge. He seemed concerned about the *intifada* but also convinced that Israel would be able to manage. Then we stopped in to talk with an Israeli official responsible for public health in the Strip. Finally, after lunch, we met an energetic civilian in charge of "resettlement, rehabilitation and absorption" of Palestinian Arabs in the refugee camps. In the Israeli perspective, "resettlement, rehabilitation and absorption" meant—in the spirit of the original U.N. resolutions—getting residents out of the 1948-1949 war camps, which had been intended as temporary responses to Arab flight from the fighting, and either repatriated in peace "when practicable" or resettled and assimilated in new, permanent residences.

So, Israel in Gaza had begun a pilot program. On what had been sandy open space in Gaza City, we saw a small new subdivision of midrise apartment buildings. Camp residents, many already second and even third generation "refugees," were given the opportunity to relocate to the new buildings and finally begin life anew.

How many families live in the apartments, I asked.

Only a few, the official admitted.

Why not more? More signed up for the program, he said, and some families from the camps actually moved in. Then the PLO murdered a few of the new residents and the program ground to a halt.

To sustain the cause, to maintain an aggrieved population and a pool of ready, resentful recruits, Yasser Arafat could not permit his people to be "rehabilitated and resettled." He needed them impoverished and confined—by Palestinian force if necessary—generation upon generation. Their condition made the Jews, the Israelis, not him, his financial backers and ideological sympathizers, look bad. So, the Israeli-built subdivision stood nearly empty.

Late afternoon and time to go. Our little convoy reassembled at the Taggart fort civil administration offices and proceeded up an empty main street in Gaza City. A few blocks along, the soldier riding with us pointed to a balcony several stories up. "Look! See that guy standing there? He's a spotter. Now watch."

The young man ducked inside. "He's going to call his friends and tell them about us," the soldier said. "They'll prepare a welcome a little farther up the street."

Welcome? For the first time since crossing from Erez, my palms began to sweat. The Subaru might be able to stop a pellet from an air rifle, but nothing more. I was already catastrophizing.

"Keep driving, but slowly," he said. Then he spoke a few words in Hebrew on his radio to the men in the jeeps.

Another few blocks and he said, "See the three guys standing at the entrance to that alley? They got the call." We rolled ahead a little more, then he shouted "stop!" and leaped out of the car. The two rent-a-jeeps also stopped, and in an instant six uniformed Israelis carrying M-16 rifles were chasing three Arabs up an alley. This left Lenny and me alone, sitting by ourselves in a Subaru with a door opened in the middle of Gaza City.

Only a minute or two later the Israelis strolled out of the alley, seemingly carefree, one carrying a Molotov cocktail—a soda bottle filled with gasoline, topped with powdered detergent (the better to spread the flames), and kerosene-soaked rag wick stuffed into the neck. The members of our welcoming committee had left it when they ran. Along with the head of our team, the soldier with the firebomb climbed into the backseat of our car. The car quickly filled with gasoline fumes. The Israelis passed the Molotov cocktail back and forth like a trophy. Both carried cigarette packs in their fatigue shirt pockets. Fortunately, neither lit up.

Thanking our escorts, taking a last look at the Molotov cocktail, we exited the checkpoint. Back in Israel we headed toward Jerusalem, all of about 40 miles northeast up into the Judean Hills. Air conditioning turned up; we nevertheless kept the windows down. The Subaru's interior reeked of gasoline fumes.

Chapter Ten:
Yitzhak Rabin, A Quandary

A Tragedy in Israel

Kings of Israel Square surrounding City Hall in Tel Aviv would be renamed Rabin Square in 1995, after the assassination there of Prime Minister Yitzhak Rabin at the end of a rally in support of the 1993 Oslo Accords with the PLO. From the September 1993 White House Rose Garden handshake between Rabin and Palestinian leader Yasser Arafat, prodded by President Bill Clinton, and Rabin's murder in October 1995, Palestinian terrorism against Israelis—including high-casualty suicide bombings—intensified. In 1994, Arafat told a meeting of Muslim leaders in South Africa the accords were a temporary maneuver to undermine Israel. He urged them to join in a pan-Islamic anti-Israeli *jihad*. Rabin threatened several times to freeze the process, which had imported Arafat and his leadership from various Arab countries to the Gaza Strip and West Bank town of Jericho to start the Palestinian Authority. But he never did.

The 1995 rally had been organized to support Oslo diplomacy among an increasingly divided Israeli body politic. Yigal Amir, a law student described as an ultra-nationalist opposed to Oslo and any concessions regarding *eretz Yisrael*, the land of Israel, shot the prime minister as he was leaving the event. Rabin's long-time rival and more recent partner, Foreign Minister Shimon Peres, assumed the premiership. Stretching an analogy, Rabin and Peres were to Israel's founding prime minister, David Ben-Gurion, what Marquis de Lafayette and Alexander Hamilton had been to George Washington, indispensable young right hands. Or in Peres' case, left hand. Unlike Lafayette and Hamilton, however, Rabin and Peres would be on the national scene for nearly half a century, much of the time in leadership roles. Rabin was primarily a military man, Peres foremost diplomatically. Politically, they dueled each other for Labor Party leadership, and with little love lost. After Rabin's murder, more suicide attacks killed more Israelis and foreign visitors. Israeli fury at the carnage helped Likud Chairman Benjamin Netanyahu defeat Peres by less than one percent in the 1996 elections.

Security personnel, overt or covert, Israeli, Tunisian, American (George Wallace would be shot on the campaign trail in 1972 and paralyzed from the waist down) or otherwise, maintain security. Until the day they don't...

... I first heard Yitzhak Rabin in person in 1980. He was to address several hundred English-speaking Labor Party supporters in a beachfront hotel at Herzliya. I got a ride from Kibbutz Ma'agan Michael with Martin Sherman, a kibbutz member who'd been able to sign out a car for the day. We drove the 25 miles south to Herzliya—that is, from northern to central Israel—and managed to get seats near the back of the already crowded ballroom. Sherman, though a *kibbutznik*—the *kibbutzim* were incubators for Israel's early socialist, Labor Zionist establishment—would move to the political right. He campaigned for retired Gen. Rafael "Raful" Eitan's Tehiya Party, (former commando leader Eitan was a secular Jewish nationalist), then earned a Ph.D. in political science and international relations, lectured for 20 years at Tel Aviv University and finally founded the often anti-establishment Israel Institute for Strategic Studies. But that lay in the unforeseeable future. Our interest as we drove south along the Mediterranean was Rabin.

He and Peres were locked in a bitter battle for the party chairmanship. Elections for the Knesset (the 120-seat parliament) would be held the next year. Chairman of the party winning the most mandates would become prime minister. But since 10 or more parties—left, right, secular, religious, Zionist, Arab—usually contested Israeli elections, no single movement ever won a majority. This necessitated unruly coalition governments. "Two Jews, three synagogues" is not just a quip, it's also an ethnic-spiritual defect. If, as Judaism first insisted, God is intimately concerned with each individual life, then who are you to tell me to compromise? Ask Him, you idiot! As the comedian Jackie Mason had it: " 'If he says one more word, I'll kill him!' You ask him, 'What is that word?' He never knows ..." And the arguments, throwing off insights and nonsense in volume after volume, never end.

Leon Uris supposedly used the young Rabin as model for protagonist Ari Ben Canaan in *Exodus,* his bestselling novel about Israel's 1948 War of Independence. The actual Rabin was a former lieutenant general (the highest rank in the country's military) and Israel's chief of staff during the Six-Day War, as well as prime minister from 1974 to '77. He campaigned as a "Labor hawk."

Peres, a Knesset member since 1959, had been a miracle-working director-general of the nascent defense ministry from 1953 to 1959, beginning at age 29. He briefly succeeded Rabin as premier in '77. Peres appealed for support as a "Labor dove." Rabin commonly was described as "stolid" and "reliable" and Peres as "charming." *The Jerusalem Post, N.Y. Post* and his son Chemi all described Peres as a life-long Francophile; his political enemies preferred the adjective "slippery."

Rabin's speaking style, certainly in English, was slow, low and unemotional, almost ponderous. His manner did not inspire. But his words convinced. As part of his stump speech and oft-stated strategic concept, he told us in Herzliya, in close paraphrase, "If I am prime minister, no future chief of staff will face what I faced on June 4, 1967—an Israel nine miles wide north of Tel Aviv, enemy artillery a few miles from the Knesset in Jerusalem, Syrian guns overlooking the Galilee. We will not come down from the Golan Heights, we will not leave the Jordan Valley, we will not retreat from Jerusalem." Israel would retain the Gush Etzion settlement bloc in Judea south of Jerusalem and widen the coastal waist above Tel Aviv into Samaria.

When Rabin spoke, one felt one could take his pledge to the bank. But Peres captured the Labor chairmanship and, in 1981, lead the party to a 0.5 percent loss at the hands of Begin and Likud.

Begin resigned in 1983. He was widely believed to be psychologically drained by Israel's losses in the inconclusive Lebanon war against the PLO—Israelis ousted Arafat and 10,000 of his gunmen from Beirut but, shielded as the latter were by the United States, the Vatican, and other countries, plus international news media, Israel could not crush them—and the death of his wife Aliza in 1982. From 1984 to 1990, Rabin served as defense minister in Likud-Labor unity governments, two-headed affairs that resulted from electoral stalemates. Late in that period I worked as publications editor for the Washington, D.C.-based Jewish Institute for National Security Affairs (JINSA). Among other things, I helped staff a members' study trip to Israel. One stop on the itinerary was Rabin's office in *haKirya*, Israel's version of the Pentagon. In Tel Aviv instead of the capital, Jerusalem, to give it a whiff of strategic depth, *haKirya* now features a modern glass-and-metal headquarters building and a roughly 50-story tall communications tower, a Seattle Space Needle-like structure that no doubt enables Israeli signal intelligence to eavesdrop throughout the Middle East. But circa 1990, the defense ministry resembled a fence-enclosed campus of low, drab concrete structures.

Our group of 15 or so gathered around a table in a sparsely furnished conference room that was part of Rabin's office suite. Coffee was served. We waited a few minutes, then Rabin entered. According to the ground rules, we had 30 minutes. I was to read members' questions from pre-written notecards Another staffer thanked the defense minister for meeting us, and I began. Rabin answered each question in that same slow, thoughtful-sounding rumble I had heard a decade before in Herzliya.

The half-hour passed in what seemed an instant. In the mini-bus for the 45-minute drive back up to our hotel in Jerusalem, I felt the same reassurance the defense minister's firm words conveyed as I had that day in Herzliya. Yet the lack of affect in how he spoke bothered me; I attributed it to the fact that Hebrew, not English, was his mother tongue.

My third opportunity to hear Rabin came a year or so later in Washington. No longer defense minister—Peres having jilted the unity government in a "dirty trick" departure meant to bring on fresh elections—Rabin nevertheless was a high-profile Knesset member. He had accepted an invitation to speak to 50 or 60 JINSA supporters gathered at a D.C. hotel. Once again, the same knowledgeable, no-nonsense words, the same unruffled if not particularly moving English speaking style. But this time, perhaps because I re-heard what I expected, nothing more, nothing less, and nothing determinative in the face of the first Palestinian Arab *intifada*, it neither convinced nor reassured. Discomfited, I began to wonder: Was I listening to boilerplate?

A little later, in the spring of 1991, I published a freelance article in *Moment* magazine. *Moment* then was a general Jewish interest bimonthly headed by Hershel Shanks, who founded and also ran *Biblical Archaeological Review* and *Bible Review*. My article was headlined "Jewish Arabists at the State Department," and it got me fired from JINSA. The piece critiqued the speeches and writings of four influential members of the Reagan and George H. W. Bush administrations' State Department and White House Middle East policy teams. The four were Dennis Ross, Richard Haass, Daniel Kurtzer and Aaron David Miller. In the article, I argued, citing the quartet's own words, that these were not bend-over-backwards Jews of old stereotypes, trying to blend into the traditionally WASP-ish diplomatic set. Rather, they were self-identifying members of the tribe who mistakenly believed they could simultaneously save Israel from what they conceived of as its anti-peace rigidity and enlighten Yasser Arafat and his fellow bone-deep Jew-haters as to the advantages of peaceful compromise with the Zionists.

JINSA board members were split over "Jewish Arabists at the State Department." The objection was less one of substance than publication in the first place. The article, especially the "rogues' gallery" of photographs illustrating it, embarrassed organizational lay leaders—the president and chairman in particular—in front of their well-placed Washington friends. The pair issued an ultimatum: "Either he goes, or we do." Staff being eminently replaceable—a lesson I had not absorbed until then, somehow having missed that particular "for all new employees" memo—in June, 1991, I went, with head-spinning dislocation.

All the way to Miami and the managing editor's job at the *Miami Jewish Tribune*. And although Shimon Shieffer, Washington correspondent for one of Israel's major dailies, would mirror "Jewish Arabists at the State Department" in his own Hebrew-language article headlined "Baker's Boys," referring to Secretary of State James A. Baker, III, our efforts did not adversely affect their subjects. Ross achieved ambassadorial rank as President Clinton's special Middle East coordinator and Secretary of State Hillary Clinton's special adviser for the Persian Gulf and Southwest Asia; Kurtzer became ambassador to first Egypt, installing a kosher kitchen in the Cairo embassy, then Israel; Haass eventually served as president of the Council on Foreign Relations; and Miller, a much sought-after commentator, worked first as vice president of the Woodrow Wilson Center and then senior fellow at the Carnegie Endowment for International Peace. As the door hit me in the butt on my way out of town, an older colleague explained, "There's nothing worse in Washington than being prematurely right."

Right or wrong, it was in the *Miami Jewish Tribune's* third-floor office—in a non-descript six-story bank building at the intersection of Biscayne Boulevard and 36th Street (at that point the western end of the Julia Tuttle Causeway across Biscayne Bay east to Miami Beach)—where I heard of Rabin's 1992 speech as newly-inaugurated premier. Having defeated Peres in another fight for party chairmanship, that June Rabin led Labor to a narrow victory over Yitzhak Shamir, Begin's successor as Likud prime minister. Rabin took office as premier for a second time, heading a coalition including the secular Meretz Party to Labor's left and Shas, an ultra-Orthodox religious party far to the right culturally but not necessarily on foreign policy.

In his speech, Rabin noted the collapse of the Soviet Union and what almost appeared now as a partnership between former Cold War enemies in Washington and Moscow. Internationally, a train of peace was beginning to roll, he said. Israel should not miss its chance to jump on board. As for the Palestinian Arabs, well, after all, one made peace with one's enemies, not with one's friends.

This was not unsentimental fact, or even campaign boilerplate, but rather a mélange of misplaced and superficial analogies or foreign policy "realist" clichés. One day soon after, a local pro-Israel activist rushed, practically breathless, into the *Tribune* office. "They're tossing 'Nine Narrow Miles' into a dumpster" at the Israeli consulate downtown, he declared. "Nine Narrow Miles" long had been a staple of Israeli government information efforts. A small, glossy pamphlet in blue with thick headlines, it showed maps of pre-'67 Israel, including the vulnerable, heavily-populated coastal waist above Tel Aviv, and the country-covering range of Arab artillery along the borders and armistice lines.

Why toss "Nine Narrow Miles?" Had geography changed? Had Arafat, or Syrian dictator Hafez al-Assad or his Ba'athist Party twin and competitor Iraqi dictator Saddam Hussein changed? Had the fanatically anti-Israel regime of Iran's ayatollahs transformed itself? One did not need access to CIA or Mossad intelligence, just passing familiarity with the daily papers to know that the answers to those questions were no, no, no, no and no.

What had changed, apparently, was Israel, or at least the psychology of the new government coalition and its backers. The formula—reflected by some but hardly all members of the Miami Jewish community—ran something like this: the Lebanon war and suppression of the first *intifada* proved "there is no military answer to the conflict"; Israel has fought hard, steadfastly and creatively for two generations, bearing countless tragic sacrifices, and so deserves peace; and, deserving peace, must have it. Now. That's it, "Peace Now!" With the tragic echoes of America's Vietnam era peace movement unheard, the subsequent deaths of hundreds of thousands of abandoned South Vietnamese, Cambodians and Laotians unheeded, Israel was nerving itself, or better, inuring itself to attempt to accommodate the PLO.

Apart from psychology, the less malleable trio of geography, ideology and diplomacy said:

The United States and its (sometimes reluctant) NATO allies had for the most part effectively contained the Soviet Union and its Warsaw Pact satellites in a 40-year plus Cold War;

That war ended with the U.S.S.R. crumbling under economic, cultural and yes, military pressure and the Warsaw Pact dissolved;

Nations made peace with—or rather, imposed it on—defeated enemies. Or, when both sides were equally exhausted, they reached truces of varying duration; and

Just because the Cold War had been brought by Washington to a successful close hardly meant the Arab-Islamic war against the Jewish state could be ended by goodwill and deft management from Jerusalem, or Washington puppeteers through Jerusalem.

Regardless, as often with human beings, reality would not be permitted to obstruct desire. Instead, Israel desired peace with the Arabs in general, the Palestinian Arabs in particular. For their own geo-strategic ambitions, American policymakers desired it and many American Jews—

more focused on domestic issues like church-state separation and abortion on demand—longed for it. So, peace there must be, and if not arriving in fact, then redefined psychologically.

In 1971, a Miami optometrist named Sanford Ziff opened a kiosk in Dadeland Mall and called it Sunglass Hut. It proved successful, so he opened more. By 1986, there were 100 Sunglass Huts with sales of $24 million annually. Ziff sold a majority interest in his business to an investment firm. He unloaded his remaining share in 1991 when annual sales of the still-growing company reached $100 million. Along the way Ziff became an important contributor to the Miami Jewish Federation and friends with Prof. Jiri Valenta at Miami University.

Valenta, in turn, was a friend of Jiri Dienstbier. A well-known foreign correspondent, Dienstbier was fired after Soviet tanks crushed Czechoslovakia's 1968 "Prague Spring" experiment of communism with a human face, including open dissent and competing political parties. For the next 20 years he could find work only as a janitor. But with the fall of the Berlin Wall and collapse of communist governments in the Soviet Union's Warsaw Pact satellites, including Czechoslovakia, Dienstbier became foreign minister in the new, democratic administration of President Vaclav Havel. If only more janitors could become foreign ministers, especially in Washington. Dreams aside, Dienstbier's rise meant I got to meet Shirley Temple.

Shirley Temple was the prototype and perhaps epitome of all childhood stage, screen and television stars to follow. It long ago became commonplace to note that this dimpled cheek, curly haired, beguilingly smiling little girl lifted America's national mood during the depths of the Great Depression. From 1935 through 1938, no other Hollywood star was a bigger draw in the United States or, from '36 through '38, the United Kingdom, than this eight- to 12-year-old girl. Her films, including "Bright Eyes" (in which she first sang "On the Good Ship Lollipop"), "The Littlest Rebel," "Poor Little Rich Girl," "Dimples," "Heidi" and "Rebecca of Sunnybrook Farm" were on as reruns when I started watching TV in the '50s.

Unlike many childhood stars when their show business careers fade, Shirley Temple made a bumpy but successful transition to adulthood and significance of a different sort. An early marriage to actor John Agar (John Wayne's co-star in "Sands of Iwo Jima") failed but her second, to Charles Black, son of the president of Pacific Gas and Electric, lasted 55 years. In 1967, she ran unsuccessfully in a Republican congressional primary, but two years later President Nixon appointed her as a delegate to the U.S. mission at the United Nations. Black went on to serve as ambassador to Ghana, first female U.S. chief of protocol and, from 1989 to 1992, ambassador to Czechoslovakia.

In the late 1980s and early '90s, some American Jewish activists and Israeli officials were looking for a second route for Soviet Jews given permission to emigrate to Israel in addition to that through Austria. Too many were "dropping out" in Vienna. Instead of going on to the Jewish state as returnees—"repatriation" to a native homeland was the only grounds at the time for a Soviet citizen to move from the workers' paradise—they were seeking asylum as refugees in the United States, Canada or in Western Europe. But if Israel were the Jewish state and ready to welcome them then they could not be refugees in need of asylum. And if they were refugees from the Soviet motherland, then why couldn't any and all Soviet citizens choose to leave their proletarian heaven?

Working with the U.S., Israeli and Czech governments, Ziff, Valenta, Miami Jewish Federation leaders and others arranged for a second route, from Moscow through Prague to Tel Aviv. As managing editor of the *Miami Jewish Tribune*, I was invited to join Ziff, Valenta and federation officials to cover the inaugural flight on the new pathway. The democratic Czech government—still staffed in part by yesterday's Communist Party apparatchiks, who eagerly pressed their newly-printed capitalist business cards on us—put us up in a former party guest house. In a quiet, well-tended Prague neighborhood on a hill overlooking the heart of the city, the in-town retreat had been converted recently to hotel use. The place was modern but sterile, all hard surfaces, wood paneled walls and marble floors. Room dimensions were oddly overlarge, as if for a bloated, variant species. A bloated species called the *nomenklatura*. I've had apartments smaller than the bathroom in my suite. Aesthetic critiques aside, being a party apparatchik obviously had been more rewarding than life as a *worker*.

I tossed and turned the night before we were to meet the inaugural flight of Soviet Jews at Prague airport. Yasser Arafat and the Palestine Liberation Organization were no happier at the prospect of more Jews escaping Moscow's grasp than Arafat's claimed uncle, Haj Amin al-Husseini, British-appointed grand mufti of Jerusalem, had been during World War II at the possibility of Bulgarian and other European Jewish children being transferred out of Nazi-occupied Europe to British Mandatory Palestine. Pro-Hitler al-Husseini, "the Palestinian George Washington," gets too little credit for propagating neo-fascist Islamism. During the Holocaust he intervened diplomatically several times to ensure Jewish children did not escape their doom. The PLO, which had pioneered attacks on airports and airliner hijackings in the late 1960s and '70s, likewise continued to object to Jewish immigration to the Jewish state.

What kind of security would the Czechs have at the airport? As yesterday's Soviet puppets, would they even be capable of deterring today's still Soviet-supported PLO? As a trained U.S. Army Reserve tire repairman, what good would I be in countering a terrorist assault?

"These rooms are huge, aren't they?" a fellow Miamian asked at breakfast.

"Too big," I said. "I kept hearing noises and couldn't tell where they were coming from."

"You probably were just dreaming," he replied through mouthfuls of food. "I didn't hear a thing."

"Uh huh," I grunted, bleary-eyed, appetite suppressed. Some people just have no imagination.

At the airport our delegation and several senior Czech officials waited in a visitors lounge. The special Aeroflot flight with more than 100 soon-to-be new Israelis would be landing from Moscow nearly on schedule. As we were ushered onto the tarmac a limousine bearing diplomatic plates and an American flag rolled up. A rear door was opened and out stepped Shirley Temple Black.

There actually was a red carpet unreeled to the spot at which the emigres would briefly deplane. We Floridians formed a reception line alongside and Ambassador Black walked briskly down it, shaking hands while talking with her Czech escorts. Dark-haired, 63, still attractive if unsmiling, no-nonsense in manner, she shook my outstretched hand. Briefly. "It's an honor to meet you," I said, in long-stored, star-struck sincerity. She looked at me, nodded—perhaps in affirmation—and moved on.

The PLO did not attack that day. A more immediate potential danger turned out to be the Aeroflot plane. Our Miami delegation joined the now former Soviet Jews on the Prague-to-Tel Aviv leg of their flight. The plane, especially the interior, looked familiar. My first commercial airline trip, in the summer of 1966, had been on American Airlines, from Cleveland to New York. We were making a family excursion for a relative's wedding (and Broadway side trip to see *Fiddler on the Roof*, my lobbying for the conflicting Rolling Stones' concert in vain). The plane likely had been a Boeing 727, that workhorse model then in service only a few years. The Aeroflot craft looked to be a copy, an old copy. Or maybe the same plane, for that matter, purchased second- or third-hand. Small cracks showed themselves along the plastic ceiling panels. Every so often water condensed and dropped onto the worn carpet. The narrow metal supports under one aisle chair bowed, tilting the seat into the walkway. The windows seemed permanently fogged.

No terrorists in their right minds would risk seizing this particular plane. Oxymoron? Anyway, the immigrants, some almost dazed at Prague, or perhaps already tired from a long first leg of their journey, were subdued enroute to Tel Aviv. We landed to a joyous official welcome at Ben Gurion International Airport. It was the kind of scene a much younger Shirley Temple would have recognized, or more likely led, singing and dancing through customs.

In September, 1992, I returned to Washington as editor of the *Washington Jewish Week*. One year after that, on Sept. 13, 1993, Rabin and Arafat signed the Oslo Accords at the White House, a beaming President Clinton at their side. That afternoon, members of my small staff at the *Jewish Week* excitedly watched the Rose Garden ceremony on the newsroom television. I'd been invited by the embassy to join a couple hundred other guest witnesses but could not bear to go. The event sounded like a charade to me, and a badly choreographed one. I sent a young reporter in my place. "This is not peace," I cautioned the staffers glued to the TV. "It might be the beginning of a process that eventually leads there, but it's not peace, not with Arafat, not now."

That night I stood under a large pavilion pitched on the grounds of the Israeli embassy at the corner of Van Ness Street and International Drive in northwest Washington, along with a couple hundred others invited to a reception to celebrate the day's signing. Rabin and Peres both spoke. Many in the crowd seemed filled with the same unwarranted anticipation I had advised my staff against. Harvard University Prof. Ruth Wisse, one of American Jewry's preeminent thinkers, shortly thereafter would call the near-euphoria sweeping much of the community "an epidemic of hope." Epidemic or hope? The former, I thought.

As the Israeli leaders talked, several veteran AIPAC hands, a long-time pro-Israel political activist and I stood off to one side in a corner of the tent. A strange thought occurred to me. "When the Jews find out what the Israelis have done, there'll be hell to pay," I said. "What does that mean?" one of the AIPACers demanded. "I don't know," I replied, but remembering the frenzied disposal of "Nine Narrow Miles" on the dustbin of some people's imagined future, I said, "Either what the Israelis have been telling their diaspora supporters about the Arabs for decades was true, or what they're telling us today is true, or both are wrong. But both can't be true."

Three years later I was at my desk at the *Washington Jewish Week*. Martin Weil, then and now a local news reporter at *The Washington Post*, called. He wanted Jewish community reaction to Rabin's assassination and was talking to a variety of sources. I chose my words very carefully; verbal, emotional and communal land mines were everywhere.

"Rabin's assassination is for Israel what John Kennedy's assassination was to this country," I said. The killing was "a subversion of Israeli democracy" and "exactly the kind of terrorism" Israel fought externally. "I think it may distort Israel's future."

I hung up with a sense of relief. After an editorial early in the Oslo delirium cautioning against both undo optimism and undo pessimism, I'd been told my name landed on the Israeli embassy's purported "enemies of peace" list. Now I was pretty sure I'd crossed that minefield without an explosion. I had managed not to criticize Rabin while implying praise in an American context. What I said seemed to me to be the truth. And it avoided that dangerously devalued word, peace.

Chapter Eleven:
Opera Bouffe with Your F.B.I.

The Man Who Knew Too Little but Heard Plenty

In the series *The F.B.I.*, broadcast by ABC Television from 1965 to 1974, agents of the Federal Bureau of Investigation were the good guys. But when real life counterparts bungled their way through a phone call to my parents in Tiffin, Ohio and then turned up in my office in Washington in 1990, they seemed kind of pathetic. So, by 2019, when Justice Department Inspector-General Michael Horowitz sautéed the bureau in his report dissecting its "Russian collusion" investigation of the 2016 Trump presidential campaign and the early days of the Trump presidency, I was not surprised.

"Is this Mr. Samuel Rozenman," the voice on the phone asked my father.

"Sam," he replied. "Who's calling."

For some reason, my father never used his full first name. His framed diploma, from Tiffin Columbian High School, class of 1938, hangs in my home office. It was awarded to Sam, not Samuel Rozenman. If you wanted to put him on guard, call him Samuel.

The agent gave his name, adding portentously, "from the FBI. Were you in an accident in Washington, D.C. recently?"

"Washington?" my father replied. "No, why do you ask?" He was wary. He also did not suffer fools lightly. On the other hand, my father once had to produce reams of paper for the Internal Revenue Service to document the fact that he, as owner-operator of Rozenman & Sons Auto Wrecking, State Route 101, Tiffin, Ohio indeed had paid every required penny of one particular year's income tax and not one red cent more. Hence, he thought the federal government operated best at a distance.

"Well, Mr. Rozenman, a Chevrolet Cavalier station wagon with Ohio tags and registered to you was involved recently in an accident on 16th Street in Washington, not far from the White House."

"It was?" my father replied incredulously. "That car is registered in my name, but my son drives it. And he hasn't said anything to me about an accident."

The reason for that was that there had not been any such accident. The agents were using a ruse, perhaps attempting to trip my father into some incriminating statement. They were behaving as bad guys, not good guys. Lt. Gen. Michael Flynn, President Trump's first national security advisor, would get a more thorough version of this manipulation-by-inquiry technique early in 2017.

"Why is the F.B.I. calling about a traffic accident?" Sam Rozenman wanted to know. This gave the agent pause.

"Well, we think another car, with diplomatic plates, might have been involved."

"You'd better speak with my son." My father was used to problems involving one his automobiles and his older son, beginning with the time I backed his cream and turquoise '63 Mercury Monterey into a light pole at a local gas station, at speed.

So, Sam, not Samuel, gave the agents my name, work address and phone number. At the time, I was publications editor of JINSA, the Jewish Institute for National Security Affairs. As noted above, JINSA then was a small think tank and educational non-profit (bigger now) aimed primarily at strengthening the U.S. and Israeli militaries and the ties between them. He also phoned me.

"I don't know why they called, Dad. There was no accident. But I did park the car on 16th Street not long ago. I had an interview at the Soviet embassy there with the Middle East desk officer."

So, it happened that some days later two FBI agents, one a tall, slender man, the other a short, stocky woman, kept an appointment at the JINSA headquarters on 17th Street, N.W. a couple blocks from Farragut Square in downtown Washington.

For anyone still surviving who remembers the Mutt and Jeff comic strip, or has an advanced degree in American popular culture—the collapse of American liberal arts studies probably dates to the awarding of sheepskins for this particular discipline in the 1970s—the pair literally were figures from that cartoon series in their disharmonious proportions. And the disharmony carried over to their wardrobes. Neither would have been permitted on the set of television's *The F.B.I.,* let alone before the cameras. The male agent's battered trench coat—he actually wore one—was long overdue at the dry cleaner. The female agent's overlarge earrings and too-short skirt shouted the question: What were you thinking?

"So, you parked the Chevy Cavalier station wagon in the 1100 block of 16th Street, N.W. opposite the Soviet embassy?" he asked.

"Yes," I confessed.

"Why?" she asked.

"Because I was on crutches then and didn't want to walk far. I couldn't believe how lucky I was to find a spot right across from the embassy," I said.

"Why were you on crutches?" he wanted to know.

"A bad ankle sprain. I'd been in Philadelphia to give a speech and had a few hours to kill, so I went jogging, Twisted my ankle on a rock. My ankle swelled up like a softball." This from the same athlete who once threw his back out warming up for a slow-pitch softball game in a Columbus Recreation Department league.

"Why did you go to the embassy?" she asked. If they were playing good cop-bad cop by alternating their questions, I couldn't tell who was who.

"Because I had an appointment to interview the embassy's Middle East specialist. I wanted to get the official Soviet view as a sort of counterpoint, a little spice from the other side, you might say, for our newsletter."

"What did he tell you?" he asked.

"That's easy," I said. "Here's the article I wrote. You can read it yourselves." I handed them copies of our bi-monthly, eight-page newsletter, *Security Affairs.*

They each spent a couple minutes reading the article. I sat still, surprised to realize I wasn't sweating, my pulse wasn't racing. I began to feel a perverse satisfaction, as if I were the one in charge of the interrogation, not the other way around.

"Well," he said, folding the newsletter and stuffing it into a coat pocket, "what else did he tell you?"

"Nothing important," I said. "Anything he had to say that was the least bit newsworthy, I included in what you just read."

"Did you tape the interview?" she asked.

"Yes," I said. "I taped it, mostly for back up, and took notes. I generally take extensive notes."

"We'd like to see them," she said. This was the first break in their he-asked, she-asked approach, two consecutive questions by the same agent.

"Like I said, there's nothing in my notes of any importance that isn't in the article. Besides, the only two people who can read my handwriting—besides myself, and then only before it gets stale after a few days—are my mother and an old girlfriend. Here, look." I flipped open the traditional 8" x 4" reporter's notebook I currently was using. They glanced at the hieroglyphic scrawl for a second and looked at each other. Unhappily, I thought.

"Is this the notebook you used for the interview?" he asked.

"No," I said. "It's the one I'm using now."

"We'd like to see the one from the interview," he said. Apparently, they now were asking two questions at a time.

I had thought about this possible request beforehand. I reviewed my Ohio University Journalism 101 Ethics lecture (don't you love oxymorons?) and tried to recall any lessons taught by Efrem Zimbalist Jr., starring as Inspector Lewis Erskine in *The F.B.I.* The FBI's founding director, J. Edgar Hoover, and Zimbalist eventually formed a mutual admiration society, Hoover citing Zimbalist's Inspector Erskine character as a model for how his real agents should look.

"I'm afraid I can't do that without violating journalistic standards and confidentiality of sources," I told the non-telegenic agents, just liked I had rehearsed mentally beforehand. "Not without a warrant. Besides, the published interview tells you everything."

They glanced at each other, then rose to leave. But before doing so, the male agent said, "We may be in touch again." They weren't, but I kept their impressive-looking business cards in my desk drawer for a long time, in the same rubber band-bound stack with that of the Soviet embassy's Middle East officer.

Had the F.B.I. agents really wanted to know more about what I'd heard regarding the Soviet Union while working at JINSA, they could have asked. It would have been revealing.

At the end of 1988 or early in 1989, Michael Ledeen spoke to a small luncheon for institute supporters. Ledeen, a historian, consultant to the National Security Council, State and Defense Departments and "neo-conservative" arch-villain to adversaries, was just back from a swing through some of the Soviet Union's communist satellites in eastern Europe. He painted a picture of an empire on its last legs. In Romania, for example, "in the middle of winter they weren't heating the main terminal at the airport in Bucharest." There was only cold water in the bathrooms. In Bulgaria, the regime was unable to replace burnt out light bulbs in public places. The shabby gray workers' paradise of Soviet communism, grayer and shabbier than ever, was crumbling.

A few months later, Georgetown University research professor Murray Feshbach, formerly the U.S. Census Bureau's long-time expert on Soviet demography, addressed a similar luncheon. He dismissed conventional wisdom of Kremlinologists from Jerusalem to Bonn, Paris, London and Washington. Except perhaps in military power, he said the Soviet Union was not a superpower roughly equivalent to the United States. "Life expectancy among those of the majority Russian ethnic population is decreasing. Rates of alcoholism and other diseases are increasing. In the military, most of the sergeants are still Russian, but more and more of the enlisted men under them are not. Increasing numbers are non-ethnic Russians, rather they are Muslims from the central Asian republics." Officials figures of economic production and growth were exaggerated and unreliable. And so on, almost all contrary to the consensus views of Soviet specialists in academia, national security, journalism and politics. If contrary to the comfortably informed consensus, then certainly almost unknown to the general public.

Yet in the late 1970s, the Columbus *Citizen-Journal* had published a wire service background piece describing a Soviet Union failing for reasons like those expounded by Ledeen and Feshbach. I'd long forgotten what sources the news agency had relied on and in any case that report seemed to have been a one-day story. But because of it what Ledeen and Feshbach said sounded vaguely familiar to me. They were, more than a decade later, confirming and detailing the old news article. A year after those luncheons, the Soviet's eastern European empire of coercion, the fearsome Warsaw Pact, fell apart, to the astonishment of the F.B.I. and most of the rest of the U.S. government. And to me. Such can be the weight of conventional wisdom. The Soviet Union itself would follow in collapse in 1991. Only then did descriptions of the former Union of Soviet Socialist Republics as "a third-world economy with a first-world military" became fashionable.

If the F.B.I., C.I.A., N.S.A., D.I.A. and other dozen or so U.S. intelligence agencies and offices wanted to hear not just from American specialists but also from someone with an insider's brutal first-hand knowledge of the Soviet system, they could have turned to another fellow who had passed through Washington, D.C. a little earlier.

The Inconvenient Natan Sharansky

Occasionally, there comes a man or woman who never hesitates to speak the truth, intelligently and profoundly. He or she does so even at the threat of prison or worse. One such was Anatoly Shcharansky. By speaking and acting, he had become a majority of one and helped demolish the Soviet Union.

Of course, he was never truly just one. Though separated by great distances, the love of his indomitable wife Avital sustained and supported him, even in those parts of his nearly nine years imprisonment spent in solitary confinement. She supported him also by recruiting countless others to his cause. And, often locked in isolation, the former child chess prodigy remained free to replay games in his mind. Then there was also the tiny Book of Psalms ready to hand. The Kremlin had no idea who and what it was up against.

Under international pressure reinforced by the Reagan administration, Moscow released *refusenik* Shcharansky in 1986.

Reunited with Avital, he Hebraicized his name to Natan Sharansky—one of the "crimes" that landed him in the *gulag* had been learning and teaching Hebrew—and immediately moved to Israel.

At the end of that year, Sharansky was in Washington, D.C. with advice for the newly-elected Congress, Americans in general and other Westerners who wanted to deal with the nuclear-armed Soviets as equals, notwithstanding their different system. I interviewed him for *Near East Report* in the Wisconsin Avenue apartment of a colleague and mutual friend.

Short but sturdy, physically sort of a bulldog of a man, he had an engaging smile, playful sense of humor, and penetrating gaze. He was the sort who would laugh at a joke and despise a lie. Sharansky worried that the West was falling for Soviet leader Mikhail Gorbachev's much-publicized campaign of *glasnost* (openness) and *perestroika* (restructuring). To Sharansky, the terms signaled a "very strong public relations campaign." Behind them were new restrictions on the 400,000 Soviet Jews who'd taken the first steps to emigrate to Israel. Congress needed to understand this and adopt a new measure reminding Moscow that progress on trade and arms control would be tied to its human rights practices.

I headlined the two-part series based on the interview "The Inconvenient Sharansky." It was obvious even then that his insistence on policy founded on principle would prove just so, inconvenient, that is, for all those in the United States and Israel who wanted to throw their arms around the heroic ex-prisoner without fighting from the same trench. "By insisting that the East-West agenda is linked to Soviet observance of human rights," the series said, Sharansky "contradicts those who believe that no matter how heavily the Soviets oppress their own and other countries' citizens [those of Soviet satellites in Eastern Europe] weapons agreements *must* and therefore *can* be reached. And his is not the quiet approach."

Regarding the Soviets, even or especially under Gorbachev, "the West wants to be deceived," Sharansky insisted. He knew why. "I remember, especially in the first months in my isolation cell—and sometimes they are threatening to kill you—your start thinking .... 'My

God, these are the same kind of people I am. Maybe we can find some common ground.' I had to remind myself, no, these people have absolutely different moral principles."

Westerners living under the nuclear threat were afraid, Sharansky acknowledged. So, they wondered, "Why shouldn't we try to find a common language with the Soviets?" But in searching for common ground on nuclear arms control such people might have been tempted to overlook the nature of the society they wanted to deal with.

If both sides disarmed the next day, open, democratic countries would need new ways to defend against "close, secret, well-organized societies with the spirit of an aggressive ideology." For Sharansky, the best way to test Kremlin intentions would be the fate of Soviet Jewry. Western governments, beginning with that of the United States, would need to stand strong. Their private citizens "must not be afraid to irritate the world" with the problem of Soviet Jewry. He wasn't. And working with Andre Sakharov—first a winner of the Lenin Prize as father of the Soviet nuclear bomb, later Nobel Peace Prize laureate as the country's premier human rights activist—*refusenik* Sharansky helped opened a crack that became a fissure. Ultimately, thanks to Western pressure, that fissure shattered the communist carapace called the U.S.S.R that suffocated Russia.

In Israel, Sharansky would spend more than a decade as a member of Knesset (parliament) and then served nine years as head of the Jewish Agency for Israel, a semi-governmental organization promoting Jewish immigration and ties between Israeli and diaspora Jewries. Along the way, he opposed "major concessions" to the Palestinian Arabs, in the words of the Associated Press, saying Israel could make peace only with a democratic Palestinian entity.

Sharansky received both the U.S. Presidential Medal of Freedom and the Congressional Gold Medal. When he was awarded Israel's $1 million Genesis Prize for a lifetime of promoting political and religious freedoms (like previous winners he donated the money to charities), he quoted President Ronald Reagan:

"Freedom is never more than one generation away from extinction. It is not passed to our children in the bloodstream. It must be fought for, protected, and handed on for them to do the same, or one day we will spend our sunset years telling our children and our children's children what it was once like to live when men were free."

An inconvenient if necessary reminder then, and today too. Our era features the expansionist, surveillance state of China aggressively seeking world domination—yet to whom financial stars like Blackrock's Larry Fink, Goldman Sach's David Solomon and J. P. Morgan Chase's Jamie Diamond still advocate selling the Leninist rope with which to hang their capitalist selves ("China Still Has One Powerful Friend Left in the United States: Wall Street," *Wall Street Journal*, Dec. 2, 2020). Contemporary culture in the Weimar West also accommodates reactionary leftists, particularly in the United States, whose neo-Marxist taxonomies threaten liberal democracy more than rightist populists. Freedom *is* never more than one generation from extinction.

If, in fact, "eternal vigilance is the price of liberty," another belief many early nineteenth century Americans thought self-evident, then "endless wars" don't end just because we tire of fighting them. As "the warrior monk" James Mattis, general and defense secretary, famously noted, "the enemy gets a vote."

Chapter Twelve:
Democracy Dies in Darkness,
Dogma and Used Needles

One Day at The Washington Post

The belief that Jews in *eretz Yisrael* (the land of Israel) are an "occupying power" conducting "the illegal Israeli occupation" is a tale told so often even Jews believe it. Sometimes otherwise intelligent Jews with first-hand experience, Israelis as well as their diaspora cousins. So when demonstrators in self-righteous orthodoxy shout "Palestine Must Be Free, From the River to the Sea!" on the streets of Europe and North America, when they paint swastikas on a synagogue in Los Angeles and a Jewish fraternity house at Vanderbilt University, when they march in Washington, D.C. after the 2020 police murder of George Floyd in Minneapolis and in the poison of intersectionality scream, "We know you Israel, you kill children too!" many who should know better stand mute.

The libelous indictment extends from the early Church to today's Internet. It seamlessly maintained and maintains that Jews killed Christ, that in medieval times Jews killed Christian children to use their blood in religious rituals (and Israeli Jews, Zionist devils, similarly "harvest the organs" of Palestinian Arabs today), that Jews started the plague of the Black Death, that more recently they have stood behind both exploitative capitalism and oppressive communism, instigated World Wars I and II (it's all there in the Hamas charter and fever swamps of Jew-hatred right and left), and lately created the HIV-AIDS and coronavirus COVID-19 pandemics. When a self-troubling world goes wrong, it looks for a scapegoat. And for more than 2,000 years, it has found the Jews. Which, except for direct attacks against the Israel Defense Forces, seems safe, since the Jews are a tiny tribe. Being tiny, facts in their favor are of diminishing value, including regarding "the occupation." Nevertheless, they must be asserted, among them:

The basic relevant provision, the League of Nations' 1922 British Mandate for Palestine, Article 6, encourages "close settlement by Jews on the land, including state lands and waste lands not required for public use." Jewish rights already had been recognized by Great Britain's 1917 Balfour Declaration and incorporated into international law by the 1920 San Remo Treaty. The United States endorsed Article 6 by signing the 1924 Anglo-American Convention, a treaty stipulating acceptance of the mandate. The League of Nations is long gone, but Article 6 remains in force. The United Nations' 1945 Charter, Article 80—sometimes known as "the Palestine article"—notes among other things that "nothing in the charter shall be construed to alter in any manner the rights whatsoever of any states or peoples or the terms of existing international instruments."

Eugene Rostow, U.S. undersecretary of state for President Lyndon Johnson—who was an authority on international law and a co-author in 1967 of United Nations Security Council Resolution 242, which outlines requirements for Arab-Israeli peace—reaffirmed this principle. In 1990, he said: "The Jewish right of settlement in the West Bank is conferred by the same provisions of the mandate under which Jews settled in Haifa, Tel Aviv and Jerusalem before the state of Israel was created."

But "illegal Israeli occupation" is an essential part of "the Palestinian narrative." So, many cling to it, never questioning its accuracy.

In 2003, early in my tenure as Washington director of the Boston-based, 65,000-member Committee for Accuracy in Middle East Reporting and Analysis, CAMERA President and Executive Director Andrea Levin and I met with *Washington Post* Foreign Editor David Hoffman. We wanted to discuss several recent examples of what we considered anti-Israel bias in *The Post's* coverage. Hoffman himself had served as the newspaper's Jerusalem bureau chief and gained respect as its Moscow correspondent. He later would win a Pulitzer Prize for his book, *The Dead Hand: The Untold Story of the Cold War Arms Race and its Dangerous Legacy.* Levin and I were barely seated when Hoffman demanded, with some vehemence, "Do you believe the West Bank and Gaza Strip are occupied?"

Apparently, representatives of a pro-Israel organization previously had tried to tell him that was not the case.

"Yes," I replied. I had dealt with this question—or accusation—many times. Too many times in the previous 18 or 19 years as editor of AIPAC's *Near East Report*, the *Washington Jewish Week* and B'nai B'rith's *International Jewish Monthly* magazine. And not infrequently in response to Jews. So, surprised by Hoffman's manner if not substance, I had an answer ready.

"They're occupied similar to the United States, Great Britain, France and the Soviet Union's occupation of Germany after World War II—a result of defeating an aggressor in war," I said. "The difference is that, unlike the Allies, Israel has historical claims to the territories."

For whatever reason, perhaps surprise, Hoffman did not pursue the issue and we turned to our agenda items. But Levin and I were struck by the fact this, of all other possibilities, was his opening, and challenging, question. "Israeli occupation"—a default defense mechanism when confronting critics of his staff's Arab-Israeli reporting. "Illegal Israel occupation!"—a core element in the libel that rises like a werewolf under every bad moon, shining in the summer of 2020 on some of the anti-racism demonstrations held in the name if not direct auspices of the Black Lives Matter! network. In its 2016 manifesto, Black Lives Matter included the obligatory left-wing superstitions about an alleged Israeli genocide of Palestinian Arabs and Israel as "an apartheid state."

We killed their children and took their blood; we killed their children and took their land. Many Jews know better, but in the face of unreason, partner of hatred, brother to violence, they hesitate to speak. So, David Hoffman, of all people, felt compelled to interrogate critics of his newspaper's anti-Israel coverage over the Jewish state's highly inconvenient yet utterly legitimate claims in its ancestral land.

I'd read *The Post* religiously—at least the "A" section with the world and national news (the much-vaunted Style section, Editor-in-Chief and Watergate star Ben Bradlee's innovation, with its seepage of cultural fluff and arrogance was instant recycle)—in a secular sense since arriving in town in December, 1980. As a young reporter in Columbus, I'd wanted to be Woodward and Bernstein, preferably Woodward, as played by

Robert Redford in the 1976 Watergate film *All the President's Men*. That even though physically I leaned more toward Dustin Hoffman's Bernstein. Either way, Woodward or Bernstein, Redford or Hoffman, I was thrilled that *The Washington Post* would be my new morning newspaper. To paraphrase blues legend B.B. King, the thrill was gone in only a month or two.

    Post coverage of Arafat and the PLO's war against Israel and its Jews functioned—consciously or not—to put readers in mind of Robin Hood and his Merry Men versus the Sheriff of Nottingham and his knout-wielding deputies. Lebanon became their Sherwood Forest and Israel a sort of Gothic *gaol*. Having just spent five months in the Jewish state, reading *The Jerusalem Post* daily, and enduring a multi-day lockdown at seaside Kibbutz Ma'agan Michael prompted by a warning about a possible landing by PLO terrorists—whose brethren had waded ashore nearby, hijacked a bus and murdered 38 men, women and children two years earlier—I'd come to that same conclusion I would arrive at later regarding Israeli diplomatic explanations pre- and post-Oslo of dealing with the Palestinian Arabs:

    Either *The Washington Post* was right and *The Jerusalem Post* was wrong, or the latter correct and the former mistaken, or both erred. But both could not be right. Having my own sources in Israel—relatives and friends—and access to other news outlets, including as a congressional staffer the daily FBIS (Foreign Broadcast Information Service) reports excerpted from Middle East media, it became plain that the paper of Watergate fame chronically misreported from the Middle East and didn't much care to correct itself. When, early in the Trump administration, *The Post* sanctified its open enlistment in the "resistance" by ostentatiously adopting a new masthead slogan, "Democracy dies in darkness," I swallowed the increased cost and began subscribing to *The Wall Street Journal*. Democracy does die in darkness. Also, in dogma.

I Left My Heart in San Francisco. But Nothing More

    It was hard to tell whether the news media stimulated America's unraveling or, by naturally obsessing over its man-bites-dog aspects, tore at what already was coming apart. Certainly, social media, substituting keystrokes for inter-personal contact, transmuted news into techno-gossip, digital graffiti and click-bait ad fodder. Anti-social in so many respects, it worked as an accelerant. In the process it profitably destroyed both attention spans and comity.

Three years before Minneapolis police asphyxiated George Floyd in 2020, before people's shouts for racial equality were hijacked by insistence on a new, intolerant aristocracy of identity groups demanding "equity," my wife and I came face-to-face with a tapestry unweaving itself. Until 2017, I told myself that the undeniable trees did not necessarily constitute a darkening forest.

In Washington, D.C. in 1967, during the March on the Pentagon, I thought an unwinding was happening only among some of my college undergraduate peers. In Miami in 1991-1992, I presumed it snared just the impoverished Haitian immigrants and wealthy "Anglo-Saxons" who lived cheek-by-jowl, third world style—the former noisily day and night on littered sidewalks, the latter comfortably behind the gates of glittering high-rises—but rarely intersected. Until San Francisco in 2017 I didn't admit to myself that things might be so far gone as to be nearly unsalvageable. In the always topographically and architecturally charming city by the bay, was licentiousness at long last discrediting liberty, good intentions serving as pretext for ever more intrusive authorities?

During the long Labor Day weekend that year Northern California baked in an unprecedented heat wave. From the drought-parched hinterland across the Golden Gate Bridge, a haze from distant fires wafted in off the horizon. Temperatures topped 100 daily until breaking our last night in town. Average for early September was 70, *The San Francisco Chronicle*—page-wise a sickly shadow of its former self, content still avant-rearguard left—reminded us. A sweatshirt purchased on a previous summer visit remained in a suitcase.

On September 2, thermometers hit 103 degrees Fahrenheit, a San Francisco record for the date. From high in the upper deck of AT&T Park, my wife, Melinda, cousin Ian Kloville and his daughter Marganit and I watched the Giants beat the Cardinals 2-1 in 10 innings. It was too hot for peanuts, popcorn or Crackerjacks but not for overpriced beer, lemonade and water. Desultory breezes eventually reached the four of us. Though sun-block coated and shaded by the stadium's overhang we glistened in the heat. In "McCovey Cove" just beyond the right field wall boats—sail, motor and kayak—gathered as usual, occupants lounging in anticipation of a home run ball, one or two sailors leaping in to cool off.

We reached the ballpark via Lyft from Golden Gate Park after a stroll through the lovely Japanese Tea Garden and lunch in the DeYoung Museum. The expansive park itself was, despite the heat, busy with joggers, bicyclists and walkers. Offerings in the museum cafeteria did not so much shout "California cuisine!" as assume it. From avocado to fennel, quinoa to yogurt, salad and soup, with appropriate wines, it was more than delicious. It was informed. I eat, therefore I am. I eat woke, therefore I'm the utmost, baby, the ginchiest.

The DeYoung, in a modernist structure with the surplus of dramatic wasted space apparently mandatory in newer public buildings— atria *uber alles*—boasted a fine collection of American art from various periods. Exhibits were intellectually defaced, however, by explanatory placards in curatorese. These repeatedly insinuated the various artists' intentional or subconscious racism, cultural ethnocentrism, colonialist appropriation and/or other benighted attitudes presumably shed by woke quinoa eaters. Such "Polly-want-a-cracker!" anachronisms, however, suggested not enlightenment but rather two-dimensional presentism.

Our Lyft driver was a young man from Houston, who said he also worked in an Apple store and, as a newly-minted city resident, attended San Francisco Community College free. In the wake of Hurricane Harvey, he'd talked to his mother in Texas. "She's safe, but the house is pretty much gone. I saw a video of the neighborhood on the TV news." I said I'd seen a picture in *The Chronicle* of Houston residents standing guard next to a hand-lettered sign reading "Looters will be shot."

"I don't know why people are so quick to resort to violence," he replied. "A lot of people are poor to begin with and might have to take what they can to survive." Our objective being to cut through traffic and get to the game in time and the driver not being particularly aggressive, I kept my eye-rolls to myself. I did not suggest he was maligning a majority of the poor, who like the majority of middle class and wealthy people, for some reason do not loot or steal. The possibility such undocumented acquisitive behavior might violate the moral-ethical imperative of the Eighth Commandment also passed unmentioned.

Adding to the weekend's abnormal climate was a chain of brush fires in mountains east of the city. The result was a non-automotive smog that diffused sunlight and clouded otherwise postcard-perfect vistas all the way across the Golden Gate, through God- and Internet billionaire-favored Marin County and into Sonoma wine country along Highway 101. Once the route of teenaged lore immortalized in song ("Black Denim Trousers and Motorcycle Boots") but now an expressway through suburb and exurb, the road took us 60 miles or so to Francis Ford Coppola's immaculate-looking winery and spa.

Besides the gift shop, tasting bar and restaurant—with artifacts from the director's many films—there wasn't much to see. No tour of the winery itself or walk through the orderly vineyards, even when under a less merciless sun. Highlights were a spit-polished Tucker automobile from Coppola's movie of the same name, revolving slowly, endlessly on a large turntable in the middle of the gift shop, and a few of the guests revolving from cabanas to the pool and back. They were nearly all women, perhaps on day trips or waiting for their men to join them later in the weekend. A few luxuriated in bikinis cut so high on the hips that they made little pretense of covering the buttocks. Sexy or slovenly, empowered or exhibitionist? Does that depend on where the tattoo is engraved, or on how many there are?

Delaying lunch, we drove out of Sonoma and back to Sausalito to eat. We wanted to see how the other half, that is, the lower upper class, lives. Slumming it, comparatively speaking, we avoided nearby Tiburon. Two-bedroom, two-bath hillside condos overlooking the bay in Sausalito went for more than $1 million. Two-bedroom, one-bath, living room/kitchen combined condos in San Francisco got more than $1 million, and the buildings weren't necessarily new. Middle class in the Bay area meant one earned six figures annually, and not just barely. Parents could send a child—or children, theoretically, if husband and wife, or husband and husband or wife and wife both earned well into six figures—to private school, Democratic Party registration notwithstanding. Or they could buy a new car and parking space and hazard public schooling.

We were a day early for the Sausalito Labor Day weekend art festival. No matter, we enjoyed a late lunch on the deck of a marina-side restaurant. It was relaxed, pleasant and affordable. Who were the help, we wondered, and where could they afford to live?

A reconditioned wooden yacht, its long black hull and cream-colored cabin accented with barn reds, gleamed on the back of a transport trailer. We watched as the driver delicately maneuvered the big rig past the restaurant toward the marina gate. He dismounted to fold in the truck cab's outside mirrors, to no avail. A small Hyundai Elantra in the last parking space before the gate denied him clearance. The teamster walked to the restaurant deck. "Anybody know whose car that is?" he said, pointing. It was ours.

U-turning the rental through the gate, we whirled back out in front of the transport. A sign on the cab advertised a marina and shipwright in Maine. Who could afford to buy such a yacht, have it reconditioned, trucked across the continent and berthed in California? Apparently more than a few people. The marina was full of boats, many smaller, many larger, some more properly called ships. If Magellan's 270-man expedition had consisted of five of the latter instead of its quintet of carracks and caravel, it would have circumnavigated the globe in one year, not three, and returned to Spain with most of its vessels and men, not one battered ship and 19 half-starved survivors.

A noon-time stroll around bustling Union Square in downtown San Francisco, past not only the pre-Covid-19 pandemic Macy's and Cheesecake Factory but also Louis Vuitton, Bulgari and Vera Wang, a Grand Hyatt and J.W. Marriott Hotel and high-rise office buildings full of high-rise workers, produced only a single man in a business suit. But what a suit!

I'd just reached a men's shop when its door swung open. "Here, let me get that for you, sir!" said a salesman, scurrying ahead of his exiting customer. The latter, 60-ish, about six-feet, two-inches tall, squarely built and silver haired, strode out. Directly ahead of me, he moved quickly through the throng of shoppers, tourists and homeless people. The city's homeless seemed to be everywhere. San Francisco had yet to begin spray bleaching its sidewalks, unlike San Diego, which was trying to combat a deadly hepatitis A outbreak. The disease spreads in unsanitary conditions, including contact with fecal matter left by those defecating along the streets. In 2015, San Francisco had begun painting a few city walls with a repellant that caused urine to spray back onto the shoes and pants of those inappropriately relieving themselves. Some of the people living on the city's sidewalks in heartless homage to personal autonomy looked imminently terminal.

The non-homeless fellow's suit was a rich navy blue, a fine fabric closely—but not too closely—tailored. Polished black shoes, white shirt, bold tie. In the teeming throng—young women in high heels, short skirts, bare midriffs, snug tops and Saks Fifth Avenue bags slung across their shoulders; out-of-towners wearing shorts, sandals and T-shirts; small Chinese women in long, loose blouses and short black pants; the tattooed, the bearded, the girls and women of all ages stuffed into yoga pants; every other person on his or her cell phone—the man in the suit was immediately noticeable. He exuded confidence and purpose. A senior vice president at Wells Fargo, chief investment strategist from Microsoft or, things rarely quite what they seem, a model from a *Gentleman's Quarterly* photo shoot? It wasn't Chinatown, Jake, but Chinatown wasn't far away.

Late that afternoon two more fellows in jackets, dress shirts and ties appeared. One was also silver haired, like that suited figure in Union Square, and though this man's was thinning and his build was more portly than squared off, his stance a bit stooped, he too expressed unspoken confidence. It was happy hour in the Leatherneck Lounge atop the Marine Memorial Club and Hotel, with its comfortable furniture, numerous conversations, fine view of downtown and countless tributes to Marines and Marine units past and present.

Who would we want making decisions: The young salespeople in the Apple iStore nearby, baseball caps on backwards, or these two geezers in clothes becoming as antique as Washington's breeches in the long-pants age of Lincoln? The youth hyper-actively explained the newest features on the latest devices, from which with the proper apps one could control the electric grid in Moldova, reroute airliners or get a hot pizza delivered in under eight minutes. The geezers, who of course also carried smartphones but who probably had others Tweet for them, not only gave the impression they knew whom to hire and fire but also that they had taken a hill or two when necessary.

On Sunday morning, what looked like the best thing about San Francisco's Contemporary Jewish Museum turned out to be closed. In the building, Wise Sons Jewish Delicatessen offered "sandwiches piled with classic deli meats … since 5771." That would be all the way back to 2011, for those not on the Hebrew calendar.

The deli said it was "dedicated to building community through traditional Jewish comfort food." No one can be in business just to make an honest buck anymore, especially in the Bay area. In the age of "relationship banking," brand-building and marketing to millennials ever in need of the next big thing, the righteous big thing, every butcher, baker and candlestick-maker sounds like the stripper Miss Electra in "Gypsy." "Ya gotta have a gimmick," she sang, "if you want to get ahead." Hers was an electrified, lighted G-string. Today it's community building, world improving, a sustainability mission, a commitment to … Never mind! Give me the damn corned beef on rye, with mustard and a half-crocked pickle. And if you expect a tip, shut up about it already!

Designed by famed architect Daniel Libeskind, the CJM described itself as "a beaux-arts-meets-modern space." Reviewers invoked the usual suspect terms like "deconstructionist" and "post-modernism." Yawn. Having already seen the DeYoung, the Contemporary Jewish Museum struck us as more warehouse-in-search-of-identity. Lacking a permanent collection, it operates as a gallery by displaying rotating exhibits, hardly a museum. We saw "The 613 by Archie Rand," the traditional 613 Jewish commandments—and you, Dear Reader, imagined there were only 10?—whimsically rendered in colorful single-panel cartoon fashion. Also whimsically rendered—a few absolutely laugh-out-loud funny, evincing a Mel Brooks'-like high anxiety sensibility—were the many actual drawings in "Roz Chast: Cartoon Memoirs." Chast had been turning out her stylistically recognizable work for *The New Yorker* since 1978. Rabbi, scholar and stand-up comic—who knew?—Joseph Telushkin, in his book *Jewish Humor*—reminds readers how anxiety, a reasonable response to 2,000 years of exile and oppression, underscored much of Jewish humor. The problem for Chast, like Woody Allen and countless others before and after, is that anxiety eventually debilitates. Inevitably there comes a point at which bloodying someone else's nose is therapeutic and, in that first shocking instant, funnier.

Then there was the CJM exhibit "Lamp of the Covenant: Dave Lane," presumably the artist's take on the *ner tamid*, the eternal light over the Torah ark in every synagogue. Lane fashioned his creation as a "six-ton work suspended high over the heads of visitors. Attached to an enormous oval of steel were antique objects: world globes, light bulbs," apple peelers, blow torches "and various other objects that suggest the unfolding marvels of the cosmos." No doubt warped by the unfolding marvel of child labor in my father's scrap yard—Rozenman & Sons Auto Wrecking, Tiffin, Ohio—the objects suggested something else to me: a long, sweaty day shoveling slag. But, hell, everyone thinks he's a critic. Or an artist, like one-name only Kutiman.

"Kutiman: offgrid offline," the museum described as "minutely edited snippets of music played by soloists found on the Internet [what was found on the Internet, the music or the soloists?] and displayed on 12 monitors that periodically join in or go silent." Kutiman was said to be "a young Israeli musician and composer [who] utilizes found audio and video from the Internet as the source of his own work." Since we spent many waking hours before video screens, minutely editing our own and others work, my wife and I took the museum's word for "offgrid offline" and skipped the installation of screens and speakers in a nearly bare space. Any more minimalist, and it wouldn't have been there at all.

Wondering what was particularly Jewish and contemporary about the Contemporary Jewish Museum, beyond Rand and Chast's cartoons, we walked through Chinatown to North Beach in search of poetry and coffee. North Beach was, and in some respects still is, the old Italian neighborhood. We stopped at Café Trieste, which doubled as a neighborhood coffee shop and tourist site. In Columbus, Indianapolis or Oklahoma City an entrepreneur would buy the place and upgrade it to look like an inviting old Italian coffee shop instead of a moldering old Italian coffee shop. And he or she would hire perky staff who didn't sidetrack your order while talking to an acquaintance. But they probably wouldn't have musicians on the sidewalk early Sunday afternoons playing to an appreciative knot of tourists and old men from the neighborhood, some smoking cigarettes and talking with their hands.

At the table next to us a young couple—he was Anglo, she Asian—with a baby in one of those expensive three-wheeled prams such couples seem to prefer, talked and divided the Sunday *New York Times*. Neither took the "A" section with its *Times'* facsimile of hard news. If the skeletal *Chronicle* was autopilot-left, superficial and predictable, the still-substantial *Times* was intelligentsia left, convoluted and predictable. The couple read it apparently untutored in media appreciation. Trump-era obsession with the other side's "fake news" obscures our decades-old general contagion of news fakes. These are unavoidable in mainstream media's Pollyannaish reporting of critical subjects such as Islamic triumphalism and unfunded and eventually unsupportable government debt, not to mention their masochistic lamentations—"but it feels so good!"—over white privilege and systemic racism. Ah, but *après moi* and my latte, *la deluge*.

The evening we visited, young waiters were speaking Italian to each other and to some customers in E Tutto Qua on Columbus Avenue near Broadway. Inside or at street-side seating, downstairs or up, windows all open to the sidewalk, it was still hot even as the sun set. Like many other businesses, not to mention residences in San Francisco, E Tutto Qua ("It's All Here") seemed to lack air conditioning. No matter; it did not want for patrons, an engaging atmosphere or good food.

Across Columbus Avenue lay poet and publisher Lawrence Ferlinghetti's City Lights Bookstore. At 19, which is to say a half a century earlier, I had discovered Ferlinghetti's *Coney Island of the Mind* and, so I thought, a powerful free verse means of self-expression and understanding. Self-expression first, understanding later. Of course, then I was a sophomore in college and girls, Batman on TV and the Vietnam war were the biggest things, in that order. In City Lights I bought another paperback copy of the poet's little collection, *Pictures from a Gone World*. In moving I've lost two previous versions. Maybe a cosmic message about a world really gone. Anyway, some of the poems held up.

North Beach and City Lights were Beat era haunts. City Lights published Allen Ginsburg's *Howl and Other Poems* in 1956. An obscenity trial followed in 1957, a judge ruling that "Howl," with its many blunt homosexual and heterosexual references, or perhaps references to blunt homo- and hetero-sex, was not obscene. Whatever, as the court might declare today, "Howl" famously begins:

"I saw the best minds of my generation destroyed by madness, starving hysterical naked/ dragging themselves through the negro streets at dawn looking for an angry fix/ angelheaded hipsters burning for the ancient heavenly connection to starry dynamo in the machinery of night..." And so on. And on. At 19 it struck me as mysteriously profound, suspiciously repellent and seriously run-on. Stream of consciousness, baby. In those days hipsters was a cool word, not a marketing cliché, and by 2017 Mr. Wikipedia would say "Howl" was considered one of America's most important literary works. By hipsters, no doubt. But reread it for yourself. See if it doesn't put you in mind of that Steven Wright joke: "When I first read a dictionary, I thought it was a long poem about everything." The more time passes, the more "Howl" reads like a short dictionary defining Allen Ginsburg's inability to distinguish between Dwight Eisenhower and Juan Peron.

Five large banners draped City Lights. They were drawn in the flat, hard, pseudo-proletarian style one sees on placards and posters of the causes *de jure*. The first four quoted poet Mahmoud Darwish: "Nothing is harder/ On the soul/ Than the smell of dreams/ While they are evaporating." The fifth exhorted: "Stop the Deportations." Under each line of text was a non-Caucasian face.

The banners lacked disclosure. In this they were consistent with agit-prop everywhere. Darwish was a Palestinian Arab supremacist and Palestinian Liberation Organization "cultural affairs" functionary when the PLO was one of the world's leading terrorist movements. His poem "Those Who Pass Between Fleeting Words" told Israelis 10 times in 52 lines to "get out." A revisionist work denying Jews' organic tie to the land of Israel, it instructed them to "pile your illusions in a deserted pit, and be gone. ... Die wherever you like, but do not die among us..."

Posters proclaiming solidarity with undocumented immigrants in general and "Dreamers" in particular were common around San Francisco then. But rhetorical hyperbole equating opposition to Trump's overturning of Obama's DACA maneuver (Deferred Action on Child Arrivals) with guerrilla resistance to Nazi occupation during World War II necessarily raised suspicion.

When lobbyists for unrestricted immigration, which is to say opponents of national identity, or at least American national identity, first pressed President Obama on legalizing Dreamers, he correctly observed unilateral action by the president would be unconstitutional. But after Congress, the legal embodiment of popular sovereignty, refused to act, he went ahead regardless. Amnesty—"deferred action [postponed deportation]"—for children infiltrated by parents themselves illegally present in the United States (and sometimes children who border-crossed on their own) became sacrosanct. Like all leftist *causes celebres*, it melded into the secular fundamentalist catechism, which like touchstones of every cult, admitted of no doubt. A wedge issue for civic deconstruction, it in many cases also is a matter of compassion.

Nevertheless, Dreamerism challenged rule of law. And rule of law is what distinguishes America from Cuba, for example. Still, humankind cannot bear too much truth, as T.S. Eliot observed. So smart money does not bet on City Lights publishing a neo-Beat epic poem on the Castro brothers' decades-old policy of imprisoning disagreeable poets and restricting emigration to the States. Those dreaming of reaching free soil and willing to risk sharks in the Florida Straits so far amount to at least 10 percent of the Cuban population. But no City Lights' poet among them?

A weekend evening near but not quite in Chinatown and a half-dozen young women lined up outside a club of some sort. They were dressed pretty much as Sports Illustrated Swimsuit issue models if the latter wore stiletto heels with Lucite platforms to the beach, which is to say these young ladies bulged out and around strategically placed Lycra Spandex straps over satin-like short shorts. Except for the tallest, prettiest of the group. Over her heels and briefs she wore nothing at all except a wide-mesh, black fishnet top. Her breasts were large, well-shaped and there for all of greater San Francisco to see. My head snapped back as we walked past. My wife asked, "Club-goers, shills for the place, or prostitutes?" True-false or multiple choice? A do-I-look-fat-in-this-fishnet trick question? I couldn't tell.

San Francisco is like Jerusalem—"builded as a city compact, together" (Psalm 122)—the latter with its seven hills, the former with its 40 or so and both urban areas featuring numerous, distinct neighborhoods. We took the Hyundai on a spin through the Mission district, the Castro and Haight Ashbury. Gentrification and genteel shabbiness contended, variety provided by an occasional residential tent. The once notorious Mission district featured the homeless, yes, but also numerous signs in Spanish and inviting corner restaurants, probably not Tex-Mex but just authentic Mex. A morbidly obese woman steered a motorized chair-scooter down the sidewalk, her tiny dog trotting beside on a red leash.

We drove through the Castro, busy long-time hub of the city's gay life. Rainbow flags adorned lampposts, their colors and patterns repeated in a crosswalk and on the sign of a nearby used car lot. Three men stood in doorway talking. Two, middle-aged and muscular, wore only red, G-string-like, fringed penis sheaths. The third man, clothed, conversed as if this were normal. Normal—now there's an increasingly hateful concept. Too much normality and one might imagine nudity as a private affair. Pondering the essentially naked men and half-naked young women, not to mention the yoga pantsed legion, we wondered if the less a society values fertility, the more it flaunts sexuality.

Haight-Ashbury affected a 50-year hang-over. It had been half a century since Scott McKenzie sang, "If you're going to San Francisco/ Be sure to wear some flowers in your hair/ Summertime will be a love-in there …" Yet "Summer of Love" posters were still on display. Tourists couldn't escape them, which may have been the point, but then neither could locals. Langston Hughes asked what happens to a dream deferred and provided powerful, unhappy answers. Nostalgia prolonged, on the other hand, curls up like a faded Peter Max poster.

Bay area streets thronged with Toyota Priuses, the electric/hybrid automotive equivalent of quinoa. They were a powerful signifier, fashionable in their ostensibly anti-fashionable way. They advertised to all and sundry that the driver practiced sustainable living, narrowing his or her carbon footprint. This was done by plugging the coal-fired Prius into an electric outlet for recharging every night. On our way back to the hotel in city traffic we watched as a black Prius in front accelerated—they can do that—pulled left partially into oncoming traffic, straddled the yellow dividing line to pass a slower-moving, hydro-carbon consuming vehicle ahead, and ducked back into our lane. Sustainability conferred its privileges.

Our last night in San Francisco we had dinner with Bob and Jane, we'll call them, relatives of a neighbor back in suburban D.C. He described himself as one of the oldest techies in Silicon Valley. Life was good and he had been considering retirement when one of the Big Four Trusts of this age—Google, Amazon, Apple and Facebook—made him an offer he couldn't refuse. Now he was commuting in a company bus filled with techies 30 years or more younger than he to a new corporate campus and—sometimes also jetting to other parts of the world—assisted this particular robber baron industry in moving to the next level of controlling what mankind consumed, read, wrote and remembered. Some capabilities were "scary," he acknowledged. And some were life-savers. Not knowing in whose archive they might eventually repose, we took no selfies with our cell phone cameras.

Early the next morning, we reversed the pioneers' journeys. What had taken them months, stretches of tedium interrupted by instances of life-threatening danger, took us a few hours of airline inconvenience. We returned to our nation's capital, where some people still imagined there was an *e pluribus Unum* nation and that they were in charge.

There had been an *e pluribus Unum* nation once, not that long before. Among other things, it featured a dominant, mostly joyous—if mostly simple—music. This sound blew outward, shaking much of the world. Then, curiously, its makers aimed the music, which had coalesced from disparate traditions, back in fragments at fragmenting audiences. In the process they kept pumping up the volume and losing the common beat. Like the members of the *Unum* itself, who began de-assimilating, retribalizing and thereby unraveling back into contending *pluribus...*

Chapter Thirteen:
Birth of the Beat

Only Rock 'n Roll, but We Liked It

... Popular music in the early and mid-1950s was Patti Page's "How Much Is That Doggie In the Window," ("The one with the waggily tail ..."); Dean Martin's "That's Amore" ("When the moon hits your eye like a big pizza pie..."); and Dinah Shore's "Love and Marriage" ("Go together like a horse and carriage ..."). In other words, torture. At least it was for a third grader being driven over town by his mother in the family's red and cream-colored Chevy Bel-Air in Napoleon, Ohio to his first piano lesson. One always went "over town" in Napoleon, population 5,000, across the wide, brown Maumee River from the south side to the larger north side with its compact if comprehensive business district. Young ears heard the tunes—issuing from the AM-only radio, station selection firmly under adult control—as auditory gauze, mentally suffocating.

Until that summer day in 1955, the day "Rock Around The Clock," by Bill Haley and His Comets blasted through the speaker. The song had reached 23 on Billboard's pop singles chart in 1954, but re-released the next year, hit number one. In 1956, director Richard Brooks used "Rock Around the Clock" as theme music for his Academy Award-nominated film *Blackboard Jungle*. The movie pitted a dedicated teacher against switch-blade carrying juvenile delinquents in an inner-city high school. It was the first to use rock n'roll for the soundtrack and drew some teenaged audiences to dance in theater aisles as the opening credits rolled, others to riot, slashing seats. Legendary disc jockey and television rock n' roll impresario Dick Clark would call "Rock Around the Clock," which ultimately sold 25 million copies worldwide, "the national anthem" of rock music.

My mother, Mollie Esther Rozenman, took a hand off the steering wheel to change the station. "No!" I shouted, to my own surprise as much as hers. "I want to hear this."

Mom had changed the spelling of her first name from Molly to Mollie to avoid any confusion with her sister-in-law, my Aunt Molly, one of my father's sisters. Mollie and Sam married in 1946, ages 21 and 25, respectively, and remained in uxorial union, mutually supportive, firmly happy until my father's death in 1993. Aunt Molly, on the other hand, had married more than once, for shorter periods and her cyclical exuberance was not often mortared by happiness. So, Mom became Mollie, not Molly.

Perhaps she thought that starting me with piano lessons—I'd wanted to play drums, if I had to take any musical instruction at all—was victory enough. Whatever the reason, she let me listen to "Rock Around the Clock." The effect was electric. Here was a sound pulsing with energy, knowing lyrics—knowing what, I wasn't sure, but however inarticulate surely esoteric and erotic. Though at that age erotic as a concept hovered outside my understanding if not my intuition. Something to do with naked women, the mysterious Ultima Thule of immature male brains. Mature ones, too. Whatever, that sound was electric and magnetic. I had to hear more.

Not long after, I bought a copy of the single, on the Decca label, and played it on the family phonograph until it bore as many scratches as grooves. Purchase of "Rock Around the Clock" would be followed by "(You Ain't Nothin' But a) Hound Dog" by Elvis Presley (flip side "Don't Be Cruel" also a hit), "Great Balls of Fire" by Jerry Lee Lewis, Buddy Holly's "That'll Be the Day" and through sixth grade and a couple dozen other 45 rpm singles. In fifth grade, during lunch period classmates and I at C.D. Brillhart Elementary School would bolt down our 30-cent cafeteria offerings, government-subsidized half-pint cartons of milk two cents extra, and rush back to the classroom. We hung a hand-lettered poster board reading "Kool Kats Klub"—yes, in complete innocence, the K.K.K.—and jitterbugged, 10-year-old boys following the lead of 10-year-old girls (how did they already know how to dance?) until the end of lunch hour. I also took control of the car radio, at least when Mom was driving. And so long as I and my younger siblings, Cathy and Martin, seemed to require babysitters, we would watch Dick Clark's Saturday night television show, sponsored by Beech-Nut Spearmint Chewing Gum ("It's Flavor-IFIC!") and featuring the latest hits, in the company of one of our two regular babysitters. Each one, Judy W. or Barb S., was a perfumed, lip-sticked junior high school nymph. At least as I saw them.

Rock n' roll became not only life's soundtrack but a sort of mental template. When, in "Dream Lover," Bobby Darin sang, "Dream lover, where are you/With a love, oh, so true/And the hand that I can hold/To feel you near as I grow old" I knew that was the way grown-up life was supposed to be. And when the Beach Boys harmonized about their 1962 Chevrolet with the 409-cubic inch engine, "When I take her to the track she really shines/She always turns in the fastest times/My four-speed, dual quad, Posi-Traction 409" I knew I had to have a car like that, someday.

So, when in fourth grade, classmate Rick Horner asked if I wanted to go to Toledo to see the Elvis Presley show, I said yes first and asked my parents second. For some reason, perhaps because Mrs. Horner would be driving, Mollie and Sam agreed. The concert was scheduled for Sunday, Nov. 22, 1956.

Presley, already a national sensation who'd appeared twice on television's *Ed Sullivan Show* and just released his first movie, *Love Me Tender*, would perform at a matinee and in the evening. Our three-person Napoleon contingent saw the matinee. Tickets were $2 and $2.50 each (roughly $19 and $24 inflation-adjusted 2020 dollars, respectively). The shows did not quite sell out the 7,500-seat Toledo Sports Arena, but according to a Presley history blog, the gross of $28,200 broke the venue's previous record of $24,000 set by Bob Hope. In any case, the rock n' roll icon drew bigger crowds in Glass City than either Vice President Richard Nixon or Democratic presidential candidate Senator Adlai Stevenson (D-Ill.) on campaign stops that year.

More enthusiastic crowds, too. About Stevenson, it must be noted parenthetically, the story goes that after an impressive speech he was told "you're the thinking man's candidate." To which he responded, "That won't do. I need a majority."

Culture leads politics and in November, 1956 Presley led culture—and for years afterward. Our seats were up near the rafters. On the floor of the arena, where circus animals, boxers or minor league hockey teams normally plied their trades, 2,000 or so temporary seats were occupied by young girls. They screamed, many rising to their feet as Elvis walked through. Only it wasn't Elvis, just a girl who'd made herself up to look like The King, complete with brushed back hair, turned-up collar and guitar slung across one shoulder. When the real Presley parted the stage curtains, in dark trousers and a loose fitting, shiny suit coat—was it gold lamè'?—the screams merged into a sustained vocal hysteria.

Every time Presley opened his mouth to sing, or swiveled his hips, more screams erupted, intensifying to a crescendo, then collapsing only long enough for another audible syllable to be heard from the star, another pelvic rotation glimpsed. Up in the nose-bleed seats, the concert sound amounted virtually to one long shriek.

Organizers had attempted to upgrade security. But as *The Toledo Blade* reported, when Elvis starting singing "Hound Dog," his closing number at the time, "it was the signal for the surge to the stage by thousands of youngsters who obediently had kept in their seats throughout the performance. They broke out and jammed down the aisles as an extra crew of 20 policemen watched helplessly." But by the time the bobbysoxers/teeny-boppers reached the stage, Presley had ducked out the back and into a waiting car. It whisked him off to his rooms at the downtown Commodore Perry Hotel, perhaps Toledo's finest at the time. Competition being mostly the Hillcrest Hotel, where the Rozenmans from Napoleon, Shankmans from Norwalk, and Silversteins from Bellefontaine—aunts, uncles and cousins—lodged annually for Rosh Hashana and Yom Kippur services at the improbably Yiddish-accented Anshe Sephard synagogue my grandfathers attended.

Presley's Sports Arena escape from nearly 2,000 frenzied fans was, in micro, what the Beatles would execute in macro as they bolted from Municipal Stadium steps ahead of a larger adoring mob swarming lemming-like over more numerous and often beefier Cleveland policemen 10 years later. I somehow missed The Beatles' hit comedy film, *A Hard Day's Night*, at its 1964 release, but when I saw the mock-documentary years later, in particular the scene of the Fab Four running from a horde of fans, I realized I had seen that movie before. Twice.

"Those Louie Louie Boys, the Kingsmen!"

If you were a teenager in the 1960s, then the sound remains embedded—thanks to endless repetition—in gray matter just above your proto-reptilian brain. Musically, the notes are C-C-C, F-F, G-G-G, F-F, C-C-C, in 4:4 time. Over and over. You can't shake it and don't want to. Written by Richard Berry and recorded by him in 1957, "Louie Louie" (no comma, according to Berry) became a regional hit around San Francisco. Berry sold the rights to Flip Records for $750 in 1959.

"Louie Louie" was a Los Angeles-area hit for Rockin' Robin Roberts and the Wailers in 1960. Then in April, 1963 the Kingsmen, a Portland, Oregon group often described as playing garage-rock, spent $50 for a studio session and recorded its version of the song, changing the tune from a ballad about a Jamaican sailor eager to get home to his girl into insistent, rock n' roll house party music with slurred lyrics and intentional, muddy background noise. The lyrics were widely regarded as unintelligible, obscene or somehow both. Countless teens, then including this writer, taped the song on reel-to-reel recorders and replayed it slowly in futile attempts at decoding. Nevertheless, "Louie Louie" was banned in many cities and the state of Indiana, and subjected to a two and a-half year F.B.I. investigation. The feds concluded they were "unable to interpret any of the wording." One hoped they did better on wire taps of mob bosses. On its release, a Boston disc jockey called "Louie Louie" the worst record of the week.

Perfect. "Louie Louie" spent December of 1963 and January of 1964 in the top ten of Billboard's Hot 100 chart, including six joyous weeks at number two. The Kingsmen's version overwhelmed a more polished simultaneous release by another Portland band, Paul Revere and the Raiders. The latter group would go on to rock n' roll big time with a string of hits, but it was the Kingsmen's "Louie Louie" that returned to the charts in 1966.

If "Rock Around the Clock" was rock n' roll's national anthem, then "Louie Louie" was the teenage bugle call of the 1960s. And it never quite died, sung, recorded or borrowed for its melody line by everyone from Otis Redding, the Beach Boys and Jan and Dean to Frank Zappa and the Mothers of Invention and Mongo Santamaria.

So, of course, Ron Zartman, Wade "Butch" Estep, Rick Bump and I piled into Dad's two-toned—turquoise roof, cream colored body—'63 Mercury Monterey, the model with the cantilevered electric rear window, and raced north one school night in 1964 on Ohio Route 53. We left Tiffin and passed Fremont, headed for Ole Zim's Wagon Shed in Gibsonburg. We were on our way to hear "those fabulous Louie Louis boys, the Kingsmen!"

Gibsonburg was a town of 2,000 people about 23 miles southeast of Toledo. Ole Zim's was a restaurant/dance hall. Hundreds of teens packed themselves in that night to hear the Kingsmen. The crowd was so dense the four of us from Tiffin could not circulate close to the stage. The congestion deprived more than a few of the northwestern Ohio high school girls present of a glimpse me, costumed as I was for the occasion in linen white jeans and a neon bright madras plaid shirt that did everything but flash.

The Kingsmen played "Louie Louie," their follow-up version of Barrett Storm's "Money," if memory serves, and an entire evening's worth of jet engine decibel level music. We left hot, sweaty, happy and hearing impaired. Driving home, we kept turning up the volume on the car radio. Nothing seemed loud enough. Plus, all the familiar rock n' roll songs being broadcast sounded slower than usual. I'd suffered a 50 percent hearing loss in one ear at age 14, apparently the long-delayed result of childhood measles, but Zartman, Estep and Bump also experienced post-performance auditory declines. It would take two days, for me at least, before my ears returned to their pre-concert norm. Something similar happened after The Who concert in Columbus' Palace Theater in 1969. Everything spoken the next day around my desk at the Ohio Development Department, tourism and information section, sounded like it was being muffled through a towel. In high school the morning after the Kingsmen show, awkward moments occurred in class when teachers called on me but their words came across as distant mumbling. In the late 1980s, "Pump Up the Volume!" became a hit example of something called British acid house music. Americans were there first, without the acid.

Live and On Stage, The Rolling Stones!

On Friday, July 8, 1966 folk singer Tom Rush was playing a small club, maybe the Chessmate Coffee House, in Detroit. In Cobo Hall downtown, The Rolling Stones—half-way through a 30-city, two-month concert tour of the United States and Canada—were headlining a super show. Warm-up acts included The Standells ("Dirty Water") and The McCoys ("Hang on Sloppy"). What to do? After work at our summer jobs—mine was driving a pick-up truck all over northwestern Ohio, northeastern Indiana and southeastern Michigan, making auto parts deliveries and retrievals for Rozenman & Sons Auto Wrecking—we journeyed two hours from Tiffin to see both performances.

So, Zartman, Estep, Bump and I—having finished our freshman year in college and our ears having recovered from the Kingsmen show at Ole Zim's Wagon Shed two and a-half years earlier—headed through Toledo to Detroit. Now college students, we watched Rush, who had a better voice and smoother way with words than many more well-known folkies, sing a few numbers. "Okay," I said, "time to go. We need to get Cobo Hall." Zartman, a particular fan of Rush, decided to stay. We couldn't dissuade him, and—even though he too had a ticket to the Stones' concert—left him behind.

We were nearly in the rafters (always get the least expensive seats; once you're inside, it's the same show, right?) and, Cobo Hall being a 12,000-seat oval, at the opposite end from the stage. If we'd really wanted to see the Rolling Stones, we should have brought binoculars. But we heard them alright, little creatures on the faraway stage. Early in the set list, which included "Not Fade Away," "The Last Time," Paint It Black" and "Under My Thumb"—an anthem of male dominance that has not survived feminism—something gave way in one of the guitars, or connecting cords and speakers. The distorting "fuzz tone" that made so much of rock n' roll a) distinctive, b) exciting, c) grating, or d) all of the above became even more distorted. But the Stones kept playing, all the way, I believe, through "19th Nervous Breakdown" and "(I Can't Get No) Satisfaction."

The other indelible moment from the show, in addition to the guitar breakdown, came just behind us, slightly above and to the right.

We'd noticed that even in jeans, loafers and short-sleeved shirts, we were, compared to much of the rest of crowd, over-dressed. Some concert-goers looked like Grateful Dead camp followers. Among them, a couple in back, both mis-attired males, holding hands. And kissing.

We'd never seen anything like that before. And didn't imagine we ever would again.

The Fab Four, The Beatles!

It was Sunday afternoon, Aug. 14, 1966. The Beatles, supported by The Cyrkle ("It's a Turned Down Day"), Bobby Hebb ("Sunny") and the bombshell Ronettes ("Be My Baby") were booked into Cleveland's cavernous Municipal Stadium downtown on the edge of Lake Erie. My sister, Cathy and our cousin, Laura Shankman, both 15, were desperate to go. More of a Rolling Stones fan, I was curious enough to agree to drive them. A Tiffin friend of mine, Jack Yaeger, decided to come along. We picked up Laura in Norwalk and made the long drive to Cleveland.

Tickets costs between $3 and $5.50, or roughly $24 to $44 today. Managers of Cleveland's new Top 40 radio station WIXY reportedly hoped the relatively low prices would generate a near-capacity crowd—something the stadium's regular summer occupants, baseball's too-often hapless Cleveland Indians, could only fantasize about in those days. The 24,000 Beatlemania sufferers who did show up, mostly girls too young to drive, disappointed the promoters but in fact constituted a very large audience for a rock n' roll show up to then.

About halfway up in the lower deck, along the first base line, we had no trouble hearing the warm-up acts, though the sound coming through the public address system made it hard tell if they were actually singing or lip-synching. Then came the Beatles. At the sight of their mop-topped idols, the audience members screamed as one. And kept screaming, pausing only to gulp another breath before collectively reopening their mouths wide enough to frighten an orthodontist.

It was Elvis all over again, giant economy-sized. And it did not matter that we were outdoors. As soon as The Beatles began to play, the screams and the stadium's sound system, geared for a single announcer intoning into a single microphone, "And now, ladies and gentlemen, our National Anthem," merged into high volume static. When the screams ebbed just enough to hear Paul McCartney's bass and Ringo Starr's drums, never mind George Harrison and John Lennon, the roar flowed again. Vocals? Are you kidding?

Disappointed at not being able to hear music in any meaningful sense, I sat back to watch the scene. The large stage occupied a big chunk of the baseball infield, centered where second base normally would have been. A four-foot high snow fence, the kind routinely unrolled along Ohio roads in winter to keep wind-blown snow from drifting across the pavement, stretched from home plate down the first and third base lines into the outfield. And at roughly eight to 10-foot intervals along the fence Cleveland policemen with arms folded stood facing the crowd.

It happened during the Beatles' fourth song, "Day Tripper." Thousands of pre-teen and teenaged girls—some reports said 2,500 but I guessed more—fueled by anticipatory or full-flush estrogen-rushes, erupted from the stands. Pack-like, they made as one for the stage. Heedless of the outnumbered cops, scoffing at their flimsy snow fence, they poured toward the stage and the objects of their adoration. In them was something like the grim determination of Pickett's Confederates marching deliberately toward Union lines at Gettysburg. Only faster, much faster. And ecstatic.

The Beatles saw them coming. They darted off, stage right, into a waiting black limousine. The car raced toward the right field bullpen—where normally the visiting baseball team's relief pitchers warmed up—and through its inner and outer gates to safety, the mob's most determined members trailing tearfully behind.

Then the real Beatles—the first quartet being a decoy—hurried down stage left and into another limousine that headed at a measured pace out the left field bullpen. The whole thing was an automotive version of the foot-powered escape scene in "A Hard Day's Night." It took 30 minutes for police, reinforced by private security guards, to clear the stage and the infield and allow the concert to resume. The band played another seven static-filled and scream overlaid tunes and then cut out for good.

Some accounts claim the Beatles hid in a backstage trailer during the disruption, but if they did, then why the second decoy limo? In any case, it was shortly after that summer's U.S. tour that the band gave up performing before audiences. The Cleveland show was said to be one of the last straws. Much safer to focus on recording studio work. That way, at least, one could hear one's guitar softly weep.

"The Supremes, Never the Same Show Twice"

Cue the *Dragnet* theme: It was late December, 1966. It was cold in Miami. My partners, Alec Berezin and Larry Shiff, and I were working the spring break watch out of tourism. Only it was winter. We somehow hadn't figured that spring break—bikini-clad girls on sandy beaches, sunny skies and warm blue water, free-flowing beer, no parents within hundreds of miles—wouldn't be happening for another three months. Our job? Get wise. *Dum-da-dum-dum.*

So it was that, with Pan American Airlines Miami-to-Nassau tickets in our pockets, we found ourselves waiting for departure, watching "The Lawrence Welk Show" on television in the south Florida home of a retired relative. Alec, from Tiffin, and Larry, from nearby Fostoria, were in their freshman year at Miami University in Oxford, Ohio. I was a sophomore at Ohio University in Athens. Our parents all were members of the Tiffin-Fostoria-Fremont B'nai B'rith chapter.

Those who imagine the '60s as an era only of youth culture and social upheaval have forgotten, or never saw "The Lawrence Welk Show." Nothing but canned corn, elevator music brought to simulated life by the most wholesome-looking singers and dancers, hokey skits overlaid by eruptions of unprovoked patriotism, and all under the baton of North Dakota-born but German-accented big band leader Welk. The show came from an alternate America in which rock n' roll, let alone Eldridge Cleaver and the Black Panthers, had never happened. A rather large alternate America. "The Lawrence Welk Show" was one of the most successful television series of all time, airing on ABC from 1955 to 1972, then from '71 to 1982 in first-run syndication. Mundane tunnel vision prevents us from seeing the parallel worlds that always exist next door.

Forced viewing of Welk, "with the luv-a-ly Lennon Sisters," as the host invariably enunciated, "brought to you by Polident [a denture adhesive] and Serutan [a laxative], Nature's spelled backwards!" should have warned us. "Spring break" on Nassau would not go as imagined. Not at all.

For one thing, it really was winter in the Bahamas. That meant cloudy skies, temperatures dipping from the 60s into the 50s and no girls on the beaches. Not any. To rate our hotel as a two-star would have been generous. To review the sandwich shops in which we chewed and re-chewed our alleged hamburgers as better than dubious would have been impossible.

But that wasn't all. We'd landed about two weeks before the Jan. 10, 1967 general elections. The Progressive Liberal Party and the United Bahamian Party were locked in battle, with the Labour and National Democratic parties far behind. Voting would take place under the new 1964 constitution, although the islands would not become fully independent from Great Britain for another nine years. On election day the PLP and UBP tied, each winning 18 seats; PLP, with help from Labour, formed the first black-led government. During the campaign's closing days and nights, as we wandered through New Providence clueless about racial tension underlying the campaign, a few firebombs would be thrown, windows smashed and beatings administered.

There was another Nassau just a few blocks away, the Bahama of tourist brochures and our imaginations—manicured landscapes, beaches and deferential service. It could be found, for example, at the British Colonial Hilton Nassau Resort, with its spacious pool, private beach, grand lobby, bar and upscale restaurants. All behind a driveway gate we could not afford to pass.

A few disappointing days and nights later we were on our way back to Miami. Airborne for no more than 30 minutes, the Pan Am flight barely had time to level off. Back in the United States after our first foreign adventure—not counting trips to Windsor, Canada across the Ambassador Bridge from Detroit, and no one from northwestern Ohio did count them, Windsor seeming like an appendix of the Motor City—we considered how to salvage our winter break fiasco. Fortunately, there was an answer. We would celebrate New Year's Eve with Diana Ross and the Supremes at Miami Beach's sparkling Deauville Hotel!

The Supremes were headlining the Dec. 31, 1966 show. They already were big-time stars. By then their hit records included "Baby

Love," "Come See About Me," "Stop! In the Name of Love," "My World Is Empty Without You" and "Back in My Arms Again."

Motown Records famously developed, groomed, choreographed and coached its artists, initially unpolished if talented African American kids from the inner city. It launched the careers of many acts, individuals and groups. None would be more successful than The Supremes. The three original members, Diana Ross, Florence Ballard and Mary Wilson came from Detroit's Brewster-Douglass public housing project. The trio, with personnel changes over the years, eventually became not just Motown's biggest act but also the country's top popular vocal group, with a dozen number one records.

A problem presented itself with our New Year's Eve plan, however. The Deauville, "Hotel of the Stars!", imposed a $5 drinks minimum per patron. That would be $39 or $40 today. Bad as the cost was to three undergraduates to whom the sight of a $20 bill was rare, the fact that none of us were of drinking age—then 21—was worse.

We showed up at the Deauville anyway. "Look," we told the doorman when the admissions line finally had carried us to the entrance, "we'll drink $5 worth of Cokes. Each."

He stared at us, appraisingly. Finally, lifting the rope with his left hand and—holding the right palm up but unobtrusively close to his front pocket—he nodded. I had never tipped, let alone bribed, anyone. But I remembered my father and Uncle Alan Shankman arguing with Uncle Max Silverstein over whether to tip the parking garage attendants at all and if so, how much at Toledo's Hillcrest Hotel one Yom Kippur break-the-fast. Dad drove a Chevy but Max, the big tipper, had a Cadillac. I forked over a dollar bill. So did Alec and Larry.

We were in!

Seated toward the back of the sweeping two-story dining and ballroom, we nevertheless had a clear view of the stage. A linen cloth draped the table, on which elegant glasses and napkins rested. This was the big time! And a far cry from our Nassau eateries.

A drum roll, a swirl of spotlights, and The Supremes glamorously appeared. Applause swept the room. After an introductory number, Diana Ross addressed the audience confidentially. Bending over the microphone a bit, as if to impart a secret, she said, "just to let you know, we do a different show every night ... We have to; our band leader drinks." The big room laughed. Two years later I would hear Ross utter the same faux confidential lines in the same way after I introduced The Supremes to about 10,000 fans at their Jan. 18, 1969 concert in Ohio University's new Convocation Center.

Not to get ahead of the story, though. At the Deauville an aggressive waiter kept bringing us Coca-Colas. We were going to meet our $5 drinks minimum—at $1 per Coke, as I remember—no matter what. I gave up midway through my third glass and handed over a $5 bill then and there. But Larry kept ordering. "If I have to pay for them, I'm drinking them!" he declared.

The Supremes had shown no signs of winding down when Larry began shifting in his seat. "Damn! I've got to piss so bad ..." "Just go to the bathroom and then sneak back in," we advised. "No," he hissed, unzipping his pants, "I'm not missing any of this." And with that, shielded by the draped tablecloth, he relieved himself on the Deauville's stylish carpet.

"My world is empty, without you, babe, Without you ..."

The Grateful Dead: Free, No Bargain

Sunday night, Nov. 25, 1968. I took a study break and walked out of the old Chubb Library at Ohio University. A sound washed in an undercurrent across the Main Green from Memorial Auditorium. It strengthened into the bass guitar and drums of a rock band. Curious, I walked across the green. No one stopped me at the door or asked for a ticket as I crossed the lobby. From the rear of the auditorium I wandered partway down an aisle.

Mem. Aud., as it was known on campus, was an aging, 2,500-seat affair complete with a large balcony. In these drafty confines Gov. Winthrop Rockefeller (R-Ark.), in a suit and tie, black Western boots and well in the bottle, memorably had declared a year or so earlier that "some of us in this room have fought and died for freedom." Rockefeller indeed had fought for freedom, rising from private to colonel and receiving a Purple Heart in World War II. But that evening at Ohio U., the grandson of John D. Rockefeller and the first Republican governor of Arkansas since Reconstruction, managed to be simultaneously hard to follow and highly entertaining.

It was also in Mem. Aud. where Marxist agitator Saul Alinsky, in a sliver of his long career schooling a generation of activists (deconstructionists a more precise but awkward term), conspired with potential followers among Bobcat undergraduates. In an avuncular manner he suggested we consider as a tactic getting the entire 15,000-member student body to spit chewed gum on campus walkways until administrators caved in to our demands, whatever they might be.

Such illuminating moments aside, the band on stage appeared large—because audience members occasionally walked around among them—seemed disorganized and looked poorly dressed. If not large— Mem. Aud. was little more than half full at the moment—the audience too appeared disorganized and poorly dressed. Who were these people, I wondered? Many did not look like students, though in Athens, Ohio, a relative pearl in Lyndon Johnson's fraying Appalachia, in the late '60s one never knew for sure.

The musicians seemed to be warming up, and taking their good old time doing so. Periodically, I caught a melody line, only for it to vanish. The sound mix never quite found a balance. Vocals—when clear enough to be singled out—emerged indistinct. Overall, the aural effect was muddy.

A review in the next day's *Athens Messenger*, the daily paper for the town and Athens County, not to be confused with the student-run *O.U. Post*, put it this way: "There's something about music that this old-fashioned listener demands, if he can be expected to dig it. A beginning, a middle and an end." But of the outfit he'd heard the night before, "there's something about 30-minute 'songs' which have no melodies, which start nowhere, end nowhere with nothing happening in between," that put him to sleep. As for "the boring light show" that left the band in the dark part of time while beams flickered aimlessly on the auditorium's big screen, it was another example of an irritating, distracting trend.

I felt the same way. After a half-hour or so, still waiting for what I mistook to be the warm-up to resolve itself into rock 'n roll, never having been hooked enough to take a seat, I walked out, joined others trickling away in search of more rewarding pursuits. In my case, that meant back to a hard, unpadded chair in the Chubb reference room. Did you know that the pottery of the early first millennium B.C.E. Israelites was less sophisticated than that of the peoples who'd preceded them in Canaan? Me neither.

Meanwhile, inexplicably, a larger stream of footloose fans kept flowing into Mem Aud.

The concert, as it was billed, did have its unforgettable scene. It was that of scores of people continuously jerking in wave-like spasms in the aisles and in front of the stage. Arthur Murray, take cover! An image of those phantasms remains etched at the back of the retina more than half a century later. Unfortunately.

Not until the next day, overhearing other students talking, did I realize I'd walked out of a free Grateful Dead concert. The San Francisco-based Grateful Dead was one of the better-known acid rock bands then influencing contemporary music, or at least expanding its psychedelic scene. The ensemble at O.U. included two drummers, apparently in the vain hope that if not alone then together they might manage one steady rock beat. According to reminiscences posted decades after on a Deadhead website, the band jammed far into the next morning to an appreciative crowd before being thrown out of Mem. Aud. by a university administrator. There is, as they say, no accounting for taste.

Roughly 25 years later, driving back to Washington, D.C. from Ohio on the Pennsylvania Turnpike with my first wife, Jill Kaplan Rozenman, and our two young children, we made our way through a long clot of slower-moving vehicles, the occupants of which generally seemed to be poorly dressed and, judging by their autos' overpacked appearance, disorganized. Bumper stickers—the dancing "Jerry Bears" or the bold, red, white and blue skull emblazoned by a lightning bolt—confirmed my suspicion: Here was a throng of Deadheads, mom, dad, kids and often dogs, campers frequently in tow, retreating from yet another show on another summertime Grateful Dead tour.

Making a pit stop at the next service plaza, we found it jammed with Deadheads. A band that in nearly 30 years had only one top ten chart hit ("Lady Grey," 1987) and for me only one "I've got to hear that song again" tune ("Truckin'," 1970)—Danny and the Juniors had two (the 1.5 million-selling gold record "At the Hop," 1957 and "Rock 'n Roll Is Here to Stay," 1958)—the Dead nevertheless retained a sub-nation of followers. It sold countless albums and perhaps even more paraphernalia. In the late 1980s the Vermont capitalists-socialists Ben Cohen and Jerry Greenfield, donors to left-wing causes and sellers in 1990 to the Unilever conglomerate, introduced their most frequently suggested flavor, Ben & Jerry's Cherry Garcia. This was cherry ice cream with cherries and fudge flakes, in tribute to the Dead's lead singer and guitarist Jerry Garcia. Garcia himself eventually lent his name to a line of men's ties, usually bright colors in abstract patterns. I still wore mine occasionally, before the 2020 Covid-19 pandemic, before people stopped going to the office, stopped going out to lunch, stopped in-person public speaking. Bold swirls of dark blue and fuchsia, the tie goes great with navy blue and charcoal gray suits. On rare occasions now when suits are worn. Unlike the concert at O.U., the tie was hardly free, but worth every penny.

I Introduce The Supremes!

Ohio U.'s chapter of the Sigma Nu fraternity somehow managed to sponsor a Supremes' concert midway through my senior year. But the show quickly loomed as more than a chance for my roommate, Glen Whitehead, and me to take our girlfriends on a double-date. *The Athena*, the university's student yearbook, typically a thick, glossy-paged, hardbound record of each year's activities, organizations, and photo gallery of graduating students, faced dire financial straits. We—I was an assistant copy editor—saw looming the grim and humiliating prospect of breaking a long annual tradition and not publishing *Athena '69*. Quite simply, not enough fellow students cared enough to subscribe.

In desperation, yearbook editors arranged with concert organizers to be able to make a 60-second pitch to the audience during the show. They tapped me to deliver the plug. Sure, I said. It would be a huge crowd, but I'd be onstage only for a minute. How bad could that be?

When you have to ask yourself that question, remember the first time you threw a grenade. Which, in the chronological insouciance of youth, I hadn't yet done.

The last warm-up act for The Supremes would be rhythm and blues singer Chuck Jackson. I was to make my way to the stage when I heard him start his 1961 hit, "I Don't Want To Cry." At the opening notes, I started down from our places high in the 13,000-seat Convocation Center. I'd rehearsed my short pitch out loud several times. I had it written on a notecard tucked reassuringly in my sport coat pocket. Since I was acting as *Athena* spokesman, I'd dressed the part, including jacket and tie, not jeans and a sweater. I thought I was ready.

I was wrong. The closer I got to the arena floor, the more I sweated. By the time Jackson flourished his final notes and bounded off the stage, I'd lost a couple of pounds in water weight. My shirt wasn't damp, it was soaked, and clung to my body.

Someone whispered, "You're next!" and I climbed the steps to the stage. It wasn't enough that I sweated so; now my knees began to feel uncertain and I realized I had a tactical problem, two in fact. First, I stood in a spot of light squinting into an otherwise dark and gigantic arena. I knew the audience was out there—I'd been part of it and just descended through it, and could hear the rustling and murmuring of countless O.U. Bobcats. But I could see no one. How would I be able to tell if my plea for the yearbook made an impression? Second, the Convo Center was round. The audience surrounded the stage in the middle of what ordinarily was the basketball floor and nearly encircled me. Whatever direction I chose to look, most of the crowd would be at my sides and back.

Holding my notecard, I began: "Before I bring out The Supremes …" As I spoke, a familiar voice, that of a colleague in student government, cut through the relative quiet: "Erich Rose!" the voice shouted. This was one of my pen-names on *The Hocking River Valley Silt*, an independent student humor magazine. For some reason the exposure of one of my secret identities (always prepare more than one, you never know) caused me to relax a little. From the arena sound system I heard myself speaking more or less calmly. As I pirouetted like a vertical rotisserie chicken to face each part of the crowd for at least a few seconds, I urged fellow students to save the *Athena*, to uphold a great O.U. tradition.

And that was it. Just before I made myself completely dizzy my 60 seconds in the spotlight mercifully ended. The mysterious someone who'd motioned me on now ushered me off. As I climbed back to my friends, I heard Diana Ross' faux whisper, "we never do the same show twice ... our band leader drinks." And whatever sources of funding materialized, or why they did so, we published *Athena '69.*

Warming Up for Woodstock, Overheating in Georgia

July 4 and 5, 1969. Anyone at the Atlanta International Pop Festival that Friday or Saturday could not have been surprised the next month by the rough beast that slouched onto Max Yazgur's farm at Woodstock in upstate New York. The scheduled performers in Atlanta included numerous stars in the rock and pop firmament. Among them: Janis Joplin; Led Zeppelin; Blood, Sweat and Tears; Canned Heat, Joe Cocker, Creedence Clearwater Revival and the Chicago Transit Authority. Inexplicably, Dave Brubeck and His Trio, with Gerry Mulligan, also were on the bill, as if jazz aficionados were about to park their rear ends on the infield dirt of the Atlanta International Raceway under a broiling Georgia sun just for another chance to hear "Take Five."

A faded poster, now a collectible, advertising the event showed tickets cost $16 each, worth around $113 today. But that conversion can't be right since there was no way I, a recent college graduate working that summer in an Atlanta men's store, could have afforded one, let alone two—the other for Donna Ross, the girl next door. Next door to my Aunt Marge and Uncle Joe Kloville.

Saturday morning, we drove the 25 miles or so from northeast Atlanta south to NASCAR's Atlanta track near Hampton, Ga., site of the festival. The closer we approached, the more clogged the roads became. Finally, we abandoned my car—a blue, basic '67 Chevy Camaro, in-line six-cylinder and three-speed manual shift—on the shoulder of the asphalt amid countless other vehicles. We joined a throng of late-comers and walked the last mile and a-half or so. Walking in temperatures well over 90 degrees with good old Southern humidity percentages not far behind.

Once inside the raceway infield, we picked our way through as much of the crowd as possible and finally found an open patch more or less in sight of the stage. There we sat on baked dirt and dried grass amidst tens of thousands. One attendance estimate went as high as 150,000. But as a spectator at more than a few Ohio State football games in 88,000-seat

Ohio Stadium (later enlarged to 110,000), I guessed 50,000, give or take. There were hippies, apprentice hippies and plain rock n' roll fans. And medical casualties.

Festival organizers were not prepared for the turnout or the conditions. A relentless summer sun radiated off the high-banked, black asphalt racetrack directly into the crowd with the efficiency of an expensive microwave. The public address system routinely interrupted the concert buzz by begging for salt tablets and pleading, "Will any medical personnel present report to aid station one" or two, three or whatever? Heat prostration apparently was more prevalent than drug overdoses. Occasionally an ambulance siren receded into the distance.

Concession stands were as sparse and as distant from our little spot of earth as the first-aid tents. The festival taking place in the pre-W.B. (water bottles) era, we heard the wait time in line to get a Coke could be up to infinity. It wasn't just pre-water bottles days, it was also before wheeled coolers full of iced beverages and snacks, before sunscreen, before easily portable beach chairs and pop-up tents. Hell, apparently before hats.

No matter. It was sex, drugs, rock and roll and watermelons in the sweated stew of fans. A young man with shoulder-length, wavy dark hair under a tall wizard's cap and carrying a star-tipped wand strolled through the crowd, smiling bemusedly. "LSD! Pot! Peyote!" "LSD! Pot! Peyote!" The "peanuts, popcorn and Cracker-Jacks!" of the aborning Woodstock Generation.

Not far behind him followed a ripe young woman. In cut-off blue jeans and wide-mesh fishnet top, wonderfully bra-less, skin glistening, hair somehow perfectly in place, she strode with an almost regal hauteur. Would life break this parents' nightmare or shamelessly reward her? An even money bet.

Around noon, Delaney, Bonnie and Friends left the stage, making way for Genya Ravan and Ten Wheel Drive. Ravan occasionally was compared to Joplin, and though the latter was much the bigger star the former was both a better singer—more polished, greater range and control—and more attractive. In the endlessly expansive and cruelly arbitrary music world, some talented performers stall permanently on the cusp, countless others forever becalmed in small clubs and piano bars. Ravan performed in a transparent top; once, though not at Atlanta, sans top altogether, revealing painted breasts.

Nine male musicians, led by Mike Zager and Aram Schefrin, comprised the rest of Ten Wheel Drive. The group was essentially a rock-jazz ensemble. I'd lugged my second-hand Pentax 35-mm camera, with its 200-mm telephoto lens, into the festival, so I had a close-up view of Ravan and the band even from our location in the crowd.

That Independence Day weekend Ravan was 29. She had been born Genyusha Zelkovicz in Lodz, Poland in 1940. That was the year the Nazis established the Lodz Ghetto, second largest in occupied Europe. The Germans imprisoned approximately 230,000 Jews there. By the time Soviet troops reached Lodz early in 1945, virtually all those who had not succumbed to disease or starvation in the ghetto had been sent to Chelmno or Auschwitz death camps. Ravan, one sister and her parents were the only family members to survive the Holocaust. They managed to immigrate to the United States in 1947.

Before Ten Wheel Drive, Ravan had formed Goldie and the Gingerbreads, one of rock n' roll's first all-female bands. After Ten Wheel Drive, she went on to play both Madison Square Garden and Carnegie Hall, work as a record producer and host a radio program about women in music. Her life was featured in the off-Broadway musical *Rock and Roll Refugee.*

Ten Wheel Drive was followed by Pacific Gas & Electric, Al Kooper and Tommy James and the Shondells. Kooper (Alan Peter Kuperschmidt), a protean rock n' roll and post-rock n' roll music presence, performed in the Royal Teens ("Short Shorts," 1958), played organ on Bob Dylan's "Like a Rollin' Stone" (1965) and formed Blood, Sweat and Tears (1967), among many other milestones. James, by the time of Atlanta, was playing pop psychedelia like "Crimson and Clover" and "Crystal Blue Persuasion." But Tommy James and the Shondells first hit was that elemental paean to male teenage lust, "My Baby Does the Hanky Panky" (it reached number one in 1966). Sing "My baby does the hanky panky." Repeat 22 times, alternating twice with "I saw her walkin' on down the

Chapter Thirteen   167

line/You know I saw her for the very first time … Hey baby, can I take you home …" By George, I think you've got it!

It was late afternoon and somewhere between Joe Cocker and Spirit, but before Led Zeppelin that evening. Donna and I, sustained only by a couple of Coca-Colas over the previous five hours or so, were through. Thirsty, hungry, lobster red and sun dazed, we straggled past countless fragrant watermelon rinds back to the car. Zeppelin and the rest of the 50,000 or 100,000 would have to manage without us.

A seven-minute mini-documentary about the festival made decades later by the *Atlanta Journal-Constitution* notes that some humanitarian, hearing about festival conditions, donated a truckload of watermelons. It may be the thought that counts, but quantity matters. Another dozen truckloads really would have helped. As for the melons that were distributed, some concert-goers added Miller Lite or Budweiser for instant beer soup. You can lead a horse to water, but that's not always what it wants.

U-turning onto the road, I drove east back toward U.S. 19. Disoriented, I turned right instead of left and headed south. Near Griffin, Ga., looking for a place to get something, anything to drink, we stumbled into a pottery shop. One of the two women behind the counter took a look at Donna, her face somewhere between pink and beet red, and said, "Oh, honey! You're overheated. Let me get you some water." She disappeared into a storeroom and returned quickly with a big jar of ice water. "Now drink it slowly," she cautioned. We drank and drank. I thanked them profusely; they refused my offer to pay. We left, somewhat revived. This time I got the car aimed north and back toward Atlanta.

The high point of Woodstock Nation, perhaps for the Baby Boomer generation, would come a few weeks later at Max Yasgur's New York state dairy farm. Yippie Abbie Hoffman, who had coined the phrase "Woodstock Nation" (he claimed he lived there, not in the United States) climbed the stage and headed for the microphones, intending to address the 300,000 or so assembled citizens. Peter Townsend, mastermind of The Who, displaying a fine counter-revolutionary instinct, stepped forward and smashed a guitar over Hoffman's head. His move anticipated by two years

The Who's hit single, "Won't Get Fooled Again," in which the quartet offered political commentary:

"I'll tip my hat to the new Constitution/ Take a bow for the new revolution/ Smile and grin at the change all around/ ... Then I'll get on my knees and pray/ We won't get fooled again/ No, no/ ...Meet the new boss/ Same as the old boss."

Nine years later, in 1978, The Who's sometimes-outrageous drummer, Keith Moon, then 31, died of a drug overdose. "He was scared of getting old," the wire services reported. He had been putting on weight—something unusual in the upper reaches of frenetic, drug-corroded rock stardom—and become quiet, a friend told reporters. Doctors had warned him to stay away from alcohol. By then Hoffman, political radical, Chicago Seven alum and counter-culture vaudevillian, was wanted on charges of dealing heroin. Ten years later, as noted above, he would kill himself.

Most of us get fooled. It's repetition by our children's generation that's depressing.

"From Hawthorne, California — The Beach Boys!"

Aug. 15, 1976. The Beach Boys, who defined the mid-'60s "California sound," played Ohio State University's St. John Arena, then the 13,000-seat home of Buckeye basketball. Although *The Citizen-Journal* had a regular music and theater critic, I happened to draw the assignment to cover the show. This meant a half-priced date; I bought a ticket for Linda, but my own came complimentary.

Again, I was high off the floor, but with a clear view of the stage below. The Beach Boys famously were three brothers, Brian, Carl and Dennis Wilson; a cousin, Mike Love; and a friend, Al Jardine. They'd formed their rock n' roll group in high school, where, also famously, music teacher Fred Morgan gave Brian an "F" on a composition. The tune, co-written with Love, was "Surfin'," which in 1961 became the Beach Boys' first hit. In 2018, Wilson, then 75, returned to Hawthorne High and got the "F" changed to an "A." For Baby Boomers at least, high school is forever.

The Columbus show featured two walls of amplifiers, a stage with a ship's hull as center-piece, and multi-colored lights suspended from faux palm trees. The Beach Boys, minus founding genius Brian Wilson but augmented by 11 other musicians including a brass section and electric piano, performed two 45-minutes sets. Between them, I interviewed Love. At 35, the oldest Beach Boy was in danger of becoming a Beach Man. Nevertheless, on stage he wore white pants, white cap, white gloves and a sparkling gold vest over a bare chest.

At intermission I trooped up a portal off the arena floor, bumped into a stagehand and spilled his drink. It didn't matter, everyone seemed relaxed; even the promotion person who wondered what day it was. Sunday, as it happened. Before I got all the way under the stands enroute to the dressing room, Love came out to meet me. He was eating a bowl of fresh strawberries with his fingers. He didn't offer me any.

I asked him about the 10,000 people in attendance, capacity with the upper balcony closed. About half of them seemed to be older than 25—cut-off for original Beach Boy fans—and the other half younger, born about the time "Surfin" was released. "We get a big cross section, and I think that's good," Love said.

The act already was 15 years old. How long could they go on? "I think as long as we're making music that people relate to, that people love."

Where was Brian? The group's founder, battling depression, would become known as rock n'roll's hermit king, staying off the road for long periods, experimenting in his home recording studio. "Brian's always been shy, retiring, and doesn't care to perform," Love said. But their leader was working in the studio on an album to be released late in the year, he reassured me. No new album would be released in the U.S.A. that year, but *Twenty Golden Hits*, a compilation of Beach Boy singles from 1963 through 1969, went gold or platinum in the United Kingdom, Germany, Switzerland and Austria, all well-known for their hot rods and surfing. Meanwhile, the group's American summer tour would draw record crowds at some stops, almost 50,000 in Pittsburgh; 62,000 in Denver.

"Surfin Safari," "Surfin' U.S.A.," "I Get Around," "In My Room,"" "Fun, Fun, Fun," their remake of the Regents' "Barbara Ann," "Good Vibrations," Chuck Berry's "Rock and Roll Music" and other hits had the crowd in St. John Arena standing on the seats and singing along.

My review was complimentary enough that Warner Bros. Records mistook me for the *Citizen-Journal's* rock critic, if that term is not an oxymoron. (Ever read a bad review of a major rock act? Didn't think so.) Once a month, for the ensuing three-plus years, until I lit out for Israel and a stab at kibbutz life, I received a post office notice telling me to pick up another box of albums, new releases from Warner's in Los Angeles. A few, like Johnny Cougar's *Chestnut Street Revisited,* were keepers. Unfortunately for those eternally seeking the next Elvis, a search as futile as that for the Fountain of Youth and for similar reasons, Johnny relapsed into John Cougar Mellencamp, then ultimately John Mellencamp, became a conventional left-leaning balladeer and, rock n' roll-wise, was never heard from again. Most of the free albums were quickly disposed of as giveaways.

There would be other shows, other interviews between Elvis in 1956 and The Beach Boys in 1976. The Who, previewing some of the music that would be included in their landmark rock opera *Tommy* (rock opera, really?) at Columbus' spacious Palace Theater, with another of those post-concert, day-long deafness experiences; The Byrds, in Chicago's Aragon Ballroom; Ray Charles, not once but twice and well worth a third; Ike and Tina Turner with the Ikettes; Dion without the Belmonts; Neil Sedaka; Fats Domino; the utterly bizarre Ohio U. Homecoming 1968 twin bill of Jose Feliciano and Led Zeppelin; the J. Geils Band; Paul Revere and the Raiders; and Martha and the Vandellas. The last were a more danceable version of the Supremes, with hits like "Heatwave," "Nowhere to Run," "Dancing in the Streets," and "Jimmy Mack."

Interviewing Martha Reeves and her companions for the *O.U. Post* in the women's locker room of Grover Center before their part in a big rock n' roll show in Athens, I found three non-Dream Girl personas. They seemed unpretentious, almost shy, not in the least products of what Joanie Mitchell called the "star-maker machinery." Or maybe they were just tired that night. Martha and the Vandellas eventually made it into the Rock n' Roll Hall of Fame; Reeves served on Detroit City Council from 2005 – 2009, and in 2007 testified before Congress, arguing for a better cut of record companies' profits to their musicians.

And then there was that show by Johnny and the Hurricanes, set up with their amplifiers on the back of a flat-bed truck in a bank parking lot one balmy summer night about 1965 or '66 in Fostoria, Ohio. Johnny Paris (John Matthew Pocisk) and his Hurricanes, high school pals from near Toledo, hit the charts with their saxophone and organ-driven instrumentals "Crossfire," "Red River Rock," and "Reville Rock." "Red River Rock" made the top ten in both the United States and United Kingdom and sold more than one million records. The Internet asserts that they played the Star Club in Hamburg, Germany in 1962 with a British band called the Beatles as their warm-up.

By the early '80s, rock n' roll, overtaken by heavy metal, disco, rap and hip-hop, had become a museum piece, best found on oldies radio stations peddling premature nostalgia to Baby Boomers moving into their '40s. Once in a while something fresh, like the Stray Cats "Rock This Town" or Cindy Lauper's "Girls Just Want to Have Fun" turned up on the radio, but not often enough. Rock n' roll always really was music for and frequently by adolescents. By the '90s my daughters commandeered the car radio from me as I had from my mother and, jumping a generation and a-half, Destiny's Child (with Beyoncé' Knowles before she was Beyoncé') and Pink ("Let's Get This Party Started") after she was in Choice, supplanted Elvis and Jerry Lee Lewis. The three-guitars-and-drums genre, once self-evidently sufficient was now for me exhausted. My parents' music replaced my own. Among others from the Great American Songbook, a Glenn Miller's Greatest Hits album, a two-disc, 40-hit Frank Sinatra compilation and You Tube videos of Jo Stafford—"See the pyramids along the Nile ..." took over.

Occasional excursions into the rock n' roll past did remain. "The Ultimate Doo-Wop Show" at Wolf Trap National Park for the Performing Arts in Vienna, Va. outside Washington, D.C. in 2011 with my fiancé, Melinda Hofstetter featured the Marcels ("Blue Moon"), Randy Safuto of Randy and the Rainbows ("Denise"), Jimmy Beaumont and Skyliners ("Since I Don't Have You")—the acts old, the audience looking older. No matter, it was all still too cool for school. Also Wolf Trap in 2019 with my wife, Melinda Hofstetter for a stop on the Stray Cats' 40th Anniversary Tour. Forty years? Couldn't be. But it was; four decades had fled somewhere. And nowhere: "Rock This Town," "Rumble in Brighton Tonight," "Stray Cat Strut"—blasts from the past.

And there was the one that got away, the original. Dennis Riley, a high school friend then working toward a Ph.D. in chemistry, and I were walking up High Street in Columbus one Sunday night around 1970. We passed a bar opposite Ohio State University. A sign beckoned: "Tonight Only! Bill Haley and His Comets!" In 1954, Decca Records, as noted above, had released Bill Haley and the Comets' "Rock Around the Clock." Irresistible jitterbugging music made not by three guitars and a drummer but a real band including a stand-up bass, saxophone and keyboard, it helped launch the rock n' roll era. "Rock Around the Clock" became a worldwide hit and embedded itself in the auditory nerves of at least two generations.

Dennis and I looked at the sign and considered. But no. Tomorrow was a workday. We kept walking and got a quick beer somewhere else. As Ral Donner, a too-close for his own good Elvis sound-alike intoned in 1961, "You don't know what you've got/ Until you lose it…"

There would be one more really big show, but only as chauffeur-chaperone. On March 19, 1999 the phenomenally successful boy band NSYNC (featuring Justin Timberlake before he was Justin Timberlake) filled Washington, D.C.'s MCI Center (before it was the Verizon Center, before it was the Capital One Arena) with 20,000 screaming teenagers, most of them girls and including my daughters. Ticketless—apparently, I didn't want one—I was confined with other parents somewhere deep within the building watching television in something called "the chaperones' room." I could still hear the rumbling bass and the screams, of course, but my life with rock n' roll—leavened as it had been by jazz and blues shows with Dizzy Gillespie, Stan Getz, Woody Herman and The Herd, John Lee Hooker, Muddy Waters and B.B. King—was over.

Except for doo-wop videos on YouTube. There, and perhaps only there, what they first called rock n' roll is here to stay.

Chapter Fourteen:
Europa, Europa, Good-bye

Only Two Places

June 30, 2018. I had a window seat on Lufthansa flight 414 from Munich to Dulles International near Washington, D.C. An hour or so into the trip I happened to glance out the window. There it was. Just like I was looking down on a giant version of the roll-down map of Europe in Mrs. Austemiller's fifth-grade geography class in Napoleon, Ohio. The image below also resembled another map—one with some national boundaries recovered post-Cold War—I'd used just that spring in teaching History 102, Western Civ. II—Europe Since 1500, at Northern Virginia Community College. The vista below was not as colorful, of course, but every bit as plain under a hazy summer sky: 35,000 feet down lay the coast of The Netherlands with the Rhine-Meuse-Scheldt delta and bay-like Marker-Meer and Ijseel-meer. Merging past the window's edge was part of Germany's North Sea coast. The sea itself—on page and screen so often dark and stormy—glimmered silver-gray and calm.

I was returning from a nine-day study mission to Poland, courtesy of Filip Jasenski, First Counselor, political section at the Polish embassy in Washington. Seven of us, representatives of Jewish and pro-Israel organizations or academics with interests in Jewish and European affairs, spent four days in Warsaw, three in Lodz and two in Krakow as guests of the Polish foreign ministry. A wonderful and jarring experience, it clanged together past and present like cymbals.

All four of my grandparents had emigrated from czarist Russia's Pale of Settlement, actually eastern Poland. My grandfathers, Morris Rozenman (then Moses Roiesman) and Louis (Lemuel) Mandel, Morris' brother-in-law Sam Liber and a friend named Browarsky arrived in Galveston, Texas on the S. S. Breslau the year before World War I erupted.

They were "Schiff Plan" or "Galveston Plan" immigrants. In the late nineteenth and early twentieth centuries German-born Jacob Schiff was one of America's leading investment bankers and top philanthropists. He publicly opposed Russian antisemitism, exemplified by the bloody pogroms of the period, and promoted Russian Jewish immigration to the United States. He put his money where his politics and Jewish solidarity were. Schiff funded, among many other charities, the Jewish Industrial Removal Office, intended to get newly-arrived Russian Jews out of New York City's Lower East Side and westward into the rest of the country. Galveston was intended as an alternative port of entry to New York.

The Schiff or Galveston Plan was meant to have secondary advantages of forestalling pressure to restrict the large, long wave of eastern European Jews coming to America, New York in particular, and resultant antisemitism that might unsettle the city's more established, earlier arrived German Jews. Forestall but not defeat. The 1924 Johnson-Reed Immigration Act not only would exclude most east Asians but also greatly reduce quotas for Italians, eastern European Jews, Poles and other Slavs. These were groups then often considered unassimilable as non-Anglo-Saxons, members of "non-white" "races." Such categories being geographically, culturally and temporally fungible, I heard myself referred to several times in 1991-'92, while working in Miami, then the capital of Latin America—at least in its own mind—as an "Anglo." My own children now are, to certain left reactionaries—examples of "white privilege." If Baby Boomers never really left high school, then anti-democratic leftists never have given up their search for "class enemies." To paraphrase Edna St. Vincent Millay, they love humanity but hate people.

So, thanks to the Schiff Plan, on Sept. 11, 1913 greenhorns Morris Rozenman, Louis Mandel, Sam Liber and Mr. Browarsky did not see the Statue of Liberty. But rather than remain dispersed out west, they like many of their cohort, began working their way east, back toward New York City. There, if the streets weren't paved with gold, at least the neighborhoods were crammed with people like themselves. Over the succeeding months, including a stint in a Colorado lead mine for Morris, they got as far as the small towns near Toledo. Sam Liber eventually pushed on into that metropolis, but knowing the Glass City already possessed a sufficient number of Jewish bakers, Rozenman, Mandel and Browarsky remained dispersed in Tiffin, Willard and Bucyrus, respectively. They grew from peddlers to scrap dealers, from scuffling new arrivals to small property owners. My grandmothers, Ettel (Anglister) Rozenman and Miriam (Grika) Mandel arrived six years later in 1919, the Great War having intervened.

Thus, I was born on Sept. 11, 1947 in Tiffin. And on Sept. 11, 2001 Americans everywhere were reminded the rest of the world still existed, regardless of the Immigration Act of 1924, its subsequent alteration in the 1952 Immigration and Naturalization Act or its overthrow by the 1965 Immigration and Naturalization Act. Whether we pulled the ladder up behind us or turned it into an escalator, on average a million people have entered the United States, legally and illegally, annually for decades. And because of that attraction, because of the underlying reasons for it, someone somewhere—speaking German, Japanese, Russian, Arabic, Farsi or Chinese—always would be murderously unhappy with the land of the free and the home of the brave.

My mother often said she'd like to see where her parents had come from. I had replied that I would too—Chemelnitz for the Mandels, Mechev for the Rozenmans—but only if someone else paid for it. Decades later, someone did. Be careful what you denigrate; it might teach you something.

In 1995 I'd taken a similar trip, that one courtesy of the German embassy in Washington and the German foreign ministry. Any earlier and I might have refused. Germany? Even expenses paid? No thanks. In 1995 I wisely accepted. Four of us, editors of American Jewish weekly newspapers, spent 10 days in the reuniting country. We were based in Frankfurt, Bonn and Berlin. Though West Germany was absorbing the formerly communist East into a merged whole, many government offices had not yet returned from Bonn, a small, pleasant city on the Rhine, to the old German capital itself. Our foreign ministry guides/minders were a young woman and a young man, both enthusiastic and accommodating, the young man noting his "half-Jewish" parental background. From small-town Ohio through Columbus to Washington, D.C. and Miami, and now Germany, an unending number of people have identified themselves to me as "half-Jewish," though I asked only once. I mean, how many African-American men did one find managing a clothing store in WASPish Upper Arlington, Ohio in the mid-1970s and wearing a Star of David around his neck? And who turned out to be active in Republican Party politics?

Once, in 1983, a tall, blonde cocktail waitress so identified herself in the presence of the Israeli deputy consul-general from Philadelphia. We were having a drink, waiting for his flight from Port Columbus to Philadelphia. "I couldn't help overhearing you talk about Israel. It sounds interesting to me. I'm half-Jewish myself," she said.

"What is this half-Jewish?" the diplomat asked me after she taken our order. "I never heard of it before I got to this country." "I've always heard of it," I said. "Scratch hard enough, and you'll find about half the people you run into here were Jewish somewhere down the line. At least some of their ancestors were."

In Germany, we were surprised to find Frankfurt, the country's financial capital, as modern and apparently prosperous as most American cities, if not more so. And cleaner. We heard foreign ministry officials in Bonn admit their policy of "constructive engagement" with the Islamic Republic of Iran was not working (though Germany and the rest of the European Union continued to pursue it, beckoned by an idealized market of 80 million Iranians. They would keep doing so, despite its never working, to and through 2015's Joint Comprehensive Plan of Action on Iran's nuclear program). And we saw remnants of the Berlin Wall. If no longer a deadly barrier, the wall's path still starkly separated busy, modern West Berlin from the dingy, threadbare East. It did so especially at night as we poked into courtyards of battered apartment blocks that could have been sets from Orson Well's *The Third Man*, had the film been set in 1949 Berlin instead of Vienna. We saw places that looked, regardless of the occasional light glimmering behind pulled shades, like post-war rebuilding barely had started.

Reminders—some echoes, some flesh-and-blood—of the Jewish past and present were never far. In Worms, for example, after a stop at the mayor's office we visited the Rashi Shul. Rashi—Rabbi Shlomo Yitzhaki—wrote his indispensable commentaries on the Hebrew Bible and Talmud in the 11th century. Their concise yet comprehensive explanations have influenced laymen and scholars ever since. The synagogue was built in 1034, destroyed in 1096 during the First Crusade, rebuilt and damaged in the pogroms of 1349 and 1615, burned in 1689 during the Nine Years' War, razed as part of *Kristallnacht* in 1938, rebuilt in 1961 using bricks and stones from the pre-Nazi structure, and firebombed in 2010.

Something we said? That thing about the one God and His Ten Commandments?

Friday evening in Berlin, we attended Shabbat services in the Pestalozzistrasse synagogue. We already had visited a Jewish school in Berlin, supported—as were facilities of other religions—by the government. It was packed with active little children, many originally from Russia or other former Soviet bloc countries.

The setting sun cast a golden light through high glass windows behind the *bimah* (altar). Services were led by Cantor Estrongo Nachama, then 75. The evening was a spiritual interlude in our tightly-scheduled itinerary, but even then it took a while for our good fortune to set in.

A photograph inside the synagogue showed Nachama in 1943, age 23, when he and his family were sent to Auschwitz. When Nachama died at 81 in 2000, a *New York Times* obituary noted that unlike his parents, sister and other relatives, he had survived in the concentration camp. "[H]is voice pleased the S.S. guards, who particularly enjoyed his rendering of 'O Sole Mio.'" "Forever marked" by his family's loss, "Nachama was an inveterate optimist of seemingly boundless energy. ... 'He was one of the absolutely critical people in terms of the rebuilding of the Jewish community in Berlin,' said Tom Freudenheim, deputy director of the city's Jewish museum."

Having heard Nachama's still beautiful voice, having seen the busy school, I caught myself thinking that just maybe Jewish life in Germany, in Europe, was still possible. Maybe. But even if possible, why? Why there?

Early in the trip we told our hosts something was missing from the official itinerary—a stop at a concentration camp site. They added Sachsenhausen, nearly the last place on our tour. Sachsenhausen, the "model" or "training" concentration camp was in Oranieburg, not far from Berlin. Administrators and guards, having learned their craft there, were deployed to put their new skills to work elsewhere in the Nazis' network of industrialized death. The place had been relatively small but with examples of the Third Reich's encompassing determination to murder not only Jews but at Sachsenhausen also political prisoners, Allied prisoners of war, Jehovah's Witnesses, Roma (Gypsies), homosexuals and others. And once in a while to get a laugh out of it.

We saw the ruins of a "medical examination room," in which inmates were, among other things, supposedly to have their height measured. A hole opened in the vertical bar to allow insertion of a gun barrel from the rear wall, so that instead of a height check, the prisoner got a bullet in the neck.

Still, this amusing means of murder was too slow, not "scalable" in today's jargon. Mass hangings were tried, but these provoked unrest among the inmates. So, at Sachsenhausen the Nazis settled on gas chambers as a more efficient means to the end of a Europe united and purified.

We got a look at Sachsenhausen's test track. This was an intentionally tortuous ring of uneven bricks and other stumble-blocks. Prisoners, sometimes with heavy packs, were forced to run tripping for miles, ostensibly testing various military footwear. Not to mention providing endless sadistic entertainment.

A line of wooden barracks stood in semi-ruin. Newly reunited, with the West paying billions of marks in absorption costs for the relatively impoverished former East, Germany was then seeking outside contributions to help maintain Sachsenhausen as an historic site. Not everyone wished to preserve the place as a memorial; we were told arsonists had destroyed some of the barracks. "He who controls the present controls the past. He who controls the past controls the future," as George Orwell so usefully noted in *1984*. Hence the compulsion to topple statues of Washington and Lincoln.

Germany helped prepared me for Poland. In Germany there was evident prosperity, at least in the western two-thirds. There also was the inescapable historical legacy. The country had been the dominant location if not always the primary force in central Europe since the early Holy Roman Empire. Whoever controlled central Europe controlled the continent and beyond, as historian Bernard Simms has argued. Hence, American participation in World War I, World War II and the Cold War, to prevent hostile militarists from dominating the continental cockpit. Europe's condition as one great, blood-soaked Jewish graveyard and Germany as chief grave-digger hung like smog. Then there was German bi-polarity; our young foreign ministry friends taking pains to describe themselves as "Rhinelanders" or "Berliners," not Germans (not yet, in 1995, at least). This while their somewhat older contemporaries strove to restore Germany to its rightful place among the nations. As a democracy, of course.

Poland proved to be very different. And similar.

Different in that historians did not claim as they did for Germany that whoever controlled Poland controlled Europe, and thereby could dominate the world. Similar in that Jewish history, centuries of it and family history too, still hung in the air. This atmospheric effect, no less real for being intangible, kept everyone, Jews and non-Jews, slightly off balance.

In Berlin, the site of the Nazi Gestapo (Secret State Police) headquarters now exists as the "Topography of Terror" documentation center and museum. In 1995, I had seen there an exhibit illustrating how German Jews were rounded up for deportation to the camps. It included a list of those slated for one particular collection. One to be seized was named A. Rosenman.

Similar also in Poland as in Germany because, whether or not most Europeans recognize it, Jewish history was and, in some ways, remains central to European history. The Nazis' insistence on killing Jews at the expense of better fighting the Allies is a glaring but by no means unique example. Spain, with its 1492 expulsion of the Jews, began its long slide from dominance. Russia, ever oppressing its Jews, never realized its U.S.-scale potential. And so on, almost endlessly; nations unable to embrace their Jews nearly always stunted themselves. Even and just so, European history with the Jews' story as part of its core still influences the Continent and nearly everyone else.

In Warsaw we stayed at the luxurious Hotel Bristol, next door to the presidential palace. This Bristol was the latest iteration of the hostelry that had stood on the spot since 1901, the original being co-owned by pianist, composer and eventually prime minister in 1919 of reborn Poland, Ignace Jan Paderewski. It survived World War II and German occupation though much of the surrounding neighborhood—later rebuilt to a pre-war look—did not. Renovated several times, the Bristol, with its glass, two-car lobby elevator, high ceilings and draped, long narrow windows imparted a grand, pre-war feeling. This feeling the big, in-room flat-panel televisions did not offset.

The hotel's location was convenient since the first meeting on our official itinerary was with aides—several quite young—to President Andrezj Duda. After breakfast in the hotel, we simply walked out the front door, turned right, walked a few paces, turned right again and, identifying ourselves at the front gate of the complex, were escorted across a corner of the large, cobblestoned courtyard and into one wing of the palace. Visible security was light, only a few uniformed guards outside, a metal detector and monitor just inside the door we entered, and what looked like a plainclothes man or two in the long corridors.

We should not have eaten breakfast. In our second-floor meeting room we found the long conference table nearly overflowing with plates of small pastries, carafes of coffee and freshly squeezed orange juice, bottles of mineral water and bowls of big, ripe strawberries. Mike Love, eat your heart out.

We could not do justice to the delicacies, however. This was our first—and perhaps would be our best—opportunity to grill government officials about legislation that reportedly criminalized speech or writings blaming Poland for collaboration in the Holocaust. In a post-trip column for *The Washington Examiner*, I noted that legislators of the ruling Law and Justice Party—conservative to some, right-wing to others—wanted to amend existing law regarding discussion of the Holocaust. "Among other things," the commentary said, "the measure barred references to 'Polish death camps.' Poles were vehement that places like Auschwitz-Birkenau were 'Nazi German concentration camps' in Poland, not Polish murder factories. In them approximately 3.2 million of Poland's pre-war Jewish population of 3.5 million—one-tenth of the country's 35 million people—

were killed. Another three million non-Jewish Poles also died in World War II."

President Duda's aides took pains to distinguish their boss' position from that of Prime Minister Mateusz Morawiecki, let alone any maverick members of parliament. They wanted to be seen as diplomats, not politicians. During the time our delegation was in Poland the amendment was modified and Morawiecki and Israeli Prime Minister Benjamin Netanyahu issued a positive joint statement with references to both Holocaust "cruelty against Jews perpetrated by Poles" and "heroic acts of numerous Poles" who "risked their own lives to save Jews."

This failed to quell the controversy. Israel's Yad Vashem Holocaust memorial and research center criticized the joint statement as underplaying Polish anti-Jewish actions. Poles, ever conscious of their country's dismemberment by Russia, Prussia and Austria-Hungary in the late 1700s and again by Nazi Germany and Soviet Russia in 1939, Germany's brutal occupation until 1945 and Soviet overlordship from the end of World War II through the fall of eastern European communism in 1989, insisted on recognition of their own victimhood. History was ever-present for the Poles just as it was for Jews, what with Vladimir Putin's Russia—though now separated from Poland by an independent Ukraine—seizing and annexing Ukraine's Crimean Peninsula and fomenting a separatist war in that country's east.

In Lodz, we stayed in the Manufaktura. Inside it was a starkly modern business hotel. The outer shell was the reclaimed red brick sprawl of what in the early 20th century had been one of Poland's major textile factories. One of Lodz's leading Jewish families, headed by Izrael Kalman Poznanski, had owned the factory. The Poznanski family's grand home in the heart of the city was a superbly appointed in-town mansion now converted to a music school. As a guide led us through the gracious and opulent rooms, we came upon a slender young woman in a simple black dress. The only thing missing was the rest of the symphony orchestra. She was playing a classical piece on piano and for a moment it could have been 1921, not 2018. For a moment.

Adjacent to the hotel was a large, three-story indoor shopping mall, as contemporary as anything in suburban Washington. Except for official meetings and lunches or dinners with Jewish community representatives, nearly every place we went in Warsaw, Lodz or Krakow seemed to feature a television showing a World Cup soccer tournament match. Poland did not get past the opening round of 32 teams, but even in the little Jewish community center in Warsaw, people watched first and second round games transfixed by the contests even though they were not a) baseball, b) basketball, c) football or d) a NASCAR auto race. Strange but true.

Warsaw was official and could seem a little formal, or heavy. It had been rebuilt from both communist stagnation and German obliteration and with Jewish history, Polish history and Jewish-Polish history draped over every third tree like Spanish moss. Perhaps nowhere could the strands be found more plainly intertwined than in POLIN, the sweeping museum to Polish Jewish history opened in 2013. The post-modern structure stands in the middle of a large, cleared urban rectangle. The rectangle is the site of the former Warsaw Ghetto.

If Warsaw was essentially rebuilt and official, then Lodz was a loaf still rising, a yeasty mix of Old Town tourism and shopping, day-to-day commerce, grit and reconstruction.

In Warsaw, the old, sprawling Jewish cemetery had been overgrown in many places by almost jungle-like vegetation. A canopy of overhanging branches cast deep shadows across long lanes of weary memorials even at mid-day. Years' worth of leaves composted themselves halfway up tombstones. Reclamation work, partly funded by cosmetics heir Ronald Lauder, proceeded grave-by-grave, far too slowly to preserve an historic city of Jewish dead from relentlessly overtaking nature. And too minutely to offset nature's auxiliary, human amnesia.

In Lodz, another sprawling old Jewish cemetery, another nearly lost city of sacrificed souls stretched for acres. It lay similarly overgrown and shadowed. But Lodz's tiny Jewish community had even fewer funds than Warsaw's for reclamation attempts. As in the capital, the graveyard was a peculiar jumble of grand family burial monuments from post-pogrom, pre-Holocaust days, more modest stones and carelessly encroaching nature. Unlike Warsaw, adjacent to the Jewish cemetery in Lodz a large, uneven open area stretched back to a masonry wall separating it from a neighborhood of apartment buildings. This bumpy urban meadow contained the mostly unidentified burial places of the Jews massacred, quickly or slowly, in the ghetto. At one edge of the mass graveyard lay a pit, perhaps 30 by 20 feet, partly sunken in on itself and grass covered. In mid-1944, more Jews were to have been shot and buried there. But orders came to dismantle the Lodz Ghetto and resume shipping the remaining inmates to their deaths at Chelmno and Auschwitz-Birkenau. So now we stood looking at nothing but an unmarked grassy depression just inside a fading red brick wall. A century hence the earth, if not humanity on it, will have healed itself.

As in Warsaw, the ghetto had not been an unseen place of removal but part of the city itself, confining several hundred thousand Jews who comprised more than one-third of Lodz's population. Street-cars ran through but did not stop. Jews, fenced in and guarded, overworked and sometimes starving, crossed major streets on pedestrian bridges to reach separate sections of the ghetto. Jew and non-Jew each saw the other. Each knew what was happening to the other.

Researching, remembering and retelling what that was is the work of Lodz's Centrum Dialogu im. Marka Edelman. That is, the Marek Edelman Center for Dialogue. Edelman died in 2009, the last surviving leader of the 1943 Warsaw Ghetto Uprising and a fighter in the city's general uprising in 1944—when Stalin parked the Red Army on the outskirts until the Nazis finished off Polish armed resistance inside.

As a youth Edelman had been a member of the socialist, anti-Zionist Jewish Labor Bund. He stayed in Poland even though Jew-hatred was increasing there and across Europe in the 1930s. Edelman later famously said, "the Bundists did not wait for the Messiah, nor did they plan to leave for Palestine. They believed that Poland was their country, and they fought for a just, socialist Poland in which each nationality would have its own cultural autonomy and in which minorities' rights would be guaranteed."

A just, socialist Poland. Minority rights will be guaranteed. Tenaciously held oxymorons that amounted to secular messianic Jewish belief. Especially so among diaspora Jews, typically a tiny minority in no position—lacking intimidating numbers or attitude let alone the sovereign power—to guarantee them. Advocate them, why not? Guarantee them? Such a belief is what my friend Juliana Geran Pilon, who as a teenager emigrated from communist Romania, calls in her book of the same name, the utopian conceit.

So, Edelman remained after World War II, literally rising from ashes to become a well-known cardiologist and eventually an advisor to the Solidarity movement as Soviet-imposed Polish communism crumbled. He stayed even after his wife, another one of the handful of Warsaw Ghetto survivors, and the couple's two children left for France in 1968. They fled the Polish communist government's "anti-Zionist" purge of the great majority of the country's remaining 20,000 or so Jews. The Jews— doctors, professors, lawyers and cultural leaders among them—were targeted as scapegoats after Israel's 1967 Six-Day War victory over the Soviet's Arab allies and for allegedly inciting Poland's pro-democracy 1968 student protests.

The "anti-Zionist" campaign cited perhaps the most notorious and most successful of anti-Jewish conspiracy theories, mother of all *deliria* about secret Jewish cabals to control the planet, the enduring late 19th century czarist fabrication, *The Protocols of the Learned Elders of Zion. The Protocols* still circulates widely in the Islamic world and, thanks to the Internet, on computers and other digital devices near you.

An exhibit at the Centrum Dialogu highlighted the communist party's "anti-Zionist, anti-imperialist" anti-Jewish onslaught. Yet Edelman still stayed on, explaining in 2001: "Warsaw is my city. It is here that I learned Polish, Yiddish and German. It is here that at school I learned one must always take care of others. It is also here that I was slapped in the face just because I was a Jew."

Not just because. Exactly because. It *was* something we said, and keep saying: Humankind can do better than its instincts; God wants us to. In reply we periodically hear: Kill the Jews! It remains a recurrently popular default. That's because, as others have understood, "kill God!" looms a bit too self-challenging even today. So, kill his messengers. Close to deicide, but so much safer psychologically.

At the Centrum Dialogu, enthusiastic director Joanna Podolska and her mostly young and similarly enthusiastic staff, explained their work. They strive to ensure that the memory of Poland's Jews and their nearly thousand-year history in the country will not be effaced like an overgrown cemetery but rather recollected in full. They intend that the Jews' history would speak to non-Jewish Poles, and that Jews and non-Jews would connect in dialogue. We learned of Poles who, discovering hidden or forgotten Jewish ancestors, began following their own family ties toward Judaism. We heard about others with no Jewish heritage but realizing that countless empty spaces, physical or intangible, dotted their country, needed to know more about the Jews who had once filled those spaces. In the centrum and on its grounds, with quiet but instructive memorials, one felt that they might succeed, at least mystically or metaphysically.

Enroute south to Krakow from Lodz was Czestochowa, home to the towering Jasna Gora Monastery with its Shrine of the Black Madonna, beloved by popes including Poland's own John Paul II. To hear that Roman Catholicism has anchored Polish identity for more than 1,000 years and stiffens Poland's spine against edicts from European Union bureaucrats in Brussels is one thing. To see the devout make their way on their knees up the long center aisle toward the Black Madonna, a perhaps 1,500-year-old icon of Mother and Child, a four-foot high bejeweled portrait on wood set amidst a museum's-worth of religious artwork, is quite another. The ancestors of such believers did not surrender, not completely, to seventeenth century Swedes or twentieth century Germans and Russians. The twenty-first century E.U. doesn't seem likely to be any more successful.

Between Czestochowa and Krakow lay Auschwitz-Birkenau.

Oswiecim, a Polish industrial town 30 miles from the medieval university city of Krakow in south-central Poland, lay at the junction of numerous European railroad routes. These would prove key to efficiently transporting more than one million Jews, men, women and children, to their deaths. Annexed into the Third Reich and given the German name Auschwitz, Oswiecim's pre-World War II Polish cavalry barracks became part of the core of the Auschwitz-Birkenau complex of overlapping concentration, slave labor and death camps—or "extermination" camps, Jews being the Nazis' "bacillus" infecting Europe. As in Internet images accompanying the 2020 pandemic pretext for antisemitism, Jews would appear as rats carrying the coronavirus to non-Jews. According to one public opinion survey, nearly 20 percent of Britons believed Jews were behind the plague. *Plus ca' change …*

Part of the sprawling Auschwitz-Birkenau enterprise was Auschwitz III with a factory belonging to the German industrial giant I.G. Farben company. During the war, during the Holocaust, the Allies bombed I.G. Farben. They chose not to bomb Auschwitz-Birkenau's death sites.

Before we walked through the main entrance gate, under the grille-work arch infamously and indelibly proclaiming "Arbeit Macht Frei" ("Work Makes Free") we were shown something closed to most visitors at the Auschwitz State Museum. This was the site's forensic laboratory. More than 70 years after the Germans fled before the advancing Red Army, taking as many of their last miserable, starving prisoners as possible, scientists—many of them young Poles—dedicated themselves to discovering whatever new they could about the place and what was committed there.

Using equipment a big-city homicide department might envy, these researchers preserved fragments of history's most notorious mass murder, preserved and tried to pry from them any new evidence about the slaughter, which also was history's most egregious mass robbery. From among the mountains of shoes (not to mention those of suitcases, and personal and household items including mocking tea sets and forlorn glasses cases snatched in the last moment) the technicians had been working on one particular women's shoe. It was a mid-heel, still almost stylish if dulled and cracked by age. Noticing a bulge under the insole, they carefully peeled back the lining. There, flattened in its hiding place, lay an envelope, old stains warning of moisture that had come and gone long ago, potentially damaging the contents. Under special lights above what looked like an operating table, they had removed and kept intact the letter within.

A woman hastily described horrors into which she only recently descended. She addressed her urgent message of warning to someone who might not have been there any longer to receive it. And though she never sent the note, never could send it, the message itself survived to be recovered three generations later. Quixotically delivered to the future, it retrieved her memory, the fact of her individual existence, from history's discards, from its concrete amnesia.

The "arbeit macht frei" entrance sign was a replica. Someone seeking amnesia or at least to induce it when it came to the Holocaust, and seeking a little profit too, had stolen the original. Found damaged and in need of repair before being returned to the gate, the sign we walked under was a temporary substitute for an icon of psychological warfare.

At Birkenau, several miles from Auschwitz I, we followed the incoming railroad tracks through the center of the long, red brick building that served as an administration office. As seen in countless photographs, the tracks ran under a two and a-half story high, glass-enclosed observation/guard tower. A quarter of a mile on, well inside the electrified, barbed-wire topped fence, was on the right side of the tracks the concrete remnant of an unloading platform. Here Jews captured from across Europe were pushed out of cattle cars for the *selektion*. Here families were separated. The very young, the old and infirm went to the left and immediate death in gas chambers further down the tracks and on the other side, their bodies as smoke up the chimneys of adjacent crematoria. Thus transformed, they were a mocking offering to their Lord by those who murdered them, supreme sacrifices as insult to their Creator. Twins and others of the damned were chosen by Josef Mengele, M.D., for a sadist's "medical" experiments. And the rest went to the right and dispersal to long, wooden stable-like barracks. Dispersed to be worked, malnourished and weakened by disease, to death.

The barracks had been jerry-built for dozens but housed hundreds each on bunk-style platforms three pallets high. Concrete-topped latrine ditches ran down the center of the narrow structures between platforms. Lucky crews emptied the latrines each day as best they could. Lucky, because they labored indoors during winter.

On Oct. 7, 1944 a group of prisoners, having smuggled small amounts of gunpower from a munitions plant within the Auschwitz network over many weeks, mutinied and blew up crematorium IV. We saw the partially sunken ruins and nearby memorial. Near the rear of Birkenau, the monument recalled the 250 mutineers killed by guards in the fighting and another 200 prisoners murdered afterward.

But it was an already familiar photograph in the entrance watchtower that left a more personal impression. A copy of the black-and-white picture hangs in the U.S. Holocaust Memorial Museum in Washington, D.C. Reproductions of the same photograph appear in numerous Holocaust histories and other texts. The image is of a *selektion*.

Near the center is a young girl in a coat and wearing a scarf. She and an older sister are among those being sent to the right, to live another day in man-made hell. Her mother, three younger siblings and an older brother, are being sent to the left. Her father too would go to the right, but when he sickened and could no longer work—he would be one of the *Sonderkommando* assigned to move corpses from gas chambers to crematoria—he would be shot and killed by the S.S. Soon after the *selektion* the girl asked another camp inmate when she would see the rest of her family again. The older prisoner pointed to the rising smoke and said, "your family is there."

The girl, not quite 14 in May, 1944 when the picture was taken, was Irene Fogel. She, her sister and an aunt survived. In 1947 they were able to immigrate to the United States. Two years later she married Martin Weiss and moved to northern Virginia.

History's quirks: Her daughter Lesley and I were members of the same congregation in Fairfax. I first heard Irene Weiss describe her tortured survival in Auschwitz-Birkenau in Lesley's living room decades before climbing the watchtower steps to look out over the semi-ruined landscape. In the tower, amidst tourists from around the world—some taking smiling selfies with their cellphones—I stared again at that picture.

I heard a little more in 2012 when Irene, a docent at the U.S. Holocaust Memorial Museum and frequent speaker in schools and at Holocaust commemorations, was one of four people honored at the Kennedy Center by the Antidefamation League at its annual "Concert Against Hate." Lesley became deputy director of the National Coalition Supporting Eurasian Jewry (formerly the National Conference on Soviet Jewry). In 2011, President Obama appointed her to the U.S. Commission for the Preservation of America's Heritage Abroad and designated her as chair in 2013. Irene Weiss, 90 at the time of this writing, lives a couple of blocks away from my wife and me. It's an easy walk on quiet suburban streets. I saw her out one sunny day during the pandemic shutdown. We exchanged waves. Americans especially—"life, liberty and the pursuit of *happiness*"—can take the easy for granted. Then we easily forget what it really is that we take for granted.

Our Polish study group arrived in Krakow in time for the final days of the 20th annual Jewish Culture Festival, one of the biggest such events in Poland. Nine days of music, exhibitions, food, tours of the pre-Holocaust Jewish Kazimierz district with its synagogues and cemeteries. Unlike Warsaw and Lodz, Krakow largely escaped destruction in World War II. Winding streets, busy with pedestrian, bicycle and motor traffic, connect Main Market Square to Wawel Hill and the Wawel Royal Castle complex. Its high walls still intact, the castle, once the home of Poland's kings, is now a major art museum.

On Friday night we were guests of the Krakow Jewish Community Center at an off-site Shabbat dinner for 700 people, many of them not Jewish. The Krakow JCC itself, made possible mostly by private and non-profit organizational funding from Western diaspora Jewry, is three narrow stories of offices and classrooms near the former Jewish neighborhood. It bustles with people and programs, including the first Jewish pre-school in the city in more than 70 years.

Saturday night, along with more than 10,000 others, we attended "Shalom in Szeroka Street," the closing, five-hour concert. Musicians, again not all Jewish, had come from Poland, Israel, the United States and elsewhere. Soloists and bands, they played all sorts of Jewish and Jewish-inflected music—klezmer, of course, but also liturgical, Chasidic, folk, pre-war cabaret and big-band. One of the Polish state television channels broadcast the show.

Who were these people in the crowd? Poland, now population 38 million, had only 7,500 individuals who identified primarily as Jews. So, they were other locals, tourists, music lovers, Jewish and non-Jewish curators of Polish Jewry's past and, at least as some envisioned, of its present and future.

Security did not seem to be a major worry. Attendees had to pass through metal detectors and a cursory bag check, but the presence of uniformed police and private guards in and around the square was light. The Szeroka Street plaza, now partly gentrified and bordered by some trendy restaurants and bars, had been the collection point for deportation from the Krakow Ghetto during the Holocaust. In the early 1990s, director Steven Spielberg had found it still dreary-looking enough to use on location in filming *Schindler's List*, which won best picture and six other Academy Awards in 1994.

It was difficult, if not impossible to imagine a Jewish Culture Festival like Krakow's in Berlin, Paris or London. Would such crowds turn out, year after year? Wouldn't security requirements be prohibitively expensive? Would public television air hours of the closing concert? No, yes, and no. So why in Poland? My grandparents, who all went to America, might have had an answer, once they surmounted their initial surprise. And in Yiddish, with more vitamins, as Isaac Bashevis Singer would have said.

Szeroka Street improves physically. Much of Europe deteriorates culturally. And America, America remains as always focused on its sprawling, if not Walt Whitmanesque then Holden Caulfieldesque self. So, survivors' stories must be made indelible. Memory can be stronger than time, and sometimes must be. Yet survivors' stories are not the only ones. They are not the majority of relevant stories from what columnist George F. Will has called modern history's black hole. The majority went up as smoke. For people who like to think well of humanity and for Jews who like to think their place fully within it, Holocaust memory contradicts. It's an oppressive recollection nearly impossible to forget, which is why so many want to, and if they can't forget, then transform, invert or trivialize.

Irene Fogel Weiss was born in a part of Czechoslovakia that later was attached to Nazi-collaborationist Hungary and is today in Ukraine. The places we are from, physically and psychically, are not always the places there now. Nor are we quite the people formed by those places.

Had the Allies bombed Auschwitz-Birkenau or the tracks leading to it, even as late as spring 1944, they could have obstructed the genocide of 400,000 Hungarian Jews. Bombing I.G. Farben at Auschwitz III demonstrated their ability to do so.

Among the Jews deported from their lives into the Nazi nightmare along with Irene Fogel and her family were Elie Wiesel and his father. The older Wiesel died in Auschwitz of starvation and disease. The younger, a teenager in the death camp, survived to become the voice of those robbed of their voices and their lives. His dozens of books, beginning with the Holocaust memoir-tale *Night*—periodically on high school reading lists to this day—proceeded through *Dawn* and *Day* to include dozens of other works such as *A Beggar in Jerusalem, The Accident, The Trial of God, Jews of Silence* and *The Oath. Night, Dawn* and *Day* emerged from Wiesel's 900-page Yiddish memoir, the title of which, in translation, was *And the World Remined Silent.*

A professor at Boston University, Wiesel received the Nobel Peace Prize in 1986. The Nobel committee called him a "messenger to mankind." Accepting the award, he said "silence encourages the tormentor, never the tormented." Wiesel campaigned for minority rights, including those of Soviet and Ethiopian Jews, and against oppression of the Kurds, Sri Lanka's Tamils, in South Africa, Nicaragua, Kosovo, Sudan's Darfur and elsewhere. But when he ran newspaper ads condemning Hamas for using children "as human shields" in its conflicts with Israel, *The New York Times* rejected the advertisement. Why? Because "the opinion being expressed is too strong, and too forcefully made, and will cause concern amongst a significant number of *Times* readers." Northeastern University journalism professor Laurel Leff titled her book on the paper's coverage of the Holocaust *Buried by The Times.* Again, *plus ca' change...*

In the mid-1970s Wiesel spoke at the old Ohio State University Hillel house. Approximately 100 people jammed into the large first-floor lounge/meeting room to hear him, many of us standing. Wiesel had married Marion Erster Rose, originally from Austria, in 1969. Their only child, Elisha, was born in 1972. At Ohio State that evening he confessed that for the longest time he had thought it was still not safe, not ethical, to bring a Jewish child into the world. But he had finally changed his mind.

In 2014, Wiesel received CAMERA's (Committee for Accuracy in Middle East Reporting and Analysis) annual EMET Award. *Emet* is Hebrew for truth. He was the keynote speaker at that year's gala fund-raising dinner. The event took place at Pier 60 (the Chelsea Piers) on the Hudson River. Where ocean liners once docked, one could stroll, drink in hand, and look down the mighty river to the Statue of Liberty, nearly ablaze in reflections from the setting sun. Then 500 of us crowded inside the ballroom of the converted dockside pavilion to hear Wiesel.

He said he had not expected antisemitism to reemerge as it was then doing. He said he was troubled that renewed Jew-hatred in the West could spread to the extent and with the toleration it was achieving.

Often, the clearest voice is not the one most listened to. In fact, its very clarity can make it unwelcome. Isaiah, Jeremiah and Ezekiel faced the same problem. More than 2,500 years ago, their voices clarified divinely inspired visions. They caused unwanted concern among those who heard them, as *The New York Times* might say.

On July 11, 2021, a "No Fear Rally in Solidarity with Jews and Israel" was held at the foot of the U.S. Capitol. Though sponsored by major Jewish organization, it attracted a pitifully few 1,000 or so participants, this author included. The rally was arranged in response to attacks on Jews in New York City, Toronto, Los Angeles and elsewhere. Pretext for the assaults was Israel's 11-day war of self-defense in May against Hamas rocket barrages from the Gaza Strip. Hamas (the Palestinian Islamic Resistance Movement, a Muslim Brotherhood derivative) is a U.S.-designated terrorist organization. Its charter calls for the destruction of Israel, an Islamic theocracy over it, the West Bank and Gaza Strip, and genocide of the Jews. Mad demonstrations in Western Europe and North America had accused Israel of "war crimes" and Jews of "supremacy" because it retaliated against Hamas aggression. One of the "No Fear" rally organizers and speakers was Elisha Wiesel.

On the way back from Poland, looking down at the North Sea coast, perhaps as the crew of a World War II B-17 or B-25 bomber would have seen it, it struck me that I was done with Europe. Besides Poland and Germany, Czechoslovakia and Croatia, I'd been to England twice, France twice, Italy once. Sure, I still would like to see the rocks of classical Greece and the rivers of Hemingway's Spain and, of course, return to a Parisian cafe. But the compulsion to do so was gone. History's corkscrew turns, bending pliable humans. Even before the Covid-19 pandemic, it always had been a mistake to imagine tomorrow would be like yesterday or assume without doubt it would be better than yesterday. After the plague, after America's racial reckoning hijacked by left intolerants, it would still be a mistake.

The times and the country of which I first was aware, into which Elvis Presley exploded and the public liked Ike, of course are long gone. The times and place in which the Stray Cats strutted, and Reagan smiled, are fading. The land where first Barack Obama and then his bookend, Donald Trump, entered the White House fragments while both men still make headlines. It does so because Americans, now too-familiar strangers to each other thanks to the endlessly misfiring nervous systems of social and communications media, tear rather than knit it.

And it's easy for them to do so in a society distracted by endless digital diversions, its self-awareness deflected by false multiculturalism. When was the last time one million Americans emigrated annually to Europe, let alone the third world, instead of the other way around, as it's been for decades? Right, never. But if Wall Street doesn't always mirror the real economy of Main Street, then America's news media doesn't always report the underlying United States, not to mention the rest of the world, any more than university humanities departments instruct on becoming more humane. The republic increasingly becomes a country peopled by those taught to revile *e pluribus unum*, to embrace the state as wards but reject the nation and responsibilities of citizenship in it.

After the 2018 massacre of 11 worshipers at Tree of Life synagogue in Pittsburgh, after the 2019 killing of one woman and wounding of several other members of the Chabad *shul* in Poway, Calif., a friend asked a question at our suburban Washington, D.C. congregation. Was it time for Jews to leave the United States? It was less the question than the person who asked that startled me. As a young woman she'd been able to immigrate to the United States from communist-ruled Poland. She recently had retired from a long career as an analyst at one of the three-letter intelligence agencies. Instead of "Of course not," I heard myself say, "Not yet."

In what occasionally seems a long, pleasant dream—countless sunny days periodically smudged by a darkling omen—one thing stands out. The fate of liberty, of the right of individual human beings to exercise free choice, hold their private property and insist on God-given personal dignity, likely will be determined in only two places. One is tiny Israel. It's the only country in which more Jews are born than die and from which the Bible—Western civilization's deed for human beings created by God each in a spark of His image—"shall go forth [as] the word of the Lord." The other is the grand, or grand until yesterday, United States of America. It struggles to continue to be the one truly revolutionary nation of "all men are created equal, that they are endowed by their Creator with certain unalienable Rights, that among these are Life, Liberty and the pursuit of Happiness." Hardly perfect, but as Lincoln correctly had it, mankind's last best hope, Americans the "almost Chosen" nation.

The rest, exhausted or frenetic, enslaved or enslaving, post- or anti-Western, anti-democratic right or left, dance haltingwise like the priests of Ba'al just before Elijah got to them.

Epilogue:
Mood Change

Seize the Day. But Which One?

This work began whimsically, and the intention was to carry that attitude throughout. But the people and events herein recalled forced an underlying message. The old Hollywood adage held that "if you want to send a message, hire Western Union" (don't ruin a film with it). Television, film, the stage and music all too often ruin themselves by reversing the entertainment-message formula. Regardless, a caution emerged here as much on its own volition as much as of this writer's. It is:

Yesterday was not just a dress rehearsal for today. It was the mother. Tomorrow will be like today, until it is not, until the moment it becomes the unexpected bastard child. If history has any laws, the first is that of discontinuous change.

Carpe diem, the Roman poet Horace advised. Seize the day. Live each one as if it were your last, Emperor-philosopher Marcus Aurelius and, nearly 2,000 years later, Apple's Steve Jobs both recommended. An early Talmudic sage, Rabbi Tarfon, put it more fully: "The day is short, the task is abundant, the laborers are lazy, the wage is great, and the Master of the house is insistent. ... It is not your duty to finish the work, but neither are you at liberty to neglect it."

Prepare. Show up. Produce. That way, at your heavenly accounting, you'll have a chance at answering the Master's question: What did you accomplish? Likewise, in the here and now, so when it comes to freedom, its defenders—always needed—will be at the barricades. The barricades opposite those increasingly thrown up by freedom's enemies, by those demanding consensus and conformity and if not that, then submission and silence. A better-known Talmudic figure, Rabbi Hillel, instructed: "In a place where there are no men [no persons of integrity], strive to be a man." Be a *mensch.*

Of course, in our allegedly post-truth Internet era—"narrative" trumping facts—distinguishing freedom's defenders from its enemies, the right side of the barricades from the wrong, can be mind-bogglingly difficult. So, Americans found in the summer of 2020, when the banner "Black Lives Matter!" obscured the reality of social unraveling in predominantly black neighborhoods across the country. Or when on Jan. 6, 2021 self-imagined defenders of democracy attacked the legislative center of that democracy. When barricades went up around the U.S. Capitol, a dangerous amount of ground already had been ceded, not only to the fever swamps of right-wing conspiracy theories but also to the censorious certainties of the "woke" left.

Still, if the past 65 peculiar years said anything comprehensible, it must have been this: Be a free, responsible individual. Be a *mensch.* It's all anyone can do. And the most.

- The end –

Portions of Chapter 12, it should be noted, first appeared in *Jews Make the Best Demons: "Palestine" and the Jewish Question* (2018, New English Review Press) and "Reflections on the Counter-Revolution in San Francisco," *New English Review* (October, 2017).

Eric Rozenman, Washington, D.C., October 15, 2021.

Index